Toward a Philosophy of
ZEN BUDDHISM

Toward a Philosophy of Zen Buddhism

Toshihiko Izutsu

PRAJÑĀ PRESS

BOULDER 1982

SHAMBHALA PUBLICATIONS, INC.
Horticultural Hall
300 Massachusetts Avenue
Boston, Massachusetts 02115
www.shambhala.com

Printed in the United States of America

Distributed in the United States by Random House, Inc.,
and in Canada by Random House of Canada Ltd

LIBRARY OF CONGRESS CATALOGING-IN-PUBLICATION DATA

Izutsu, Toshihiko, 1914–
    Toward a philosophy of Zen Buddhism.
    Reprint. Originally published: Tehran: Imperial Iranian Academy of
    Philosophy, 1977. (Publication/Imperial Iranian Academy of Philosophy ;
    no. 26)
    Includes bibliographical references and index.
    ISBN 0-87773-757-6 (pbk.)
    ISBN 1-57062-698-7
    1. Zen Buddhism—Philosophy—Addresses, essays, lectures.   I. Title.
    II. Series: Publication (Prajna Press) ; no. 26.
BQ9268.6.197   1982   81-84344
294.3'4   AACR2
BVG 01

Contents

Preface

I have entitled this book 'Toward a Philosophy of Zen Buddhism' on the conviction that Zen is possessed of innate philosophical possibilities. This conviction of mine is based on the view that at the original point of all *Philosophiren* in any form whatsoever, there is, and there must be, a peculiar reality-experience. The empiricist philosophy, for instance, is based on, and originates from, an 'empirical' experience of reality. The empiricist type of thinking begins by observing reality just at the level at which man encounters the external world through what is regarded as the 'normal' exercise of his cognitive faculties, sensation and perception being considered the most fundamental forms of cognition. The empiricist philosophy takes form when one starts to reflect upon one's own perceptual experience in a rational and analytical way.

Zen also has its own peculiar experience of reality, which is remarkably different from the 'empirical' one. Not that Zen 'transcends' at one stroke – as is often said – the empirical dimension of reality. Quite the contrary; the world of Zen at its ultimate stage is also a world of sensation and perception which is no less 'empirical' than the world as seen by the empiricist. 'The ordinary way – that precisely *is* the Way', or 'the willow is green and the flower is red'. The point is rather that sensation and perception as activated in Zen experience assume quite a different significance as they function quite differently from the same faculties of sensation and perception as they are activated on the level of the so-called 'normal' cognitive experience. Hence the peculiarity of the Zen experience of reality. And naturally the peculiar noetic experience produces, or is capable of producing, a unique type of ontology. What, then, is the nature of the noetic

experience peculiar to Zen? This is one of the main problems
I am going to deal with in this book.

It will have become clear that by the phrase 'philosophy of
Zen' I mean the philosophization or philosophical elaboration of the Zen experience. By no means do I want to assert
that there is some such thing as the 'philosophy of Zen'
already established as a definite type of philosophical thinking and its result, and that I am going to expound it in an
objective and descriptive way. What I intend to talk about in
this book is the philosophical *potential* hidden in the Zen
experience of reality.

Zen does not like to be associated with philosophy in the
ordinary sense of the word, for 'philosophy' implies rational,
discursive thinking and conceptualization. In this sense Zen is
not merely non-philosophical; it is, more positively, anti-
philosophical. To many of those who are already familiar with
Zen, the expression 'philosophy of Zen' will simply sound like
a straightforward contradiction in terms. In fact, the Zen
student is always rigorously admonished not to fall into the
pitfall of conceptualization and ratiocination. He is to grasp
the 'truth' directly through an act of spiritual realization,
away from all entanglements of thought. The intricacies of
conceptual thinking about the 'truth' are of such a nature that
they inevitably induce the Zen student to deviate from the
right path, thereby closing the door to the 'real' – as Zen
understands it – experience of reality. And, as a matter of fact,
there have occurred in the past not a few cases of philosophical distortion of Zen, i.e., the rational or intellectual manipulation of Zen ideas by those 'philosophers' who have no
experiential grasp of them.

Thus it is not without reason that Zen tends to entertain a
violent aversion toward philosophization and talking about
Zen experience in rational terms. For the world of Zen is a
world of silence. It is a world of an extraordinary experience
which defies thinking and linguistic description. It is a world
where all words are ultimately reduced to Silence. The reason
why it is so will be fully explained in the following pages.

Philosophically, the Silence is the metaphysical Oneness of
absolute non-articulation, the reality before it is articulated
into myriads of forms – 'your own Face which you had prior to

the birth of your father and mother', as Zen often says. But the non-articulated does not remain eternally non-articulated.

Zen 'silence' is a silence pregnant with words. It naturally expresses itself – it cannot but express itself – in language. Out of the depths of the Silence there emerges language. The emergence of language out of the Zen awareness of reality may ontologically be described as an event of the self-articulation of the non-articulation. Thus Silence turns into language. The primordial oneness of non-articulation articulates itself 'out' and comes into the dimension of words. It is language viewed in this light that really matters and alone counts in the eyes of Zen – I mean, the special kind of language which emerges directly out of the Zen experience of reality as the self-articulating activity of the non-articulated. But such a language may very well be subjected to an intellectual analysis and elaborated into a peculiar form or forms of philosophy. A philosophy of this kind – the only justifiable one from the Zen point of view – must be a result of philosophizing out of the very midst of Zen awareness. It must be actualized as the self-philosophization of Zen, i.e., Zen reflecting upon its own self. And as such, Zen has, as I said at the outset, remarkable potentials for creating philosophical thought.

It will have been understood that the problem of 'articulation', whether metaphysical or linguistic, is of supreme importance for Zen philosophy. Articulation is the very center and crux of the whole matter. And the present work turns round this central problem. The problem of the metaphysical or ontological articulation of reality is dealt with in Essay IV, while its linguistic or semantic aspect is thematically discussed in Essay III. Essay IV deals specifically with the problem of how and in what sense the Zen language – the language which emerges directly out of Silence – yields 'meaning' in such a way that it may allow itself to be developed into a philosophy.

The articulation of reality, however, is realized to be a philosophical problem of such a serious nature only when one has had a glimpse into the nature and structure of the Zen experience of reality itself, on the understanding of which alone can the true meaning of 'articulation' become understandable. This and the other related problems are discussed in Essays I and II.

It must be observed further that Zen Silence, when it expresses itself, does not necessarily express itself in a verbal form. That is to say, the Zen language is not necessarily verbal; it can assume divergent forms. Pictorial language, for example, is one of the most remarkable forms of Zen language. This aspect of Zen is elucidated in Essays VI and VII.

It will be clear that the present work is not a systematic and objective presentation of the philosophical ideas of Zen. It is rather a modest attempt at letting Zen experience philosophize itself. To what extent I have succeeded in doing so, however, is not for me to judge. I only hope that this attempt of mine has not resulted after all in adding one more 'useless entanglement' to the mass of already existing conceptual entanglements.

This book consists of seven Essays, all of which were originally independent papers or lectures which I prepared on different occasions. Sincere thanks are due to the editors of the books and journals who have given me permission to republish these papers in the present form. I would also express here my deep gratitude to Peter L. Wilson for his excellent editorial work.

T. Izutsu
Tehran
10 March 1977

Essay I

THE TRUE MAN WITHOUT ANY RANK

— The Problem of Field Awareness in Zen —

Note: This Essay was originally an Eranos lecture delivered at Ascona, Switzerland, in 1969, and published in Eranos-Jahrbuch XXXVIII, 1971, Zürich under the title: 'The Structure of Selfhood in Zen Buddhism'.

1 Zen and the Problem of Man

Buddhism may properly be said to have been concerned from its very historical beginning with the problem of Man, and that exclusively. The starting-point of Buddha's search after the Truth was provided by the disquieting miseries of human existence as he observed them around himself. And the doctrines which he developed after his attainment to enlightenment were through and through human, humane and humanitarian. Buddhist philosophy which began to develop shortly after his death was also 'human' in the sense that it was seriously concerned with the concept of 'non-ego' as one of its most fundamental problems. Here again we observe Man being made an object of philosophical consideration in the particular form of the problematic of 'ego'.

This anthropo-centric tendency of Buddhism was greatly fortified by the rise and development of the Zen sect. By making the actual experience of enlightenment the pivotal point of the world-view, Zen raised, or reformulated, the traditional problem of Man as the problem of the absolute selfhood. We must observe in this connection, however, that Zen raises the question in a very characteristic way. Instead of posing his question concerning Man in an Aristotelian form: 'What is man?', the Zen Buddhist directly begins by asking: 'Who am I?'[1] What is at issue is not the classical problem of the nature of Man in general, but an infinitely more personal and intimate one of *who* is this very human subject who, existing as he does here and now in a time-space system, raises the question about his own self. It is only natural that the image of Man obtained on the basis of such an attitude should be something totally different from an image of Man which forms itself in the mind of an objective observer who would approach the problem by first asking: 'What is man?'

Every one of us, as a human being, has self-consciousness and is conscious of other human beings surrounding him. Hence it naturally comes about that at the level of ordinary existence all of us possess a more or less definite idea as to what kind of a thing man is. The classical Western philosophy going back to Aristotle elaborates and defines this common-sense image of man as a 'rational animal'.

The image of Man peculiar to Zen Buddhism emerges exactly when such a common-sense image of man, be it pre-philosophical or philosophical, is smashed to pieces. The ordinary image of man on which our daily life is based, and on which our social life is carried out, does not, according to the typically Zen conception, represent the true reality of Man. For man, as pictured in such a way, is but a 'thing' in the sense that it is nothing but an objectified man, i.e. man as an object. Such cannot be a true picture, because according to Zen, Man in his true reality is, and must be, an absolute selfhood.

Without tarrying on the plane of common-sense or empirical thinking, where the primary experience of Reality, including even the absolute ego, in its pure 'is-ness'[2] is necessarily broken up into objectified pieces, Zen proposes to grasp Man directly as an absolute selfhood prior to his being objectified into a 'thing'. Only then, it maintains, can we hope to obtain a true image of Man representing him as he really is, that is, in his real, immediate 'is-ness'.

The image of Man peculiar to Zen is thus derived from a dimension which absolutely transcends the bifurcation, so characteristic of the human intellect, of the subject and object. As will be easy to see, such an image of Man can never be obtained as long as we pursue the question in the form of 'what is man?' The question must necessarily and inevitably take on the form of 'who am I?' Otherwise expressed, Man must be intuited in his most intimate subjectivity. For, no matter how far we may go searching after our own 'self' on the plane of intellectual analysis, the 'self' goes on being objectified. However far we may go in this direction, we always end up by obtaining the image of our 'self' seen as an object. The 'self' itself, the real subjective subject which goes on searching after itself, remains always beyond our reach, eluding forever our grasp. The pure subjectivity is reached only when man steps beyond the ken of the dichotomizing activity of intellect, ceases to look at his own 'self' from the outside as an object, and *becomes* immediately his own 'self'. The *Zazen*, 'sitting cross-legged in meditation', is a way specifically devised in order that the subject might delve ever deeper into its own interior so that the bifurcated 'self' – the 'self' as dichotomized into the 'self' as subject and the 'self' as object – might regain its own original unity. When, at the extremity of such a unity, man becomes truly himself and turns into a pure and absolute selfhood, when, in other words, there remains absolutely no distinction any longer between the 'self' *qua* subject and the 'self' *qua* object, an epistemological stage is reached where the 'self' has become so perfectly identified with itself and has so completely become one with itself that it has transcended even being a 'self'. The precise point at which the 'self' becomes one with it-'self' in such an absolute man- ner has come to be known, in accordance with the technical terminology of Dōgen,[3] as 'the-mind-and-body-dropping- off ' (*shin jin datsu raku*). This is immediately followed by the next stage – to be more strictly exact, it is a stage which is actualized at the very same moment as the actualization of the first one – that of 'the-dropped-off-mind-and-body' (*datsu raku shin jin*). This second stage refers to the experiential fact that the moment the mind-and-body, i.e. the 'self', falls off into Nothingness, there is resuscitated out of the Nothingness the same mind-and-body, i.e. the same old 'self' itself, but this time completely transformed into an absolute Self. The 'self' thus resuscitated from its death to itself carries outwardly the same mind-and-body, but the latter is the mind-and-body that has 'dropped off', that is, transcended itself once for all. The image of Man in Zen Buddhism is an image of Man who has already passed through such an absolute transformation of himself, the 'True Man without any ranks' as Lin Chi[4] calls him.

It is evident that such an image of Man as has just been sketched implicitly occupied in Zen Buddhism a place of cardinal importance throughout its entire history. This is evident because from the very beginning Zen centered around the radical and drastic transformation of Man from the relative into the absolute selfhood. The peculiar image of

Man was but a natural product of the special emphasis which Zen laid on the experience of enlightenment.

Explicitly, however, and in terms of the history of *thought*, the concept or image of Man did not occupy a key-position in Zen Buddhism prior to the appearance of Lin Chi. Before him, Man had always remained in the background. The image had always been there implicitly, but not explicitly. 'Man' had never played the role of a key-term in the history of Zen thought before Lin Chi. Rather, the real key-terms had been words like Mind, Nature, (Transcendental) Wisdom, Reality (or Absolute – *dharma*) and the like, all of which were directly or indirectly of an Indian origin and which, therefore, inevitably had a strong flavor of Indian metaphysics.

With the appearance of Lin Chi, however, the whole picture begins to assume an entirely different, unprecedented aspect. For Lin Chi sets out to put Man at the very center of Zen thought, and to build up around this center an extremely vigorous and dynamic world-view. The image of Man as absolute selfhood which, as we have seen, had always been there implicitly – hidden, so to speak, behind the scenes – was suddenly brought out by Lin Chi into the dazzlingly bright light of the main stage. At the same time we witness here the birth of a *thought*[5] which is truly original and indigenous to the Chinese soil.

Lin Chi's thought is characteristically Chinese in that it puts Man at the very center of a whole world-view, and that, further, his conception of Man is extremely realistic to the extent of being almost pragmatic. It is pragmatic in the sense that it always pictures Man as the most concrete individual who exists at this very place and at this very moment, eating, drinking, sitting and walking around, or even 'attending to his natural wants'. 'O Brethren in the Way', he says in one of his discourses, 'you must know that there is in the reality of Buddhism nothing extraordinary for you to perform. You just live as usual without ever trying to do anything particular, attending to your natural wants, putting on clothes, eating meals, and lying down if you feel tired. Let the ignorant people laugh at me. The wise men know what I mean to say'.[6]

The pragmatic Man, however, is not at all an ordinary 'man' as we represent him at the level of common-sense thinking, for he is a Man who has come back to this world of phenomena from the dimension of absolute Reality. His is a two-dimensional personality. He, as a most concrete individual, living among the concretely existent things, does embody something supra-individual. He is an individual who is a supra-individual – two persons fused into a perfect unity of one single person. 'Do you want to know who is our (spiritual) ancestor, Buddha (i.e. the Absolute)? He is no other than yourself who are here and now listening to my discourse!' (Lin Chi)[7] The world-view presented by Lin Chi is a very peculiar view of the world as seen through the eyes of such a two-dimensional person. But in order to have a real understanding of the nature of this kind of world-view, we must go back to our starting-point and try to analyze the whole problem in a more theoretical way. In so doing, our emphasis will be laid on two cardinal points: (1) the epistemological structure of the process by which such a double-natured person comes into being, and (2) the metaphysical structure of the world as it appears to his eyes.

II   The Functional Relationship between Subject and Object

The most fundamental philosophical assertion made by Zen at the outset is that there is a functional relationship between the subject and the object, the knower and the known. Zen begins by recognizing a very close correlation between the state of consciousness of the subject and the state of the objective world which the subject perceives. This correlation between subject and object is of an extremely subtle, delicate, and dynamic nature, so much so that the slightest move on the part of the subject necessarily induces a change on the part of the object, however slight it might be.

The observation of this point, trivial though it may appear at first glance, is in reality of paramount importance for a right understanding of Zen Buddhism, whether practical or philosophical. For both the practice of Zen in its entirety and its philosophical elaboration hinge upon such a relationship between subject and object. It is no less important to observe that in this correlation between subject and object, or the ego and the world, Zen – and, for that matter, Buddhism in general – always recognizes the former, i.e. the subject or the ego, to be the determining factor. The particular state in which the perceiving subject happens to be, determines the state or nature of the object perceived. A particular existential mode of the subject actualizes the whole world in a particular form corresponding to it. The phenomenal world rises before the eyes of an observer in accordance with the latter's inner mode of being. In brief, the structure of the subject determines the structure of the world of objective things.

Consequently, if we feel, vaguely or definitely, that the world as we actually observe it is not the real world, that the phenomenal things which we see are not being seen in their true reality, then we will have to do something about the very structure of our own consciousness. And that exactly is what Zen Buddhism proposes that we should do.

A famous Zen master of the T'ang dynasty, Nan Ch'üan[8] (J.: Nan Sen), is said to have remarked, pointing with his finger to a flower blooming in the courtyard: 'The ordinary people see this flower as if they were in a dream'. If the flower as we actually see it in the garden is to be likened to a flower seen in a dream, we have only to wake up from the dream in order to see the flower as it *really* is. And this simply means that a total personal transformation is required on the part of the subject, if the latter wants to see the reality of things. But what kind of transformation? And what will be the reality of things seen by us after such transformation?

What Nan Ch'üan himself wants to convey by his statement is quite clear. He means to say that a flower as seen by the ordinary people under normal conditions is an *object* standing before the perceiving *subject*. This precisely is what Nan Ch'üan indicates by his expression: 'a flower seen in a dream'. Here the flower is represented as something different from the man who is looking at it. The flower in its true reality, however, is, according to Nan Ch'üan, a flower which is not distinguished, which is not distinguishable, from the man who sees it, the subject. What is at issue here is a state which is neither subjective nor objective, but which is, at the same time both subjective and objective – a state in which the subject and object, the man and the flower, become fused in an indescribably subtle way into an absolute unity.

In order, however, to go a step further towards the core of the problem with which we are dealing here, we must replace Nan Ch'üan's words into their original context. It is found in a celebrated textbook of Zen Buddhism, *Pi Yen Lu*.[9] It reads as follows:

Once the high official Lu Kêng (J.: Riku Kô)[10] was holding a conversation with Nan Ch'üan, when Lu remarked: 'Sêng Chao[11] once said: "The heaven and earth (i.e. the whole universe) is of one and the same root as my own self, and all things are one with me". This I find pretty difficult to understand'. Thereupon Nan Ch'üan, pointing with his finger at a flower blooming in the courtyard, and calling Lu's attention to it, remarked: 'Ordinary people see this flower as if they were in a dream!'

The whole context clarifies Nan Ch'üan's intention. It is as though he said, 'Look at that flower blooming in the court-yard. The flower itself is expressing with its very existence the fact that all things are completely one with our own selves in the fundamental unity of ultimate Reality. The Truth stands there naked, wholly apparent. It is, at every moment and in every single thing, disclosing itself so clearly and so straightforwardly. Yet, alas, ordinary people do not possess the eye to see naked Reality. They see every thing only through veils'.

Since, in this way, ordinary people see everything through the veils of their own relative and determined ego, whatever they see is seen in a dreamlike fashion. But they themselves are firmly convinced that the flower as they actually see it as an 'object' in the external world *is* reality. In order to be able to say that such a vision of the flower is so far away from the true reality that it is almost a dream, they must have their empirical ego transformed into something else. Only then will they be able to assert with full confidence with the monk Chao that the object is no other than the subject itself and that the object and the subject become fused in an indescribably subtle and delicate way into one, and ultimately become reduced to the original ground of Nothingness.

The mysterious fusion of subject and object which the monk Chao talks about requires a great deal of further eluci-dation before it will disclose to us its real meaning. This will be done in detail presently. For the time being let us be content with simply pointing out that even a flower in the garden will appear differently in accordance with different stages in which the mind of the observer happens to be. In order to see in a single flower a manifestation of the metaphysical unity of all things, not only of all the so-called objects but including even the observing subject, the empirical ego must have undergone a total transformation, a complete nullification of itself – death to its own 'self', and rebirth on a totally different dimension of consciousness. For as long as there remains a self-subsistent 'subject' which observes the 'object' from out-side, the realization of such a metaphysical unity is utterly inconceivable. Otherwise, how is it possible that a flower, remaining always a concrete individual flower here and now, be your own self, or, for that matter, be the same as anything else? Thus, to come back to our earlier simple statement, the world discloses itself to our eyes in exact accordance with the actual state of our consciousness.

Even without going to the utmost degree of spiritual experience such as has been mentioned in connection with Nan Ch'üan's remark on a flower in the courtyard, the same type of correlation between subject and object is easily observable at the level of our daily life. For that purpose let us begin by making a very commonplace observation. It is a matter of ordinary experience that the world, or anything in the world, appears differently to different persons in accordance with different points of view or different interests they happen to have with regard to the things. The fact is not without some philosophical significance.

Bertrand Russell, for instance, has actually made an observation of this sort the starting-point for an exposition of his philosophical ideas in his *The Problems of Philosophy*.[12] In ordinary life, we often speak of *the* color of a table, assuming that it is of one definite color everywhere and for everybody. On a closer scrutiny, however, we find that such is not the case. There is, he argues, no definite color which is *the* color of the table. For it evidently appears to be of different colors from different points of view. And no two persons can see it from exactly the same point of view. Moreover, 'even from a given point of view the color will seem different by artificial light, or to a color-blind man, or to a man wearing blue spectacles, while in the dark there will be no color at all'.

What Zen Buddhism tries to bring home to us at the very first stage would seem structurally no different from this kind of daily experience. However, there is in fact a fundamental difference between the two positions. The Zen Buddhist is not interested in the shifting viewpoints from which an object may be looked at, while the 'subject' remains always on one and the same level of daily experience. Rather, he is thinking of two totally different dimensions of consciousness; that is, he is interested in a sudden, abrupt shift on the part of the perceiving subject from the dimension of daily consciousness to that of supra-consciousness.

The fact that one and the same thing seems different in accordance with different points of view at the level of daily consciousness is of no vital concern to the Zen Buddhist. His problem lies elsewhere, or is of a different order. For he is concerned with the validity or invalidity of the law of identity, '*A* is *A*', which constitutes the primary basis of human life at the empirical level of existence. The Zen Buddhist questions the very validity of the proposition: 'an apple is an apple'.

In the view of a Zen Buddhist, personal and individual differences and discrepancies in the sensory experience of things, are but events occurring all in one and the same epistemological dimension, that of daily or just normal mental activity. And this dimension is the one in which our intellect or reason exercises at ease its natural functions: identification, differentiation and combination. The ultimate principle governing our entire mental activity in this dimension is 'discrimination'. Buddhism calls this basic function of the human mind *vikalpa*, the 'discriminating cognition', in contradistinction to *prajñā*, 'transcendental or non-discriminating cognition'.

One and the same apple for example may very well appear differently to different persons. But, after all, the apple remains an apple. An apple *is* an apple, in accordance with the law of identity ('*A is A*'). And it cannot be something other than an apple, i.e. a non-apple, in accordance with the law of *non*-contradiction, ('*A* is not non-*A*'). However great the individual differences may be in the sensory experience of a thing, the thing is not supposed to step out of its own limited region. If, in the presence of an object, one person obtains the visual image of an apple while another sees a cat, for instance, one of them must be in a state of hallucination.

The very first step taken by the *vikalpa* in the exercise of its natural function is to identify or recognize a thing as itself (the recognition of *A* as *A*) by discriminating or distinguishing it from all other things (all non-*A*s). An apple must be recognized and established as an apple. This identification based on discrimination is the basis and starting-point for all subsequent stages of mental activity. Without this basis, the whole world of our normal empirical experience would crumble to pieces and things would irremediably fall into utter disorder.

But, as we have remarked above, Zen Buddhism begins

exactly by pointing out the questionability of the law of identity. To look at an apple as an apple is to see that thing from the very outset in the state of a particular delimitation. To see *A* as *A* is to delimit it to *A* -ness and put it into a fixed, unchangeable state of identity in such a way that it cannot be anything other than *A*. Thus the normal empirical approach to the world is, scholastically, nothing other than outspoken 'essentialism' in that it recognizes as the most basic and self-evident fact that *A* is *A* because of its *A* -ness, i.e. its 'essence' of being *A*.

The *A* -ness, or so-called 'essence' of *A* is understood in this sense, that is, in the sense of the solidly fixed ontological core which unalterably determines the essential limits of a thing, was known in Buddhism in general as *svabhāva*, 'self-essence' or 'self-nature'. All schools in Buddhism, from the earliest periods of its philosophical development, consistently fought against this type of approach to the world, and denounced it as *lokavyavahāra*, 'worldly habit'.[13] A dictum which was recognized already in primitive Buddhism to be one of the three basic tenets of Buddha's teaching, runs (in Pali): *Sabbe dhammā anattā*, i.e. 'All things are ego-less', meaning that nothing of all existent things has a *svabhāva*, i.e. self-subsistent and permanently fixed essence.

But here again Zen Buddhism recognizes the primacy of the state of the mind, and sees the determining factor in the particular structure of the perceiving subject. Each one of the things of the world, whether internal or external, is seen to have its own solidly fixed essence because the mind so sees it, because the mind 'essentializes'. Essences are perceived everywhere by the mind, not because they are objectively there, but simply because the mind is by nature productive of essences. It is the mind that furnishes a thing with this or that particular essence. Even in the domain of daily experience, we sometimes become aware of the fact that we are actually giving various 'essences' to one and the same thing. An apple, for example, is not necessarily always seen as an 'apple'. In fact, it is sometimes seen as a 'fruit'; sometimes as a special 'form', or 'mass of color'. Sometimes we do treat an apple simply as a 'thing'.

The Zen viewpoint, however, insists on going still further. For no matter how many essences a thing may assume in our view, it will always remain in the domain of essentialist cognition. According to Zen, it is not enough that an apple should not be seen *as* an apple; it should not be seen *as* anything whatsoever. Positively stated, an apple should be seen without any delimitation. It must be seen in its indetermination. But in order that the apple be seen in such a way, we as the subjects of cognition must see the apple with *wu hsin* (a Chinese technical term meaning literally 'no-mind'). Only when we approach anything with the 'no-mind' does the thing reveal to our eyes its original reality. At the ultimate limit of all negations, that is, the negation of all the essences conceivable of the apple, all of a sudden the extraordinary reality of the apple flashes into our mind. This is what is known in Buddhism as the emergenc of *prajñā*, transcendental or non-discriminating consciousness. And in and through this experience, the apple again manifests itself *as* an apple in the fullest density of existence, in the 'original freshness of the first creation of the heaven and earth'.

All this is actualized only through our actualizing the state of 'no-mind'. The actualization of the 'no-mind' itself is the pivotal point of the whole system. In the following section we shall take up this problem as our special topic.

III   Consciousness and Supra-Consciousness

At the end of the preceding section mention was made of the 'no-mind' as the subjective source or basis for the non-essentialist type of world view. The 'no-mind', *wu hsin* (J.: *mu-shin*), which may be translated in a more explanatory manner as a 'mind which is no mind', 'mind which exists as a non-existent mind', or 'mind which is in the state of Nothingness', is not to be understood in a purely negative sense as the mind in the state of torpidity and inertness or sheer ecstasy.[14] Quite the contrary, the 'no-mind' is a psychological state in which the mind finds itself at the highest point of tension, a state in which the mind works with utmost intensity and lucidity. As an oft-used Zen expression goes: the consciousness illumines itself in the full glare of its own light. In this state, the mind knows its object so perfectly that there is no longer any consciousness left of the object; the mind is not even conscious of its knowing the object.

The 'no-mind' has in fact played an exceedingly important formative role in the cultural history both of China and Japan. In Japan the main forms of fine art, like poetry, painting, calligraphy, etc., have developed their original types more or less under the influence of the spirit of the 'no-mind'. Many an anecdote, real and fictitious, has been handed down to us: for example, of black-and-white painters whose brush moves on the surface of the paper as if of its own accord, without the artist's being conscious of the movement the brush makes; or of master musicians who, when they play the harp, feel that it is not they themselves who play the music, but that it is as though music played itself.

The example of a master musician absorbed in playing his harp will be good enough to give at least some idea as to what kind of a thing Zen Buddhism is thinking of when it talks about the 'no-mind'. The musician is so completely absorbed in his act of playing, he is so completely one with the harp and music itself, that he is no longer conscious of the individual movements of his fingers, of the instrument which he is playing, nor even of the very fact that he is engaged in playing. In reference to such a situation, no one would say, except figuratively or in a loose sense, that the musician is 'unconscious'. For he *is* conscious. Rather, his consciousness is at the utmost limit of self-illumination. The aesthetic tension of his mind runs so high throughout his whole being that he himself is the music he is playing. Paradoxical as it may sound, he is so fully conscious of himself as identified with music that he is not 'conscious' of his act of playing in any ordinary sense of the word. In order to distinguish such a state of consciousness from both 'consciousness' and 'unconsciousness' as ordinarily understood, we will use the word 'supra-consciousness'.

These and similar cases of 'creative' activity that are known not only in the Far East but in almost every culture in the world are instances of the actualization of the 'no-mind' at the level of ordinary life. But at this level, the actualization of the 'no-mind' is but a sporadic and rather unusual phenomenon. What Zen purports to do is to make man cultivate in himself the state of 'no-mind' in such a systematic way that it might become his *normal* state of consciousness, that he might begin to see everything, the whole world of Being, from the vantage point of such a state of consciousness.

It is to the supra-consciousness thus understood – not in its limited application to aesthetic experience, but as developed into the normal state of an absolute Selfhood – that the famous words of the Diamond Sutra refer:[15]

> *Evam apraṣṭhitam cittam utpādayitavyam*
> *Yanna kvacit praṣṭhitam cittam utpādayitavyam*
>
> (One should never let an abiding mind emerge;
> A mind thus non-abiding one should let emerge.)

The *praṣṭhitam cittam* 'abiding mind' means a mind abiding by something, i.e. sticking to 'objects'. Instead of letting, the Sutra says, such an 'essentializing' consciousness emerge, one should raise a mind that does not adhere to any 'object' in its essential delimitation. This is tantamount to saying that it is not enough for us to suppress the rise of, or nullify, the object-making consciousness; we should more positively let a particular kind of mind emerge which, though fully conscious of itself as well as of external things, does not recognize any self-subsistent essences in them. This is what we would call supra-consciousness. And this is no other than the 'no-mind' with which we started our discussion in the present section.

The preceding explanation may have succeeded in at least giving a vague general idea regarding the nature of the supra-consciousness. But it has certainly clarified neither its philosophical structure nor the psychological process by which one reaches such a state of the mind. So let us go back once again to the daily level of ontological experience and begin by analyzing the structure of cognition that is typical of that level, with a view to understanding on the basis of that analysis the fundamental metaphysico-epistemological make-up of the supra-consciousness.

IV   The Structure of the Empirical Ego

From the point of view of Zen Buddhism, the 'essentialist' tendency of the empirical ego is not admissible not only because it posits everywhere 'objects' as permanent substantial entities, but also, and particularly, because it posits itself, the empirical ego, as an ego-substance. It not only sticks or adheres to the external 'objects' as so many irreducible realities, but it clings to its own self as an even more irreducible, self-subsistent reality. This is what we have come to know as the 'abiding mind' (*praṣṭhitam cittam*). And a whole world-view is built up upon the sharp opposition between the 'abiding mind', i.e. the 'subject' and its 'objects'. This dichotomy of reality into subject and object, man and the external world, is the foundation of all our empirical experiences. Of course even common-sense is ready to admit that the phenomenal world, including both external things and the personal ego, is in a state of constant flux. But it tends to see within or behind this transiency of all things some elements which remain permanently unchangeable and substantial. Thus is created an image of the world of Being as a realm of self-identical objects, even the so-called 'subject' being strictly speaking in such a view nothing but one of the 'objects'. It is precisely this kind of ontological view that Zen Buddhism is firmly determined to destroy once for all in order to replace it by another ontology based upon an entirely different sort of epistemology.

For a better understanding of the world-view which is peculiar to the supra-consciousness, let us, first, take up the normal type of world-view which is most natural and congenial to the human mind, and analyze its inner structure at a philosophical level.

Two stages or forms may conveniently be distinguished within the confines of such a world-view. The first is typically represented by Cartesian dualism standing on the fundamental dichotomy of *res cogitans* and *res extensa*. As a philosophy, it may be described as an ontological system based on the dualistic tension between two 'substances' that are irreducible to one another. As a world-view, it may appropriately be described as one in which man, i.e. the ego, is looking at things from the outside, he himself being in the position of a spectator. He is not subjectively involved in the events that take place among various things before his own eyes. Man is here a detached onlooker confronting a world of *external* objects. A whole ontological scenery is spread out before him, and he, as an independent personal 'subject', is merely enjoying the colorful view on the stage of the world. This is a view which is the farthest removed from the reality of the things as they reveal themselves to the eyes of the supra-consciousness.

The second stage may conveniently be represented by the Heideggerian idea of the 'being-within-the-world', particularly in the state of the ontological *Verfallenheit*. Unlike the situation we have just observed in the first stage of the dichotomous world-view, man is here subjectively, vitally involved in the destiny of the things surrounding him. Instead of remaining an objective spectator looking from the outside at the world as something independent of him, man, the ego, finds himself in the very midst of the world, directly affecting them and being directly affected by them. He is no longer an outsider enjoying with self-complacency what is going on on the stage of the theatre. He himself *is* on the stage, he *exists* in the world, actively participating in the play, undergoing an undefinable existential anxiety which is the natural outcome of such a position.

The common-sense world-view at this second stage is far closer to Zen than the first stage. Yet, the empirical world-view, whether of the first or the second stage, is strictly speaking totally different from the Zen world-view with regard to its basic structure. For the empirical world-view is a world-view worked out by the intellect that can properly exercise its function only where there is a distinction made between *ego* and *alter*. The whole mechanism stands on the conviction, whether explicit or implicit, of the independent existence of the ego-substance which stands opposed to external substantial objects. Whether the subject be represented as being outside the world of objects or inside, this very basic Cartesian opposition is, from the standpoint of Zen, something to be demolished before man begins to see the reality of himself and of so-called external objects.

In truth, however, even in the midst of this empirical view of the things there is hidden something like a metaphysical principle which is, though invisible, constantly at work, ready to be realized at any moment through the human mind to transform the normal view of the world into something entirely different. This hidden principle of the metaphysico-epistemological transformation of reality is called in Buddhism *tathâgata-garbha*, the 'Womb of the absolute Reality'. But in order to see the whole structure from this particular point of view, we shall have to submit it to a more detailed and more theoretical analysis.[16]

The epistemological relation of the ego to the object in the ordinary empirical world-view may be represented by the formula: $s \rightarrow o$, which may be read as: *i see this*.[17]

Thus the grammatical subject, s, represents the ego-consciousness of man at the level of empirical experience. It refers to the awareness of selfhood as *Da-sein* in the literal sense of 'being-there' as a subject in front of, or in the midst of, the objective world. The i is here an independently subsistent ego-substance. As long as the empirical ego remains on the empirical dimension, it is conscious of itself only as being there as an independent center of its own perception, thinking and bodily actions. It has no awareness at all of its being something more than that.

However, from the viewpoint of Zen which intuits everywhere and in everything the act of the *tathâgata-garbha*, the 'Womb of the absolute Reality', there is perceivable, behind each individual i, Something whose activity may be expressed by the formula $(S \rightarrow)$ or $(I\ SEE)$ the brackets indicating that this activity is still hidden at the empirical level of self-consciousness. Thus the structure of the empirical ego, s, in reality, that is, seen with the eye of Zen, must properly be represented by the formula:

$$(S \rightarrow) s$$
or: $(I\ SEE)$ *myself.*

As we shall see later in more detail, the empirical ego, s, can be the real center of all its activities simply because that hidden Principle, $(S \rightarrow)$, is constantly functioning through s. The empirical ego can be selfhood only because every subjective movement it makes is in truth the actualization here and now of that Something which *is* the real Selfhood. The nature of the activity of $(I\ SEE)$ may best be understood when it is put side by side with its Islamic parallel presented by the *irfān* type of philosophy which finds an explicit reference to the same kind of situation in the words of God in the Qur'ân: 'It was not you who threw when you did throw: it was (in reality) God who threw'.[18] The important point, however, is that this state of affairs is at this level still completely hidden to, and remains unnoticed by, the empirical ego. The latter sees itself alone; it is totally unaware of the part between the brackets: $(S \rightarrow)$.

Exactly the same applies to the 'objective' side of the epistemological relation (represented in the above-given formula by the small o). Here again the empirical ego has the awareness only of the presence of 'things'. The latter appear to the ego as self-subsistent entities that exist independently of itself. They appear as substances qualified by various properties, and as such they stand opposed to the perceiving subject which sees them from outside. Viewed from the standpoint of the above-mentioned *prajñā*, the 'transcendental cognition', however, a thing rises as this or that thing before the eyes of the empirical ego simply by virtue of the activity of that very same Something, $(S \rightarrow)$, which, as we have seen, establishes the ego as an ego. A thing, o, comes to be established as the thing, o, itself as a concrete actualization of that Something. It is properly to be understood as a self-manifesting form of the same *tathāgata-garbha*, the 'Womb of the absolute Reality' which is eternally and permanently active through all the phenomenal forms of the things.[19]

Thus the formula representing the inner structure of o must assume a more analytic form:

$$(S \rightarrow) o$$
or: $(I\ SEE)$ *this.*

This new formula is so designed as to indicate that here, too, *o* is the only thing which is externally manifested, but that behind this phenomenal form there lies hidden the activity of (*S* →), of which the empirical ego is still unaware.

In this way, the so-called subject-object relationship or the whole epistemological process by which a (seemingly) self-subsistent ego-substance perceives a (seemingly) self-subsistent object-substance, and which we have initially represented by the formula *s* → *o*, must, if given in its fully developed form, be somewhat like this:

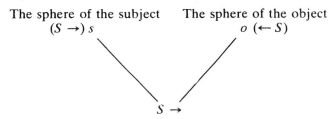

In this last formulation, the *s* or the empirical ego, which is but a particular actualization of (*S* →), is put into a special active-passive relation with the 'object' or *o*, which is also a particular actualization of the same (*S* →). And the whole process is to be understood as a concrete actualization of *I SEE*, or *S* → without brackets. But even in the *I SEE* there is still noticeable a faint lingering trace of ego-consciousness. Zen emphatically requires that even such an amount of ego-consciousness should be erased from the mind, so that the whole thing be ultimately reduced to the simple act of *SEE* pure and simple. The word 'no-mind' to which reference has been made refers precisely to the pure act of *SEE* in the state of an immediate and direct actualization, that is, the eternal Verb *SEE* without brackets.

We now begin to notice that the reality of what has been expressed by the formula: *i see this*, is of an extremely complicated structure at least when described analytically from the viewpoint of the empirical ego. The real metaphysico-epistemological situation which is covertly and implicitly indicated by the formula *s* → *o*, turns out to be something entirely different from what we usually understand from the outward grammatical structure of the sentence. And the primary or most elementary aim of Zen Buddhism with regard to those who, being locked up in the magic circle of ontological dichotomy, cannot see beyond the surface meaning of *s* → *o* or *i see this* as suggested by its syntactic structure ('subject' → 'act' → 'object'), consists in attempting to break the spell of dualism and remove it from their minds, so that they might stand immediately face to face with what we have symbolically designated by the Verb *SEE*.

We may do well to recall at this point that Buddhism in general stands philosophically on the concept of *pratītyasamutpāda* (J.: *engi*) i.e. the idea that everything comes into being and exists as what it is by virtue of the infinite number of relations it bears to other things, each one of these 'other things' owing again its seemingly self-subsistent existence to other things. Buddhism in this respect is ontologically a system based upon the category of *relatio*, in contrast to, say, the Platonic-Aristotelian system which is based on the category of *substantia*.

A philosophical system which stands upon the category of *substantia* and which recognizes in substances the most basic ontological elements, almost inevitably tends to assume the form of essentialism.

What is meant by essentialism has roughly been outlined in an earlier context. Just to recapitulate the gist of the essentialist argument for the purpose of elucidating, by contrast, the nature of the position taken by Zen Buddhism, we might remark that the essentialist position sees on both the 'subjective' and 'objective' sides of the *s* → *o* type of situation self-subsistent substances, the boundaries of each of which are inalterably fixed and determined by its 'essence'. Here *o*, say, an apple, is a self-subsistent substance with a more or less strictly delimited ontological sphere, the delimitation being supplied by its own 'essence', i.e. apple-ness. In the same manner, the ego which, as the subject, perceives the apple is an equally self-subsistent substance furnished with an 'essence' which, in this case, happens to be its I-ness. Zen Buddhism summarizes the essentialist view through the succinct dictum: 'Mountain is mountain, and river is river'.

The position of *pratītyasamutpāda* stands definitely against this view. Such a view, Buddhism asserts, does nothing other than reflect the phenomenal surface of reality. According to the Buddhist view, it is not the case that there does exist in the external world a substance with a certain number of qualities, called 'apple'. The truth is rather that Something phenomenally appears to the subject as an 'apple'. The phenomenal appearance of the 'apple' as an 'apple' depends upon a certain positive attitude on the part of the subject. Conversely, however, the very fact that 'apple' phenomenally appears as such to his eyes, establishes man as the perceiving ego, the subject of cognition. Zen describes this reciprocal relationship or determination between the subject and the object by saying: 'Man sees the mountain; the mountain sees man'.

The reality in the true sense of the word, therefore, is Something lying behind both the subject and object and making each of them emerge in its particular form, this as the subject and that as the object. The ultimate principle governing the whole structure is Something which runs through the subject-object relationship, and which makes possible the very relationship to be actualized. It is this all-pervading, active principle that we want to indicate by the formula $S \rightarrow$, or rather in its ultimate form, the Verb *SEE*.

But again, the word 'something' or 'ultimate principle' must not mislead one into thinking that behind the veils of phenomena some metaphysical, supra-sensible Substance is governing the mechanism of the phenomenal world. For there is, according to Zen, in reality nothing beyond, or other than, the phenomenal world. Zen does not admit the existence of a transcendental, supra-sensible order of things, which would subsist apart from the sensible world.[20] The only point Zen Buddhism makes about this problem is that the phenomenal world is not just the sensible order of things as it appears to the ordinary empirical ego; rather, the phenomenal world as it discloses itself to the Zen consciousness is charged with a peculiar kind of dynamic power which may conveniently be indicated by the Verb *SEE*.

Thus what is meant by *SEE* is not an absolute, transcendental Entity which itself might be something keeping itself beyond, and completely aloof from the phenomenal things. Rather, what is really meant thereby in Zen Buddhism is a dynamic field of power in its entirety and wholeness, an entire field which is neither exclusively subjective nor exclusively objective, but comprehending both the subject and the object in a peculiar state prior to its being bifurcated into these two terms. The verbal form itself of *SEE* may, at least vaguely, be suggestive of the fact that, instead of being a thing, be it an 'absolute' thing or be it a 'transcendental' substance, it is an *actus* charging an entire field with its dynamic energy. In terms of the previously introduced basic formula we might say that the whole process of *i see this* is itself the field of the Act of *SEE*. The real meaning of this statement, however, will be made clear only by our analyzing in more detail the basic inner structure of this dynamic field. That will be our task in the following pages.

V. 'The Whole World is One Single Mind'

We have observed in the foregoing that the basic formula $s \rightarrow o$, or i *see this*, which is designed to describe schematically the epistemological relation between the perceiving subject and the object perceived, conceals in reality a far more complex mechanism than appears at first sight. For, according to the typically Buddhist analysis, at the back of s there is concealed $(S \rightarrow)$; at the back of o there is also $(S \rightarrow)$. And the whole thing, as we have observed, is ultimately to be reduced to the very simple, all-pervading and all-comprehensive act of *SEE*.

It often happens that this *SEE*, which is in Zen understanding nothing other than the absolute or ultimate Reality, makes itself felt in the mind of a man living in the empirical dimension of existence. The first symptom of the ultimate Reality breaking into the empirical dimension is observable in the fact that the man in such a situation begins to feel uneasy about the nature of the reality as he actually sees it. Although he is still completely locked up in the dichotomous world-view, he somehow begins to entertain a vague feeling that the true reality, both of himself and of the external things, must be something of an entirely different nature. He vaguely notices at the same time that he is actually undergoing all the tribulations and miseries of human existence simply because he cannot see the reality as he should. This phenomenon, of decisive importance both religiously and philosophically, is called in Chinese Buddhism *fa hsin* (J.: *hosh-shin*), meaning literally the raising of the mind, i.e. the raising of a deep and strong aspiration toward the enlightenment of Buddha. Philosophically, it is to be understood as the very first self-manifestation of the metaphysical $S \rightarrow$.

Once this beginning stage is actualized, the *Dasein* as it is naturally given loses, subjectively as well as objectively, its

seeming solidity. It is felt that the *Dasein* in its empirical form
is not the real form of Being, that it is but a pseudo-reality.
Urged by an irresistible drive pushing him from the pseudo-
reality towards what he thinks to be the real reality, whatever
and wherever it might be, man betakes himself to this or that
way of possible salvation. Here Zen Buddhism proposes 'sitting cross-legged in meditation' as the most authentic way for
cultivating a special eye to see reality as it really is in its
original such-ness.

The 'sitting cross-legged in meditation' is a somato-
psychological posture by which the naturally centrifugal tendency of the mind might be curbed, and turned toward the
opposite, i.e. centripetal, direction until finally the pseudo-
ego loses itself in the realization of the true Selfhood which we
have indicated by the formula $S \rightarrow$.

Zen asserts that this kind of somato-psychological posture
is an absolute necessity for the realization of the true Selfhood, i.e. the state of absolute subjectivity, because the real
'self' is never attainable through a purely mental process, be it
representation, imagination, or thinking. For it is not a mere
matter of cognition. The question is not 'knowing' one's own
true self, but rather 'becoming' it. Unless one 'becomes' one's
own self, however far one may proceed along the successive
stages of self-cognition, the self will not turn into an absolute
Selfhood. For the real self will go on receding ever further; it
will forever remain an 'object', an object known or to be
known. The self as a known object, at no matter how high a
stage the cognition may happen to be, cannot by nature be
pure subjectivity. In order to realize the self in a state of pure
and absolute subjectivity, one has to 'become' it, instead of
merely 'knowing' it. But in order to achieve this, the whole
unity of 'mind-body' – as suggested by the above-mentioned
expression of Dōgen – must 'drop off'. The 'sitting cross-
legged in meditation' is, as Zen sees it, the best possible, if not
the only possible, way of achieving, first, the unity of 'mind-
body', and then the unity itself 'dropping off'.

The expression: 'the mind-body dropping off' means, in
the more traditional Buddhist terminology, one's experiencing with his total being the epistemological-metaphysical
state of Nothingness (Sanscrit: *śūnyatā,* Ch.: *k'ung,* J.: *kū*).

But the word 'Nothingness' as used in Zen Buddhism must be understood in a very peculiar sense.

'Nothingness' in this context, to begin with, refers to the last and ultimate stage in the actualization of Zen consciousness, at which the self, ceasing to set itself up as an 'object' for itself, 'becomes' the self itself, and that so thoroughgoingly that it *is* no longer even its own self. It is in fact one of the most fundamental philosophical tenets of Zen Buddhism that when a thing – anything whatsoever – becomes its own self thoroughgoingly and completely, to the utmost extent of possibility, it ends by breaking through its own limit and going beyond its determinations. At this stage, *A* is no longer *A* ; *A* is non-*A*. Or, to use a terminology which is peculiar to Zen, 'mountain is not mountain'. However, to this statement Zen adds – and this is the most crucial point – that when a thing, by becoming its own self so thoroughgoingly, breaks through its limitations and determinations, then paradoxically it is found to be its own Self in the most real and absolute sense.

This process may conveniently be described in terms of the traditional logical language in the following way.[21] One may note that, thus described, the logic of Zen discloses a remarkable originality which would clarify to a great extent the most characteristic form of thinking in Zen. As in the case of the traditional Aristotelian logic, the starting-point is furnished by the law of identity, '*A* is *A* ', which, as we have seen above, constitutes the logical basis of metaphysical essentialism. The law of identity signifies for Zen Buddhism too that a thing, whatever it be, is identical with itself. To express this empirical truth, Zen says: 'Mountain is mountain'.

Thus outwardly at least, there is no difference noticeable here between the Aristotelian logical system and Zen logic. Implicitly, however, already at this initial stage Zen takes a view which considerably differs from the Aristotelian position. For in the law of identity (*A* is *A*) Zen recognizes a characteristic sign of the self-complacency of normal *bon sens*. From the point of view of Zen, the formula: '*A* is *A* ', instead of being a description of a well-grounded observation of the structure of reality, is but a logical presentation of the illusory view of reality seen through the veil of *Māyā*, which is the natural outcome of man's casting upon each of the things of the world the narrow spotlight of the discriminating intellect.

The basic difference, however, between the ordinary type of logic and Zen logic comes out with an undeniable clarity at the next stage. For the former naturally develops the law of identity into the law of non-contradiction (A is not non-A), while the latter develops it into a glaring contradiction, asserting: 'A is non-A'. Zen refers to this contradictory stage by the dictum: 'Mountain is not mountain'. It must be borne in mind, however, that when Zen makes an assertion of this kind, it does not do so in the same epistemological dimension as that of 'A is A'. As long as one remains at the level of 'A is A', i.e. the level of empirical experience, one would never be able to say at the same time, 'A is non-A', unless one goes out of one's mind. This fact will become evident beyond any doubt when one encounters a more strange-looking expression like: 'The bridge flows on; the river does not flow'.[22] Otherwise expressed, the making of an assertion of this sort presupposes on the part of the person the actualization of a total transformation of consciousness in such a way that he is thereby enabled to witness A as it 'becomes' A itself to such an extent that it breaks through its own A-ness, and begins to disclose to him its formless, essenceless, and 'aspect'-less aspect.

Thus understood, the formula: 'A is non-A' will have to be more analytically paraphrased as: 'A is so thoroughgoingly A itself that it is no longer A'. Metaphysically, this is the stage of *chên k'ung* (J.: *shin kū*), the 'real Nothingness'. Here A is not A in the positive sense that it is absolutely beyond the determinations and delimitations of A-ness, that it is something infinitely more than mere A.

The third stage which immediately follows – or rather we should say: which establishes itself at the same time as – the stage of 'A is non-A' is again 'A is A'. That is to say, at the final stage, we apparently come back to the initial stage. 'Mountain is (again) mountain'. Or, as a more popular Zen adage goes: 'The flower is red, and the willow is green'. In spite of the formal identity, however, the inner structure of 'A is A' is completely different in the two cases. For at the last stage 'A is A' is but an abbreviated expression standing for 'A is non-A; therefore it is A'. The Diamond Sutra, to which reference has already been made, describes this situation by saying: 'The world is not a world; therefore it deserves to be called *world*', or 'A thing – anything whatsoever – is not a thing; therefore it deserves to be called *thing*'. This stage is technically known in Mahayana Buddhism as *miao yu* (J.: *myō u*), 'extraordinary Being'. The Chinese word *miao*, meaning literally 'subtle', 'extraordinary', 'miraculously good', is intended to suggest that reality is being seen or experienced here in an unusually elevated dimension, that it is not the world of Being as it is grasped by the discriminating activity of our relative intellect, although outwardly, that is, seen through the eyes of an ordinary man locked up in the limited sphere of empirical experience, it is still the same old world of ours which has nothing extraordinary about it. For it is the common ordinary world which has once lost itself in the abyss of Nothingness and which, then, has taken rise again in its phenomenal form.

What actually happens in the human consciousness between the stage of '*A* is non-*A*' and the next stage, that of '*A* is (again) *A*', crucially determines the nature of Zen Buddhism. The whole thing centers around the total nullification of all individual things in Nothingness and their rebirth from the very bottom of Nothingness again into the domain of empirical reality as concrete individuals, but completely transformed in their inner structure. And the rise of this kind of consciousness in a concrete individual human mind is what is known in Buddhism as *prajñā* which might be translated as 'transcendental cognition', 'non-discriminating cognition' or Supreme Knowledge. We now see that translation, in whatever way it may be made, is, in a case like this, merely a make-shift. For 'non-discriminating' is but an aspect of this type of cognition; nor does 'transcendental' do justice to its reality, because the latter in its ultimate form is, as we have just seen, a matter of the most concrete and empirical experience which is actualized in the dimension of daily life.

The most important point to note about the rise of the *prajñā* is that it consists in a complete, total transformation occurring in the ego-structure of the subject. Formulated as: ['*A* is *A*' → '*A* is non-*A*' → '*A* is *A*'], the whole process might look as if it referred purely to the objective structure of the world. But in truth it concerns, primarily and directly at least, the subjective aspect of reality. The three logical stages reflect the three basic stages in the process of the birth and establishment of the *prajñā*-type of cognition, although, to be sure, each of these subjective stages does imply the presence of a corresponding ontological dimension.

Thus the key-word Nothingness in this context refers first and foremost to the nullification of the selfhood, the ego, conceived and represented as a self-subsistent entity. The core of the ego which has hitherto been distinguishing itself from all others, is now broken down and becomes nullified. But the nullification of the empirical ego as conceived by Zen Buddhism cannot be achieved by a total annihilation of consciousness. The epistemological Nothingness about which Zen talks is not to be confused with the state of sheer unconsciousness.

True, the awareness of *myself* as appears in the above-introduced formula (*I SEE*) *myself* is no longer there. In this sense, and in this sense only, the epistemological Nothingness is a region of unconsciousness. However, in place of the awareness of the empirical ego, there is actualized here the absolute Awareness itself, which we have expressed above by the formula: $S \rightarrow$ or *SEE*, and which has not been activated in the domain of the empirical ego. Zen often calls it an 'ever-lucid Awareness' – *liao liao ch'ang chih,* a phrase attributed to the second Patriarch of Zen Buddhism, Hui K'o (J.: E Ka, 487-593). Strictly speaking, there is in this absolute Awareness no trace even of *I*, so that the formula $S \rightarrow$, or *I SEE* must, as we have observed earlier, ultimately be reduced to *SEE* alone. Far from being 'Nothingness' in the negative sense of the term, it is an extremely intense consciousness, so intense indeed that it goes beyond being 'consciousness'.[23]

In exact correspondence to the total transformation of the subject, there occurs on the side of the 'objects' also a drastic change, so much so that they cease to subsist as 'objects'. It is but natural, because where there is no 'subject' confronting 'object', there can be no 'object' remaining. All things at this stage lose their essential delimitations. And being no longer obstructed by their own ontological limits, all things flow into one another, reflecting each other and being reflected by each other in the limitlessly vast field of Nothingness.[24] The mountain is here no longer a mountain, the river is no longer a river, for on the corresponding subjective side, 'I' am no longer 'I'.

There is here no ego that sees and recognizes a thing as 'something'; nor is there any thing to be seen or recognized as such. For the 'object', whatever it may be, is no longer an object, because it has been deprived of all delimitations. The whole Being at this stage has turned into a vast, limitless space of Void in which nothing may be grasped as something definite. Man directly experiences in such a situation the whole world of Being as Nothingness.

But this very description of Nothingness clearly tells us that the Nothingness which is experienced in this way is by no means 'nothing' in the purely negative sense as the word is liable to be understood. On the 'subjective' side – if we still want to hold fast to the subject-object distinction – the experiencing of Nothingness does not mean our consciousness becoming completely vacant and empty. Quite the contrary; consciousness here is its own self in its pristine purity, a pure Light or sheer Illumination, being illuminated by itself and illuminating itself. It is the *SEE* of which mention has often been made.

But this Illumination, through illuminating itself, illumines at the same time the entire world of Being. This means that on the 'objective' side too, things are not simply reduced to 'nothing' in the negative sense of the term. True, at this stage none of the individual existents exists self-subsistently. But this is not the same as saying that they are simply nil. On the contrary, they are there as concrete individuals, while being at the same time so many actualizations of the limitless, 'aspect'-less aspect of an ever-active, ever-creative Act. But this Act, for the Zen consciousness, is no other than the Illumination of the *SEE* itself which we have just established as the 'subjective' side of the experience of Nothingness.

Instead of describing the *SEE* as Light or Illumination, Zen often refers to this simple Verb *SEE* by the term *hsin*, the Mind. And it often speaks of all things being the products of the Mind. It will have been understood by now that this and other similar assertions are not made on the basis of an idealist view which would reduce everything to 'thought' or 'ideas'. For the Mind as understood by Zen is not the minds of individual persons. What is meant by the word Mind is Reality before it is broken up into the so-called 'mind' and 'thing';

it is a state prior to the basic dichotomy of 'subject' and 'object'. Curiously enough, be it remarked, the word *hsin* ('mind') in this context is exactly synonymous with the word *wu-hsin* ('no-mind') which we encountered in an earlier context. The Mind understood in this sense is often called the *hsin fa* (J.: *shin bō*), the Mind-Reality.

As will be explained fully later, the 'mind' as understood in the ordinary sense is, in the view of Zen, but an abstraction, that is, the 'subjective' aspect of the Mind-Reality grasped as an independent factor and posited as an individual, self-subsistent psychological principle. When, therefore, Zen asserts that 'all things are but one mind', it does not mean that the mind as ordinarily understood produces or creates all things out of itself. It simply wants to indicate how out of the Mind-Reality there emerges what we ordinarily recognize as subject and object. The 'mind' as understood in the ordinary sense is in this view only an element indistinguishably fused with its 'objective' counterpart into the unity of the Mind-Reality as a totality.

It often happened, however, in the course of the history of Buddhism that the Mind-Reality was confused with the 'mind'. As a concrete example of this confusion, let us examine the famous anecdote concerning the great Zen master Fa Yen Wên I (J.: Hō Gen Mon Eki, 885-958), the founder of the Fa Yen school, a remarkably philosophical mind, who had been famous before his experience of enlightenment for upholding the idealist position generally known as the 'Mind-Only' - Theory. The theory, put in a nutshell, holds that the whole world of Being is nothing but a grand manifestation of one single 'mind', and that all that exist are nothing but so many products of one single act of 'cognition'.[25]

Once Fa Yen was travelling with two companions in search of the Truth, when they happened to take shelter from rain in a hermitage belonging to a great Zen master of the age, Ti Tsang Kuei Ch'ên (J.: Ji Zō Kei Jin, 867-928). They did not know, however, who he was.

Against the background of the drizzling rain, the three young men discussed with enthusiasm, self-conceit and self-satisfaction, the problems raised by the famous dictum of the monk Chao: 'The heaven and earth (i.e. the whole universe) is of one and the same root as my own self, and all things are one with me',[26] while Ti Tsang listened to them silently. Then suddenly he asked, 'Are the mountains, rivers, and the earth one and the same thing as the self, or different?' 'One and the same', Fa Yen replied. Thereupon, the aged Zen master, without saying anything, put up two fingers, gazed intently at them, then retired to his own room.

As the rain stopped, the three young men were about to leave, when all of a sudden the master Ti Tsang, pointing at a stone in the courtyard said to Fa Yen, 'I understand that you hold the doctrine of the whole world being one single mind. Is, then, this stone inside the mind or outside?' 'Of course it is in the mind', replied Fa Yen. Thereupon Ti Tsang remarked, 'What a cumbersome burden you have in your mind! Due to what kind of network of causes do you have to carry about in the mind such a heavy stone?'

Fa Yen, who did not know what to say, decided to stay there to put himself under the spiritual guidance of Ti Tsang. There Fa Yen learnt that all the philosophical ideas and theories that he had studied were absolutely of no avail if he wanted to obtain the final ultimate answer to the most ultimate existential question. A month or so had passed when one day, having been driven by Ti Tsang into a logical *impasse* and having finally confessed, 'O Master, I am now in a situation in which language is reduced to silence and thinking has no way to follow!', he heard his master remark, 'If you still are to talk about the ultimate Reality, see how it is nakedly apparent in everything and every event!' Fa Yen is thereupon said to have attained enlightenment.

This final remark of Ti Tsang discloses the Zen understanding of the thesis that 'the entire world of Being is but one single mind'. The thesis in this understanding means first and foremost that the self – which at this stage will more properly be written Self – directly and immediately sees its own self reflected on all things as 'two mirrors facing each other without there being between them even a shadow of a thing'.

Thus for a Zen master like Ti Tsang, the dictum: 'all things are but one mind' simply refers to a peculiar state of awareness in which the so-called 'object', a mountain for instance, and the so-called 'subject', i.e. a man, stand face to face with each other like two mirrors reflecting one another, there being absolutely nothing between the two. Since both are like lucid mirrors facing each other, one never can tell which is active and which is passive. In fact each of the two is both active and passive, reflecting and being reflected. There is no distinction to be made here between the 'subject' and the 'object' – 'the man sees the mountain, the mountain sees the man', as the above-mentioned Zen saying puts it. Note that there is no place even for the word 'and' between 'the man sees the mountain' and 'the mountain sees the man'. The man, i.e. the 'mind', immediately sees its own reality being reflected – or more strictly we should say: being actualized – in the mountain. But by this very act of the mind, the mountain, on its part, recognizes its own reality as it is actualized in the mind. And throughout the entire process, not a single thing, neither the mind nor the mountain, is objectified. For the whole thing, including the mind and the mountain, the 'subject' and the 'object', is a single act of *SEE*, one single act of the Mind-Reality. This, however, is not to assert that the act of *SEE* is pure 'subjectivity' because where there is absolutely no objectification of anything, there can be no subjectification of anything either.

But such a situation is not certainly anything which one could expect to actualize in the dimension of ordinary empirical experience. It actualizes, if at all, only in an extraordinary – so it appears to common sense – dimension of consciousness. Thus Fa Yen himself later developed his own idea about this point in his celebrated poem entitled 'The Whole World is One Single Mind' as follows:

> The whole world is but one single Mind. And all that exist are but one single Cognition. Since there is nothing but Cognition, and since all are but one Mind, the eye is able to recognize sounds and the ear colors. If colors do not enter into the ear, how could sounds touch the eye?

And yet the field of the Mind is so limitlessly vast and infinitely flexible that it may, and does, happen that the eye responds specifically to colors, and the ear to sounds. Then it is that the empirical world takes its rise out of the depths of the Mind. He goes on to say:

But when the eye is adjusted to colors, and when the ear responds to sounds, all existent things are discriminated and recognized. If all things were not thus distinguishable from one another, how could one see their dream-like existences? But of all these mountains, rivers and the great earth, what is there to change?, what is there not to change?

It is of utmost importance to note that the two different dimensions, i.e. that of the empirical world and that of Nothingness, are actualized at one and the same time in this single act of *SEE*. It is not the case that one witnesses this at one time and experiences that at another. Rather, one sees the Apparent in the Real, and the Real in the Apparent, there being no discrepancy between them. This is why many of the famous Zen sayings, poems and paintings look as if they were simply objective descriptions of Nature. Thus the Zen master Chia Shan Shan Hui (J.: Kas-san Zen-ne, 805-881) – 'Shan Hui of the mountain Chia' –, when asked 'How is the landscape of the mountain Chia (Chia Shan)?', replied:

> Monkeys have already gone home behind the blue peaks
> Embracing their young to their breasts.
> A bird has alighted before the deep-green rocks,
> Carrying a flower-petal in its beak.

Our Fa Yen is related to have remarked once on this poem: 'For thirty years I have mistakenly regarded this as a description of the external landscape!'

Does this remark of Fa Yen mean that the poem in truth is to be taken as a symbolic presentation of an inner landscape? Definitely not. He is trying to say something entirely different. In fact, the things of Nature like the monkeys, bird, blue peaks, green rock, flower-petal etc., are not symbols for 'something-beyond'. They *are* so many concretely real things. And the poem in this sense *is* a concrete description of external Nature. The important thing here to remark is that the natural landscape is seen with the eyes of the *SEE*. All the events that are described – the monkeys going home and the bird alighting, holding a flower in its beak – are regarded as the Eternal-Present evolving itself on the empirical axis of time and space. 'What is there to change?, what is there not to change?'

The relation between the Eternal-Present and the Time-Space dimension of existence in Zen consciousness is a very subtle and mobile one. It is mobile in the sense that the delicate equilibrium of the mutual interaction of the two dimensions one upon the other is ready to tilt at any moment to either direction. Thus it is now the Eternal-Present that is more prominently in view; the very next moment the Time-Space axis may protrude itself and hide the Eternal-Present behind it. In order to make this particular situation understandable, Zen sometimes has recourse to expressions that may be regarded as approaching symbolism. Then, instead of just throwing out upon the canvas of language bits of external Nature – as was the case with the description of the mountain landscape by Chia Shan – Zen describes certain things of Nature which are put into particular relations with one another in such a way that the description of Nature itself might graphically reproduce the aforementioned subtle and mobile relation between the two dimensions of Reality. The following verses are but one example:

> The shadows of the bamboos are sweeping the staircase,
> But there is no stirring of even a mote of dust.
> The moonlight is piercing to the bottom of the deep river,
> But there is not even a scar left in the waters.

The shadows of the bamboos are actually sweeping the staircase. That is, there is motion and commotion in the empirical dimension of the world. But no dust is stirred up by this phenomenal movement. That is, the supra-phenomenal dimension of Reality is eternally calm and quiet. It must be remarked that the commotion of the Apparent and the non-commotion of the Real are not actually separable one from the other. They actualize themselves simultaneously. That is to say, the non-commotion of the absolute dimension of Reality is actualized precisely through the commotion of the phenomenal dimension of the same Reality. The phenomenal commotion and the absolute tranquility are but two aspects of one single Reality. The act of *SEE* is of such a nature.

This delicate relation between the Apparent and the Real, Multiplicity and Unity in the act of *SEE* comes out still more clearly in some Zen sayings which have specifically been devised to visualize it. The Zen master Yung An Shan Ching

(J.: Ei An Zen Shō), for example, when asked, 'What is the one single color?', replied, 'Easy to recognize are the white particles in the snow; difficult to distinguish are the black (molecules) of soot in the ink'.[27] By this he wanted to indicate that the snow which from afar appears as one single mass of white color is found to contain, if examined closely, an infinite number of white particles each one of which is an individual, self-sufficient entity. In the same manner, in a cake of Chinese ink which appears to be a solid piece of black material, there are an infinity of individual molecules of soot.

Likewise Shao Shan Huan P'u (J.: Shō Zan Kan Fu), when asked, 'What is the aspect of the absolute Unity?', replied, 'A snowy heron flies away into the white sky; the mountain is far away and deep blue is its color'.[28]

More celebrated is the saying of Tung Shan Liang Chieh (J.: Tōzan Ryōkai, 807-869), the founder of the Ts'ao Tung (J.: Sō Tō) sect: 'Snow heaped up in a silver bowl, and a white heron hidden in the light of the full moon'.

The picture of a white thing, or an infinite number of white things, in the very midst of a broad white field, visualizes the subtle and mobile relation between the sensible and the supra-sensible. Metaphysically it refers to the *coincidentia oppositorum* that subsists between Mutliplicity and Unity – Multiplicity being in itself Unity, and Unity in itself Multiplicity. *Rūpaṃ śūnyatā, śūnyataiva rūpaṃ. Rūpān na pṛthak śūnyatā, śūnyatāyā na pṛthag rūpaṃ:* 'The sensible is Nothingness, Nothingness is the sensible. The sensible is no other than Nothingness; Nothingness is no other than the sensible'.[29]

The word 'Nothing' in this passage refers to the same thing as what is meant by the word *Mind* or *SEE* about which we have been talking. Since the reality itself which is at issue is of a contradictory – so it seems from the viewpoint of our common sense – nature, we are forced, in trying to describe it, to have recourse to a contradictory use of words, saying for instance, that the Mind is sensible and not sensible, transcendental and not transcendental at one and the same time.

The Mind-Reality can by no means be said to be purely sensible; it *is* transcendental in the sense that it transcends the limits of the empirical ego. For the Mind in the sense of *SEE* is the self-actualizing activity of the Cosmic Ego. But, again, it cannot be said to be purely transcendental, because the activity of this Cosmic Ego is actualized only through the consciousness of a concrete individual person. We must go further and say that the activity of the concrete individual 'mind' is itself the *actus* of the transcendental Mind. There is thus, properly speaking, absolutely no distance between the sensible and the transcendental. And yet there is a certain respect in which they *are* distinguishable from one another; that is, the individual 'mind' is most concretely individual, while the Cosmic Mind is really (i.e. non-metaphorically) absolute and transcendental. And the Mind-Reality in its real sense is a contradictory unity of these two aspects.

This peculiar structure of the Mind-Reality is indicated by Lin Chi in the following way:

> What do you think is Reality? Reality is nothing other than the Mind-Reality. The Mind-Reality has no definite form. It permeates and runs through the whole universe. It is, at this very moment, in this very place, so vividly present. But the minds of the ordinary people are not mature enough to see this. Thus they establish everywhere names and concepts (like the 'Absolute', the 'Holy', 'enlightenment', etc.), and vainly search after Reality in these names and letters.[30]

The sentence: 'It is, at this very moment, in this very place, so vividly present', refers to the individual and sensible aspect of the Mind-Reality. The Mind-Reality, cosmic and all-pervading as it is, necessarily and invariably actualizes itself in the individual minds of individual persons. This point is made clear by the following words of Lin Chi:

> O Brethren, the Mind-Reality has no definite form. It permeates and runs through the whole universe. In the eye it acts as sight; in the ear it acts as hearing; in the nose it acts as the sense of smell; in the mouth it speaks; in the hand it grasps; in the foot it walks. All these activities are originally nothing but one single Spiritual Illumination, which diversifies itself into harmonious correspondences.[31] It is because the Mind has in this way no definite form of its own that it can so freely act in every form.[32]

The contradictory unity of the most concretely individual-present and the most transcendentally absolute-eternal in the *actus* of the Mind or *SEE* is given by Lin Chi a very original description in the following passage:

O venerable Friends, (instead of being caught in the net of phenomenal things), you should grasp directly the Man who is pulling the wires of these shadowy phenomena behind the scenes. If you but realize that the Man[33] *is* the ultimate Source of all Buddhas, (you will immediately see that) any place in which you actually are at the present moment *is* the ultimate and absolute place for you, o Brethren!

(You are now listening to my discourse.) It is not your material bodies that understand the discourse. Do your spleen, stomach and liver understand the discourse? No! Does the empty space understand the discourse? No! What, then, is the one that is actually understanding my discourse? It is no other than you yourself who are thus undeniably standing before me. I mean by 'you' that fellow who, without having any definite visible form, is luminous by himself, illuminating himself. It is this very fellow who is actually listening to this discourse of mine and understands it. If you but realize this point, you are on the spot the same as our spiritual ancestor Buddha. Then, everything you do, in all time without interruption, will be in perfect conformity with Reality.[34]

The inner structure of the Mind is thus extremely elusive, at least to the discriminating intellect. Consequently the word 'mind' as used in Zen texts could be very misleading. There is in any case always noticeable in the actual usage of the word a subtle interplay of the sensible and the supra-sensible orders of things. As a telling example of this point we shall mention a celebrated anecdote concerning the debut of the sixth Patriarch Hui Nêng (J.: E Nō) into the world of Zen Buddhism in southern China.

At that time Hui Nêng was still concealing his identity for some political reasons – so we are told. One day he sat in a corner of a temple in Kuang Chou listening to a lecture being given on a Buddhist Sutra. All of a sudden the wind rose, and the flag at the gate of the temple began to flutter. This immediately induced some of the monks in the audience into a hot debate. It started by one of them remarking, 'Look! The flag is fluttering!' 'No', another objected, 'it is not the flag that is moving. It is the wind that is moving!' An endless discussion ensued as to what was *really* moving, the flag or the wind. At last Hui Nêng could not restrain himself any longer. He said, 'It is not that the wind moves. Nor is it the case that the flag moves. O honorable Brethren, it is in reality your minds that are fluttering!'

This remark of Hui Nêng about the 'fluttering' of the 'mind', as it stands, is liable to lead one into thinking that he was speaking of the individual mind or the individual consciousness of a concrete person. Furthermore, this interpretation seems in fact to suit the situation very well. It does give a certain amount of insight into an important aspect of the Zen world-view. One might find this kind of explanation interesting or curious, and being satisfied, go no further. But that will be fatal to the real understanding of the Zen world-view.

The truly delicate point about this is that such an interpretation of the situation here in question is not entirely wrong either. For it *is* partially true, though not totally. In order to obtain a total understanding of the matter, we have to begin by taking the word 'mind' as it was used by Hui Nêng in the sense of the Mind or *SEE* having reference to both the empirical and transcendental dimensions of the Zen awareness. It is the Mind taken in this sense that *really* moves.

This last statement implies first of all that in the empirical dimension, the mind of the individual person is set in motion. And the movement or 'fluttering' of the concrete and individual mind on the empirical level of experience becomes actualized in the fluttering motion of the flag in the wind. Here again, be it remarked, there is properly speaking absolutely no room for the word *and* to be inserted between the three factors of the movement. The utmost we can say by way of description is this: By the very movement of the mind, the flag-wind is set in motion. The movement of these three things is in fact one single movement.

This, however, is still but a partial description of the Reality. For, according to the typical Zen understanding which we have explained earlier, there can be no fluttering of the individual 'mind' unless there be at the same time the fluttering of the Mind. A simultaneous fluttering motion occurs in the two dimensions, sensible and supra-sensible. And since there is no connecting *and* between these two dimensions except in rational analysis, the fluttering of the Mind in reality is the fluttering of the individual consciousness. And the fluttering of the Mind of this nature is actualized in the phenomenal world as a total phenomenon of 'a man being conscious of a flag fluttering in the wind'.

As the flag flutters, the whole universe flutters. And this

fluttering is an *actus* of the Mind. But here again we find ourselves faced with a paradoxical situation – 'paradoxical' from the viewpoint of common sense. For the 'whole universe' in this understanding is nothing other than the Mind. Since the Mind is in this manner an absolute whole for which there is no distinction of the 'inside' and the 'outside', and beyond which or apart from which there can be nothing 'else' conceivable, the fluttering of the Mind is no fluttering at all. There is in reality absolutely no movement here. As we have observed before, the Eternal-Present is eternally calm and tranquil in spite of all the motions of the Mind on another dimension.

This 'paradoxical' structure of Reality is beautifully and concisely pictured in the famous saying of P'ang Yün (J.: Hō On):[35]

> Lovely snow flakes! They are falling on no other place.

It is snowing hard. It is snowing in big beautiful white flakes. Each one of these flakes, considered individually and as a phenomenon pertaining to external Nature, is certainly falling from the sky to the earth. However, at a metaphysical-epistemological stage at which both the snow and the ego-spectator are fused into the original unity of the Mind so that the whole universe has turned into the snow, the snow flakes have no place upon which to fall. As an external landscape, the snow flakes are falling. But as an inner landscape of the Mind, there is no falling, no movement, for the whole universe cannot fall toward any other place. Motion can take place only in a 'relative' world. It is meaningless to speak of the motion of a thing in a dimension where there is conceivable no 'outside' system of reference which the thing may be referred to. If, even then, we are to use the 'image' of falling, we would probably have to say that the snow flakes, i.e. the Mind, is falling toward their own place, i.e. the Mind. But evidently such a falling is no falling at all.

Exactly the same idea is expressed by Huang Lung Hui Nan (J.: Ō Ryū E Nan, 1001-1069)[36] through a similar imagery:

> 'The drizzling spring rain! It has been falling from last evening, through the whole night until dawn. Drop after drop, it falls. But it is

falling on no other place. Tell me, if you can! To what place does it fall?' Then, without waiting for an answer, he himself replied: 'It drops upon your eyes! It is penetrating into your nose!'

It is highly significant that Huang Lung combines here two contradictory statements. On the ōne hand, he says, the rain is falling on no other place, and, on the other, he states that it is falling upon the nose and eyes.

The rain does not fall anywhere, to begin with, because in the cosmic landscape of the Mind, the whole universe is nothing other than Rain. If the *whole* universe is Rain, it will be but natural that the latter should find no 'other' place upon which to fall. The entire universe which is no other than the Mind (i.e. *SEE*), is Raining. And since the universe in its entirety is Raining, the Rain, if it falls at all anywhere, cannot but fall to its own self. That is to say, Raining in this particular situation is the same as non-Raining. Yet, on the other hand, it is also true that the rain is actually falling upon the bodily eyes and penetrating into the bodily nose of an individual person. Otherwise there would be no awareness of the 'falling and not-falling' of the Rain in the cosmic dimension of the Mind. The bodily eyes and nose of an individual concrete person are the only *loci* where the Mind-Rain can actualize itself here and now.

What precedes is to be considered a lengthy paraphrase of the Zen interpretation of the 'Mind-Only'-Theory as represented by the extremely terse dictum: *I chieh hsin* (J.: *Issai shin*), 'all things are Mind'. It will have been understood by now that a dictum of this sort does not mean that the whole universe comes into, or is contained in, the 'mind'. It simply means that the whole universe *is* in itself and by itself the Mind.

A monk once asked the famous Zen master Chang Sha Ching Ch'ên (J.: Chōsha Keishin, Ninth century): 'How is it possible to transform the mountains, rivers, and the great earth (i.e. the whole universe) and reduce them to my own mind?' The master answered: 'How is it possible, indeed, to transform the mountains, rivers and the great earth and reduce them to my own mind?' The question and the answer are exactly identical with each other, word for word. But they arise from two entirely different dimensions of awareness. The monk who asks the question understands the 'all things are Mind' at the empirical level, however philosophically elaborated it may be, wondering how it is at all possible for the whole universe to be reduced to one single mind. Note that the word 'mind' itself is taken in the sense of the empirical ego. Chang Sha's answer is a rhetorical question. He means to say: It is absolutely impossible to reduce the whole universe to one single mind, because the whole universe *is* from the beginning the Mind, there being no discrepancy between them. There is, in this understanding, no opposition between the mountains, rivers and the great earth as 'external' Nature and the mind as the 'internal' domain. There is no 'mind' to assimilate the external Nature into its own 'inner' unity.

VI   The Field Structure of Ultimate Reality

We are now in a position to analyze more theoretically the basic structure of Zen epistemology. For that purpose we propose to introduce the concept of 'Field' into our exposition. In fact, what we have been discussing in the foregoing under the key-term 'Mind' may philosophically be represented as a peculiar kind of dynamic Field, from which one could obtain *through abstraction* the perceiving 'subject' and, again *through abstraction*, the object perceived. The 'Field' thus understood will refer to the original, unbroken unity of the whole, functioning as the epistemological *prius* of our experience of the phenomenal world.

We must remember in this connection that the philosophical thinking of Zen – and of Buddhism in general – is based on, and centers around, the category of *relatio* instead of *substantia*. Everything, the whole world of Being, is looked at from a relational point of view. Nothing is to be regarded as self-subsistent and self-sufficient. The 'subject' is 'subject' because it is relative to 'object'. The 'object' is 'object' because it is relative to 'subject'. In this system there is no such thing as *Ding an sich*. The *an sich* is most emphatically denied. For a *Ding* can be established as a *Ding* only when it is permeated by the light of the 'subject'. Likewise there is no 'mind' or 'subject' which has no reference to the sphere of *Dinge*. And since the 'subject' which is thus essentially relative to the 'object', is, as we have seen earlier, both the individual 'mind' and the universal Mind, the whole thing, i.e. the Field itself, must necessarily be also of a relational nature. It is in fact a Relation itself between the sensible and the supra-sensible.

Viewed in the light of this consideration, what we ordinarily call and regard as 'mind' (or 'subject', 'consciousness', etc.) is nothing more than an abstraction. It is a concept or image which is obtained when we articulate, whether consciously or unconsciously, the originally non-articulated Field into an active and a passive sphere, and establish the former as an independently subsistent entity. Likewise the 'object' or 'thing' is an abstraction taken out of the whole non-articulated Field by a kind of abstractive inflection of the latter towards the 'passive' sphere.

Zen, however, does not want to remain content with this observation. It goes further and insists that we should attain to a stage at which we could witness the originally non-articulated Field articulating itself freely, of its own accord, and not through the dichotomizing activity of our intellect, into either the 'subject' or the 'object'. It is important to note that in this self-articulation of the Field, the whole Field is involved, not this or that particular sphere of it. Instead of being an abstraction, the 'subject' or the 'object' in such a case is a total concretization or actualization of the entire Field. Thus – to go back to the particular system of formulation which we used in the earlier part of this paper – if the total Field in its original state of non-articulation is to be represented by the formula: *SEE*, the same total Field in its articulated state may be formulated as: *I SEE THIS* (all words being in capital letters). This last formula must remain the same, whether the whole Field actualizes itself as the Subject or as the Object. Thus in this particular context, the Subject or *I* means *I* (= *I SEE THIS*). Likewise, the Object or *THIS* means (*I SEE THIS* =) *THIS*.

At this stage, when I say, for example, 'I', I do not thereby mean my empirical ego. What is meant is rather the 'I' as a concrete actualization of the entire Field. The 'I' at this stage *is* actually 'I', but it is an infinitely dynamic and mobile kind of 'I' in the sense that it is an 'I' that can at any moment be freely turned into 'THIS' and reveal itself in the latter form. In the same way, 'THIS' is not fixedly 'THIS'. It is a 'THIS' that is ready at any moment to change into 'I' and begin to function as an aspect of, or in the form of, 'I'. All this is possible simply because each 'I' and 'THIS' is in itself a total actualization of the same entire Field.

This dynamic relation between the Subject and Object is admirably described in the following anecdote which in the course of history has come to count among the most important of all Zen *kōans*. The story brings onto the stage two prominent figures in the Golden Age of Zen Buddhism. One is Ma Tsu Tao I (J.: Ba So Dō Itsu, 709-788) and Pai Chang Huai Hai (J.: Hyakujō Ekai, 720-814). Pai Chang, who is destined to become later one of the greatest Zen masters, is in this story still a young disciple of Ma Tsu. The anecdote as it is recorded in the *Pi Yen Lu*³⁷ reads:

> Listen! Once, Ma Tsu was on his way to some place, accompanied by Pai Chang, when all of a sudden they saw a wild duck flying away above their heads. Ma asked, 'What is it?' Pai answered, 'A wild duck'. Ma, 'Where is it flying to?' Pai, 'It has already flown away!' Thereupon the Master grabbed the nose of Pai Chang and twisted it violently. Pai cried out in pain, 'Ouch!' The Master remarked on the spot, 'How can you say that the wild duck has flown away?!'

The young Pai Chang is here looking up at the wild duck as it flies away. The wild duck exists as an object independently of Pai Chang who is looking at it . In his eyes, it is as though the bird were subsistent by itself, and it is as though the self-subsistent bird flew away and disappeared beyond the horizon. It is only when he has his nose grabbed and twisted that it dawns upon his mind like a flash that the wild duck is not an 'object' existing independently of the activity of his mind, and that the bird is still there with him, or rather, as his own self. The entire Field comprising both himself and the bird, becomes alive and reveals itself nakedly to his eyes. Pai Chang is said to have attained enlightenment on that occasion.

The anecdote presents an interesting example of the emphasis turning from the 'objective' aspect of the Field (represented by the wild duck) towards its 'subjective' aspect (represented by Pai Chang himself) in such a way that, as a result, the dynamics of the Field in its entirety is realized on the spot.

In the next anecdote, on the contrary, which is as a Zen kōan probably even more famous than the preceding one, the emphasis is concentrated upon the 'objective' sphere of the

Field. Otherwise expressed, we witness here the whole Field of *I SEE THIS* becoming reduced to the single point of *THIS*, and standing as such before our own eyes. The kōan is known as the cypress-tree-in-the-courtyard of Chao Chou (J.: Jō Shū),[38] and is recorded in the famous kōan-collection *Wu Mên Kuan* (J.: *Mu Mon Kan*).[39] It reads:

> Listen! Once a monk asked Chao Chou, 'Tell me, what is the significance of the First Patriarch's coming from the West?' Chao Chou replied, 'The cypress tree in the courtyard!'

The monk asked about the significance of the historical event of Bodhidharma coming all the way from India to China. His intention apparently was to grasp from the inside the significance of this event so that he might participate existentially in the living world of Zen. The answer given by Chao Chou took a very abrupt and unexpected turn to disconcert the monk: 'The cypress tree in the courtyard!'

The inner mechanism of this statement is just the same as that shown in the anecdote of the wild duck and Pai Chang. Only the energy of the Field is this time inflected towards the opposite direction. Chao Chou abruptly puts under the monk's nose the whole Field of Reality in the most vividly real and concrete form of a cypress tree. In other terms, instead of presenting the Field as *I* (/*I SEE THIS*) – as Ma Tsu did with Pai Chang – Chao Chou presents it as (*I SEE THIS* =) *THIS*. This indicates that the 'cypress tree' as presented by Chao Chou is not *simply* or *only* a cypress tree. For it carries here the whole weight of the Field. The cypress tree, a real and concrete cypress tree as it is, stands before our eyes as something growing out of the very depths of Nothingness – the Eternal-Present being actualized at this present moment in this particular place in the dimension of the temporal and phenomenal. In a single cypress tree in the courtyard there is concentrated the whole energy of the Field of Reality.

As Niu T'ou Fa Jung (J.: Go Zu Hō Yū 594-657) remarks:[40]

> 'A mote of dust flies, and the entire sky is clouded. A particle of rubbish falls, and the whole earth is covered'.

And Hung Chih Chêng Chüeh (J.: Wanshi Shōgaku, 1091-1157):[41]

'The Reality (i.e. the Field) has no definite aspect of its own; it reveals itself in accordance with things. The Wisdom (i.e. *I SEE*) has no definite knowledge of its own; it illumines in response to situations. Look! the green bamboo is so serenely green; the yellow flower so profusely yellow! Just pick up anything you like, and see! In every single thing *IT* is so nakedly manifested'.

In the philosophical view of Zen a 'concrete' or 'real' thing in the true sense of the term is of such a nature. What we usually regard as a concrete thing – the 'primary substance' of Aristotle – is, from the point of view of Zen, nothing but an abstract entity, not 'reality'. A really concrete individual must be, for Zen, an individual-concrete which is permeated and penetrated by the absolute-universal, or rather which *is* the absolute-universal. A cypress tree is an individual particular; it is *THIS*. But through being *THIS*, it cannot but be an actualization of *I SEE THIS*. The cypress tree is here the focus-point of the Field of Reality. We now understand what is really meant by Lin Chi when, as we have earlier observed, he states that 'the Mind-Reality permeates and runs through the whole universe', but that it is actualized in 'the concrete person who is actually listening to his discourse'. Lin Chi presents the whole thing in the form of Man, the 'subject' in the sense of the master of the whole Field of Reality, the absolute Selfhood. Chao Chou presents it in the form of the Cypress Tree, the 'object' in the sense of the absolute center of the selfsame Field, From whichever direction one may approach, one invariably ends by encountering the Field itself.

What is most important to remark about this problem is that seeing the cypress tree in the courtyard as an actualization of the Field does not mean seeing 'something', say, the transcendental Absolute, beyond the concrete thing. Following Hua Yen (J.: Kegon) philosophy which reached its perfection in China, Zen emphatically denies Something Metaphysical lying at the back of the Phenomenal.

Quite the contrary, Zen 'absolutizes' the Phenomenal itself. The cypress tree in its concrete reality *is* the Absolute at this very moment in this very place. It is not even a 'self-manifestation' of the Absolute. For the Absolute has no space 'other' than itself for manifesting itself. And such is the structure of the 'objective' aspect of the Field.

VII   The Zen Image of Man

The foregoing section will have made it clear that the Reality as Zen conceives it may best be represented as a Field saturated with energy, a particular state of tension constituted by two major sources of force, the Subject and the Object, the word Subject being understood in the sense of *I* (= *I SEE THIS*), i.e. as an actualization of the whole Field, and the word Object in the sense of (*I SEE THIS* =) *THIS*, i.e. again as an actualization of the same Field. We have also observed how the balance of forces is delicately maintained. The Field itself never loses itself, toward whichever of its two spheres its inner energy be inflected. But the actual – i.e. conscious – point at which the balance is maintained is found to be constantly moving through the entire Field, from the point of pure subjectivity to the point of pure objectivity.

Four major forms are clearly distinguishable in this structure.

1.   Sometimes it is as though the Field maintains perfect stability, without there being any particular salient point in the entire Field as the center of the stability. Then the whole Field maintains itself in a state of extreme tension, a state of absolute and universal Illumination, an Awareness where there is nothing whatsoever for man to be aware of. There is in this state neither the 'subject' nor the 'object'. Both *I* and *THIS* disappear from the surface of the Field. This is a state about which Zen often says: 'In the original state of Reality there is absolutely nothing whatsoever'. It is also often referred to as *Oriental Nothingness* in the philosophies of the East.

2.   But, sometimes, out of this eternal Stillness, there suddenly arises a glaring consciousness of the Subject. The

energy that has been evenly saturating the entire Field is now aroused from the state of quietude, gushes forth toward the 'subjective' sphere of the Field, and ends by being crystallized into the Subject. Then, the Field in its entirety is actualized in the luminous point of *I*. Nothing else is visible. The whole world is nothing other than *I*. In such a state, the Zen master would say: 'I alone sit on top of the highest mountain', I alone; nothing else, nobody else. The important point here, however, is that the 'I' is not an empirical ego. The 'I' is a subjective crystallization of the entire Field. Thus the dictum: 'I alone sit on top of the highest mountain' implies that the whole universe is sitting on top of the mountain with the man, or in the form of an individual man.

3. Sometimes, again, the energy aroused from its stability flows toward the 'objective' sphere of the Field. Then it is the Object that is alone visible – the stately Cypress Tree towering up in the midst of the limitless Void – although the same amount of energy that could at any moment be crystallized into the Subject is also being mobilized in the appearance of the Object.

4. Finally the Field may go back again to its original state of Stillness, with the difference that this time both the Subject and the Object are given their proper places in the Field. Superficially we are now back to our old familiar world of empirical experience, where 'the flower is naturally red and the willow is naturally green'. With regard to its inner structure, however, this old familiar world of ours is infinitely different from the same world as seen through the eyes of the purely empirical ego. For our old familiar world, this time, reveals itself in its pristine purity and innocence. The empirical world which has once lost itself into the abyss of Nothingness, now returns to life again in an unusual freshness. 'Here we realize', Dōgen[42] observes, 'that the mountains, the rivers, and the great earth in their original purity and serenity should never be confused with the mountains, rivers, and the great earth (as seen through the eyes of the ordinary people)'. The same idea is expressed in a more poetic way as:

> Though the wind has fallen off, flower-petals are falling still,
> As a bird sings, the mountain deepens its silence and stillness.

'The wind has fallen off', that is, the entire world of Being has fallen into the eternal quietude of Nothingness; and yet 'flower petals are falling still', that is, all things are still vividly and concretely maintaining themselves in their original empirical commotion. 'As a bird sings', that is, precisely because of this colorful presence of things in the empirical dimension, 'the mountain deepens its silence and stillness', that is, Nothingness makes itself felt in its unfathomable depth.

Someone asked the great Zen master of the Lin Chi school in the Sung dynasty, Hsü T'ang Chih Yü (J.: Ki Dō Chi Gu, 1185-1269), 'Tell me, what is the significance of the First Patriarch's coming from the West?'[43] He answered:

> Deep is the mountain, no guest is coming.
> All day long I hear the monkeys chattering.

The dynamic structure of the Field which is thus constituted by the very peculiar tension between the *I* (= *I SEE THIS*) and the (*I SEE THIS* =) *THIS*, and which is actualizable, as we have just explained, in four principal forms was most clearly recognized by Lin Chi who formulated them into what is now usually known as the Four Standards of Lin Chi.

The expression 'Four Standards' means four basic standards by which a Zen master might measure the degrees of the spiritual perfection of his disciples. It is noteworthy, however, that this particular expression, or this particular understanding of the matter, did not originate from Lin Chi himself. It does not necessarily represent his own understanding of the issue. The expression has its origin rather in the historical fact that in the course of the development of the Lin Chi school, the four states as described by Lin Chi came to be used very often by the masters in measuring the depth of the Zen consciousness of the disciples. Lin Chi's intention was, I believe, primarily to establish theoretically the four principal forms which the same Field of Reality can assume, and thereby to indicate the dynamic structure of the Field.

Let us give in translation the relevant passage from the *Lin Chi Lu*.[44]

Once at the time of the evening lesson, the Master told the monks under his guidance the following:

'Sometimes the man (i.e. the 'subject') is snatched away (i.e. totally negated) while the environment (i.e. the 'object') is left intact. Sometimes the environment is snatched away, while the man is left intact. Sometimes the man and the environment are both snatched away. Sometimes the man and the environment are both left intact'.

Thereupon one of the monks came forward and asked, 'What kind of a thing is the-man-being-snatched-away and the-environment-being-left-intact?'

The Master answered, 'As the mild sunshine of the springtime covers the entire earth, the earth weaves out a variegated brocade. The new-born baby has long-trailing hair; the hair is as white as a bundle of yarns'.[45]

The monk asked, 'What kind of a thing is the-environment-being-snatched-away and the-man-being-left-intact?'

The Master answered, 'The royal command pervades the whole world;[46] the generals stationed on the frontiers do not raise the tumult of war'.

The monk asked, 'What kind of a thing is the-man-and-the-environment-being-both-snatched-away?'

The Master answered, 'The two remote provinces have lost contact with the central Government'.

The monk asked, 'What kind of a thing is the-man-and-the-environment-being-both-left-intact?'

The Master answered, 'As the King looks down from the top of his palace, he sees the people in the field enjoying their peaceful life'.

It is commonly held that of those four states, the last, i.e. the state in which both the man and the environment are left intact, represents the highest degree of the Zen consciousness. Ontologically it corresponds to what Hua Yen (J.: Kegon) philosophy calls the 'metaphysical dimension of the unobstructed mutual interpenetration among all things and events' (J.: ji-ji muge hokkai), a metaphysical dimension in which the world of Being appears as an infinitely huge network of gems, each one of which illumines and reflects all the others. And in the Hua Yen school, too, this 'dimension' is considered to be the object of the highest and ultimate vision of Reality. But from the standpoint of a Zen master like Lin Chi, each one of the four states that have just been described is in itself a form of the total actualization of the Field. The Field, in other words, is of such a mobile and delicately flexible nature that if emphasis is laid on the 'subjective' side, the whole thing turns into the Subject, while if on the contrary emphasis is laid on the 'objective' side, the whole thing turns into the Object. Similarly, if nothing is seen, there is neither Subject nor Object. But if the emphasis is evenly diffused all over the Field, there is the Subject, there is the Object, and the world is seen as a vast, limitless Unity of a multiplicity of separate things. And whichever of these outer forms it may assume, the Field always remains in its original state, that of *I SEE THIS*.

Thus the Field is not to be confused with the purely 'objective' aspect of the world of Being, i.e. Nature conceived as something existing outside the 'mind'. Nor is it to be confused with the purely 'subjective' consciousness of man. That which establishes the 'subject' as the 'subject' (or consciousness as consciousness) and the 'object' as the 'object' (or Nature as Nature) is something that transcends – in a certain sense – this very distinction between 'subject' and 'object' and manifests itself, by self-determination, now as the Subject and now as the Object.

It is on such an understanding of the Field of Reality that Lin Chi founds his characteristic image of Man. For him, Man *is* the Field. Man, in his view, is a personal, human actualization of the Field. And in fact there is absolutely no other type of actualization for the Field. The dynamics of the Field of Reality which we have analyzed is realizable only through the individual man, through the inner transformation of his consciousness. Man, in this sense, is *the* locus of the actualization of the whole universe. And when the actualization really takes place in this locus, the 'man' is transformed into what is called by Lin Chi the 'True Man without any ranks'. As a total actualization of the Field, the True Man embodies the dynamics of the Field. Now he may realize himself as the *I* (= *I SEE THIS*); now he may be the (*I SEE THIS* =) *THIS*; again, he can be Nothingness, that is, sheer (*I SEE THIS*); and he can also be the nakedly apparent *I SEE THIS*. He is completely free. Lin Chi refers to this kind of freedom which characterizes Man as the direct actualization of the Field when he speaks of 'Man's becoming the absolute Master of the place, in whatever place he may happen to be'.[47]

Thus Lin Chi's image of Man, if looked at from the common-sense viewpoint proves to be something extremely difficult to grasp. It is difficult to grasp because it presents 'man' in a contradictory way. The image must necessarily take on a contradictory form, because the Field of Reality which forms its basis is itself a contradictory unity of the sensible and the supra-sensible.

The image of Man presented by Lin Chi is not primarily an image of the sensible 'man' who sees with his eyes, hears with his ears, speaks with his tongue and so on and so forth – in short 'man' as the self-conscious empirical ego. Rather it is the image of the supra-sensible Man who, existing above the level of empirical experience, activates all the sense organs and makes the intellect function as it does. And yet, on the other hand, this supra-sensible, supra-empirical Man, cannot actualize himself independently of the empirical 'man'.

Thus man, inasmuch as he is a *total* actualization of the Field of Reality, is on the one hand a Cosmic Man comprehending in himself the whole universe – 'the Mind-Reality', as Lin Chi says, which pervades and runs through the whole world of Being' – and on the other he is this very concrete individual 'man' who exists and lives here and now, as a concentration point of the entire energy of the Field. He is individual and supra-individual.

If we are to approach Man from his 'individual' aspect, we shall have to say that in the concrete individual person there lives another person. This second person in himself is beyond all limitations of time and space, because the Field, of which he is the most immediate embodiment, is the Eternal Now and the Ubiquitous Here. But always and everywhere he accompanies, or is completely unified with, the concrete individual person. In fact Lin Chi does not admit any discrepancy at all between the two persons. Whatever the individual man does is done by the universal person. When, for instance, the former walks, it is in reality the latter that walks. The universal person acts only through the limbs of the individual person. It is this double structure of personality that Lin Chi never wearies of trying to make his disciples realize by themselves and through themselves.

But in most cases his disciples get simply confused and dismayed. For, the moment they try to turn their attention to the universal person in themselves, he disappears. When they walk naturally, he is there with them; he is walking with them; or rather it is he who is walking by their feet. But the moment they become conscious of their own act of walking while they are walking, the universal man is no longer there; he has already receded to where they know not. This seemingly strange phenomenon is due to the very simple fact that paying attention to something, turning the spotlight of consciousness toward something means objectifying it. The universal man, being the absolute Selfhood, i.e. pure subjectivity, must necessarily cease to be himself as soon as he is put into the position of an 'object'.

Despite this difficulty Lin Chi with extraordinary stringency requires his disciples to grasp immediately, without ever objectifying it, this absolute unity of the two persons in themselves.

> One day the Master took his seat in the lecture hall and said: 'Over the bulky mass of your reddish flesh (i.e. the physical body) there is a True Man without any rank. He is constantly coming in and going out through the gates of your face (i.e. your sense organs). If you have not yet encountered him, catch him, catch him here and now!'
>
> At that moment a monk came out and asked, 'What kind of a fellow is this True Man?'
>
> The Master suddenly came down from the platform, grabbed at the monk, and urged him, 'Tell me, tell me!'
>
> The monk shrank for an instant.
>
> The Master on the spot thrust him away saying, 'Ah, what a useless dirt-scraper this True-Man-without-any-rank of yours is!' And immediately he retired to his private quarters.

The monk 'shrank for an instant', that is, he prepared himself for giving an adequate answer. But in that very instant, the discriminating act of thinking intrudes itself; the True Man becomes objectified and is lost. The True Man, when he is represented as an 'object', is nothing more than a 'dried up dirt-scraper'. The Master grabbed at the monk with violence, urging him to witness on the spot the True Man who is no other than the monk's true self. The Master resorted to such a seemingly violent and unreasonable behaviour because he wanted the monk to encounter the True Man in his pure subjectivity, without objectifying him. The monk, however, failed to do so. He did objectify his own True Man by attempting, if only for a fraction of an instant, to *think about* him instead of *becoming* or simply *being* the True Man. But once objectified in this way, the True Man is no longer 'without any rank'; he is qualified by all sorts of determinations and delimitations in terms of time and space. The 'now' is no longer the Eternal Now as it is actualized at this very moment. The 'here' is no longer the Ubiquitous Here as it is actualized in this very place.

The image of the True Man as given in the passage which we have just read; namely, the image of Someone coming into the fleshy body and going out of it at every moment, is in reality a rhetorical device. The truth is that it is wrong even to talk about two persons being unified into one person. The two persons whom our analytic intellect distinguishes one from the other and which the rhetorical device presents as (1) the bulky mass of reddish flesh and (2) the True Man transcending all temporal and spatial determinations, are in reality absolutely one and the same person. The True Man as understood by Lin Chi is the sensible *and* super-sensible person in an absolute unity prior even to the bifurcation into the sensible and the super-sensible.

What constitutes the most salient feature of Lin Chi's thought in terms of the history of Zen philosophy is the fact that he crystallized into such a lively image of Man what we have been discussing in the course of the present Essay, first under the traditional Buddhist key-term, 'No-Mind' or 'Mind' and then under the modern philosophical key-term 'Field'. As we have often pointed out, Lin Chi's entire thinking centers around Man, and a whole world-view is built up upon the basis of the image of the True Man. What he actually deals with under the name of Man is, objectively speaking, almost the same as what is usually referred to in Mahayana Buddhism in general by such words as Reality, Nothingness, Is-ness, Mind, etc. But his particular approach to the problem casts an illuminating light on one of the most characteristic traits of Oriental philosophy; namely, the decisive importance given to the subjective dimension of man in determining the objective dimension in which the Reality discloses itself to him. And in particular, it brings home to us the fact that, according to Zen, the highest dimension of Reality, i.e. Reality in its pristine and unblemished originality, becomes visible to us only and exclusively at the extreme limit of our own subjectivity, that is, when we become through and through ourselves.

Notes

1. It is highly significant in this connection that one of the leading Zen masters of the present age, Mumon Yamada, has produced a book entitled 'Who Am I?', *Watashi-wa Dare-ka?* (Tokyo, 1966). The book is a modern interpretation of the First Part of the 'Sayings and Doings of Lin Chi'. In this work the author raises and discusses the problem of Man as formulated in this personal form as one of the most pressing problems which contemporary men must face in the present-day situation of the world.

2. Or 'suchness' *(tathatā)* as the Buddhists would call it.

3. Dōgen (1200-1253) is one of the greatest Zen masters Japan has ever produced. His major work *Shōbōgenzō* is a record of his deep reflections on matters pertaining to Man and the world from the Zen point of view. Besides, it is perhaps the most philosophical of all works written by the Zen masters, whether of China or Japan.

4. Lin Chi I Hsüan (J.: Rinzai Gigen, d. 867). A disciple of the famous Huang Po (J.: Ōbaku, d. 850), and himself the founder of one of the so-called Five Houses of Zen Buddhism (the Lin Chi school), Lin Chi was one of the greatest Zen masters not only of the T'ang dynasty but of all ages. His basic teachings, practical and theoretical, are recorded in a book known under the title of 'The Sayings and Doings of Lin Chi' (*Lin Chi Lu*, J.: *Rinzai Roku*), a work compiled by his disciples after his death. In the present paper, all quotations from this book are made from the modern edition by Seizan Yanagida, Kyoto, 1961.

5. We would like to put emphasis on the word 'thought', because insofar as the personal experience of enlightenment is concerned, we cannot see any real difference among the representative Zen masters. Lin Chi's teacher, Huang Po, for instance, was evidently as great (if not greater) a master as Lin Chi himself. But the *thought* which Huang Po develops in his work, *The Transmission of the Mind*, is admittedly fairly commonplace, showing no particular originality of its own.

6. *Lin Chi Lu*, 36, p. 60.

7. *Ibid.*, 28, p. 40.

8. Nan Ch'üan P'u Yüan (J.: Nan Sen Fu Gen, 748-834).

9. J.: *Hekigan Roku* ('Blue Rock Records'), a work of the eleventh century (Sung dynasty), *Kōan* No. 40.

10. Lu Kêng (764-834) was a high official of the T'ang dynasty who occupied a very important position in the administrative machinery of the central government. In Zen Buddhism he was a lay disciple of Nan Ch'üan.

11. Sêng Chao (J.: Sō Jō, 374-414), known as 'the monk Chao'. A Taoist at first, he later turned to Mahayana Buddhism under the direction of the famous Kumārajīva (344-413) who came from Central Asia to China in 401 and who translated many of the Buddhist Sutras and theoretical works on Buddhism from Sanscrit to Chinese. The monk Chao is counted among the greatest of Kumārajīva's disciples. Chao, though he died at the age of 31, left a number of important works on Buddhist philosophy. His interpretation of the concept of Nothingness or 'Void' in particular, which was Taoistic to a considerable extent, exercised a tremendous influence on the rise and development of Zen in China. He is rightly regarded as one of the predecessors of Zen Buddhism.

12. Bertrand Russell: *The Problems of Philosophy*, Oxford, 1954, pp. 8-9.

13. A similar opposition against philosophical 'essentialism' is observable in the relation of Taoism to Confucianism. See my Eranos paper on *The Absolute and the Perfect Man in Taoism* (Eranos-Jahrbuch XXXVI, 1967) pp. 384-411 in particular.

14. This latter psychological state is called in Zen 'dwelling in the cave of devils under the mountain of darkness'. Zen never wearies of reminding us that we should avoid falling unconsciously into such a cave.

15. *Vajracchedika Prajñāpāramitā Sūtra*. This Sūtra, first translated from Sanscrit into Chinese by *Kumārajivā* cf. above, note 12), exercised a tremendous influence on the philosophical elaboration of Zen Buddhism, particularly from the time of the sixth Patriarch of Zen, Hui Nêng (J.: E Nō, 638-713). The Sūtra centers around the Nothingness and 'egolessness' of all things.

16. In the following analysis we shall utilize certain fomulae – with some modifications – that have been ingeniously devised by Professor Tsūji Satō for the purpose of clarifying the basic structure of reality as it appears to the eye of enlightenment. See his *Bukkō Tetsuri* 'Philosophical Principles of Buddhism' (Tokyo, 1968).

17. In this and the following formula, the words written entirely with italicized small letters (like *i, see, this*) shall refer to things and events pertaining to the dimension of ordinary consciousness, while those written with capital letters (like *I, SEE, THIS*) shall refer to the dimension of

60 Toward A Philosophy of Zen Buddhism

supra-consciousness. And the word *SEE* is supposed to be a literal translation of the Chinese word *chien* appearing in the celebrated phrase *chien hsing* 'seeing into one's nature'.

18. *Qur'ân*, VIII, 17. This passage expresses exactly the same idea as the famous Tradition which God Himself is the speaker and which runs: 'I am his ears, his eye-sight, his tongue, his hands, and his feet. Thus it is through Me that he hears; it is through Me that he sees; it is through Me that he speaks; it is through Me that he grasps; and it is through Me that he walks'. For an *'irfanic* discussion of these expressions see Ibn 'Arabī: *Fuṣūṣ at Hikam* (ed. 'Afīfī, Cairo, 1946), p. 185.

19. This statement might look at this stage quite an arbitrary one. We shall be in a position to discuss its validity only at the end of our analysis of the whole process. Here the statement must be accepted as it is as a merely phenomenological analysis of Zen psychology.

20. As the famous passage of the *Prajñāpāramitā* Sutra declares: "The sensible is Nothingness, Nothingness is precisely the sensible".

21. Cf. Hideo Masuda: *Bukkyō Shisō-no Gudō-teki Kenkyū*, 'Studies in Buddhist Thought as a Search after the Way', Tokyo, 1966, pp. 219-221. For a more elaborate philosophical treatment of this aspect of Buddhism, cf. Keiji Nishitani: *Shūkyō towa Nani-ka*, 'What is Religion?' I, Tokyo, pp. 135-187.

22. A famous saying of Fu Ta-Shih (J.: Fu Dai-shi, 497-569), the understanding of which has often been considered by Zen masters as a standard by which to judge the depth of Zen consciousness of the disciples.

23. This point deserves special notice because the word *Nirvāna* which denotes the same thing as what we here call the subjective Nothingness, has often been misunderstood to mean a total annihilation of consciousness.

24. The field of Nothingness thus conceived is comparable with the metaphysical *Chaos* of the Taoist Chuang Tzŭ (cf. my paper on Taoism, Eranos-Jahrbuch XXXVI, 1967, pp. 389-411).

25. Chinese: *San chieh wei hsin, wan fa wei shih*, lit. 'the three regions (of the world of Becoming) are but one single mind, and the ten thousand existents are but one single cognition'.

26. Quoted above, cf. note 11.

27. The distinction between the two phrases 'easy to recognize' and 'difficult to distinguish' is purely rhetorical, a phenomenon which is very common in Chinese prose and poetry. The sentence simply means that both the white particles in the snow and the black molecules of soot in the ink are 'easy to recognize *and* difficult to distinguish' at one and the same time.

28. That is to say: there *is* the mountain, but it is so deeply blue that it is hardly distinguishable from the blue sky.

29. From the *Prajñā Pāramitā Sutra* referred to above.

30. *Lin Chi Lu* (*op. cit.*), 33, p. 55. Concerning Lin Chi, see above, note 4.

31. 'Six harmonious correspondences' are (1) sight which is constituted by the correspondence between the eye and visible things, (2) hearing based on the correspondence between the ear and sounds, (3) smell based on the correspondence between the nose and odors, (4) taste based on the correspondence between the tongue and flavors, (5) touch based on the correspondence between the tactile sense and touchable objects, and (6) 'cognition' based on the correspondence between the intellect and concepts-images.

32. *Op. cit.*, 31, p. 48.

33. As we shall see later, the 'Man' in the thought of Lin Chi is no other than the Mind-Reality conceived in a very peculiar way.

34. *Op. cit.*, 30, p. 45.

35. P'ang Yün (the eighth century) was one of the foremost and most distinguished of all the lay-disciples of Zen. The anecdote containing this saying is found in the above-mentioned *Pi Yen Lu*, (J.: *Hekigan Roku*) No. 42.

36. Huang Lung was a great Zen Master in the school of Lin Chi, and the founder of a sub-sect known after his name as Huang Lung school.

37. *Op. cit.*, No. LIII.

38. Chao Chou Tsung Shên (J.: Jōshū Jūshin).

39. No. XXXVII.

40. Niu Tou, a famous Zen master in the T'ang dynasty. He was first a Confucianist, and later turned to Buddhism. He became the founder of an independent school in Zen Buddhism.

41. An outstanding figure in the Ts'ao Tung (J.: Sō Tō) school, famous for the strong emphasis he laid on the importance of 'silent-illumination' (*mo chao*, J.: *moku shō*) as the best method for attaining enlightenment.

42. See above, note 4. The quotation is from his *Shōbōgenzō*, Book XXV, *Kei Sei San Shoku* 'The Voice of the Valley and the Color of the Mountain'.

43. We have earlier encountered the same question in the anecdote concerning Chao Chou's cypress tree in the courtyard.

44. *Op. cit.*, 25-26, pp. 34-35.

45. The new-born baby with long white hair, i.e. baby-old man, being an impossibility, symbolically indicates the seeming non-existence of the man as the 'subject'.

46. The whole energy of the Field is crystallized into One Man.

47. *Op. cit.*, 36, p. 60.

Essay II

TWO DIMENSIONS OF EGO CONSCIOUSNESS

Note: This is the first of three public lectures ('Ego Consciousness in Eastern Religions') delivered in New York at Hunter College Playhouse, Oct. 30 – Nov. 6, 1975, as part of the general program for the one hundredth anniversary of Jung's birth under the auspices of the C. G. Jung Foundation. It has been published in *Sophia Perennis*, Vol II, Number 1, Spring 1976, Tehran, Iran.

I The First Person Pronoun 'I'

In dealing with the topic of the two dimensions of ego-consciousness in Zen, it might be thought more in line with Jungian psychology to use the word 'Self' instead of the word 'Ego' to designate what I am going to explain as ego-consciousness in the second or deeper dimension. But there is a reason why I prefer in this particular case to use one and the same word, 'ego', in reference to the two dimensions of consciousness which I shall deal with in this Essay. For it is precisely one of the most important points which Zen makes that the empirical I which is the very center of human existence in our ordinary, daily life and the other I which is supposed to be actualized through the experience of enlightenment are ultimately identical with one another. The two 'egos' are radically different from each other and look almost mutually exclusive in the eyes of those who are in the pre-enlightenment stage of Zen discipline. From the viewpoint of the post-enlightenment stage, however, they are just one and the same, In the eyes of the truly enlightened Zen master, there is nothing special, nothing extraordinary about what is often called by such grandiose names as Cosmic Ego, Cosmic Unconscious, Transcendental Consciousness and the like. It is no other than the existential ground of the ordinary, commonplace man who eats when he is hungry, drinks when he is thirsty, and falls asleep when he is sleepy, that is, in short, the ordinary self which we are accustomed to regard as the subject of the day-to-day existence of the plain man.

But let us start from the beginning. The starting-point is provided by our ego-consciousness as we find it in the pre-enlightenment stage. Historically as well as structurally, Zen has always been seriously concerned with our consciousness of ourselves. Indeed, it is not going too far to say that the problem of how to deal with ego-consciousness is *the* sole and exclusive problem for Zen Buddhism. Says Dōgen,[1] one of the greatest Zen masters of Japan in the thirteenth century A.D.: 'To get disciplined in the way of the Buddha means nothing other than getting disciplined in properly dealing with your own I'. That is to say, an intense, unremitting self-inquiry exhausts the whole of Buddhism. It constitutes the first step into the Way of the Buddha and it constitutes the ultimate end of the same Way. There is no other problem in Zen.

Another Japanese Zen master of the 15th century, Ikkyū,[2] admonishes his disciples in a similar way saying: 'Who or what am I? Search for your I from the top of your head down to your bottom'. And he adds: 'No matter how hard you may search after it, you will never be able to grasp it. *That* precisely is your I'. In this last sentence there is a clear suggestion made as to how the problem of ego-consciousness is to be posed and settled in Zen Buddhism.

Our ordinary view of the world may be symbolically represented as a circle with the ego as its autonomous center. With individual differences that are clearly to be recognized, each circle delimits a certain spatial and temporal expanse within the boundaries of which alone everything knowable is knowable. Its circumference sets up a horizon beyond which things disappear in an unfathomable darkness. The center of the circle is occupied by what Karl Jespers called *Ich als Dasein*, i.e. the empirical ego, the I as we ordinarily understand it.

The circle thus constituted is of a centrifugal nature in the sense that everything, every action, whether mental or bodily, is considered to originate from its center and move toward its periphery. It is also centripetal in the sense that whatever happens within the circle is referred back and reduced to the center as its ultimate ground.

The center of the circle comes in this way to be vaguely represented as a permanent and enduring entity carrying and synthesizing all the disparate and divergent elements to be attributed to the various aspects and functions of the mind-body complex. Thus is born an image of the personal identity underlying all mental operations and bodily movements, remaining always the same through all the intra-organic and extra-organic processes that are observable in the mind-body complex. Linguistic usage expresses this inner vision of personal identity by the first person pronoun 'I'.

In our actual life we constantly use the first person pronoun as the grammatical subject for an infinite number of predicates. Long before the rise of Zen, Buddhism in India had subjected this usage of the first person pronoun to a thoroughgoing scrutiny in connection with the problem of the unreality of the ego, which, as is well known, was from the beginning the fundamental tenet of Buddhist philosophy and which, insofar as it was an idea distinguishing Buddhism from all other schools of Indian philosophy, was for the Buddhists of decisive importance.

We often say for instance 'I am fat' or 'I am lean' in reference to our bodily constitution. We say 'I am healthy' or 'I am ill' in accordance with whether our bodily organs are functioning normally or not. 'I walk', 'I run', etc., in reference to our bodily movements. 'I am hungry', 'I am thirsty', etc., in reference to the intra-organic physiological processes. 'I see', 'I hear', 'I smell', etc., in reference to the activity of our sense organs. The first person pronoun behaves in fact as the grammatical subject of many other types of sentences, descriptive or otherwise.

Under all those propositions with the first person pronoun as the subject there is clearly observable the most primitive, primal certainty of 'I am'. This primal certainty we have of our 'I am', that is, the consciousness of ego, derives its supreme importance from the fact that it constitutes the very center of the existential circle of each one of us. As the center sets itself into motion, a whole world of things and events spreads itself out around it in all directions, and as it quiets down the same variegated world is reduced to the original single point. The spreading-out of the empirical world in all its possible forms around the center is linguistically reflected in the sentences whose grammatical subject is 'I'.

The most serious question here for Zen is: Does the grammatical subject of all these sentences represent the real personal subject in its absolute suchness? Otherwise expressed:

Does the first person pronoun appearing in each of the sentences of this sort indicate pure subjectivity, the true Subject as understood by Zen Buddhism? The answer will definitely be in the negative.

The nature of the problem before us may be clarified in the following way. Suppose someone asks me 'Who are you?' or 'What are you?' To this question I can give an almost infinite number of answers. I can say, for example, 'I am a Japanese', 'I am a student', etc. Or I can say 'I am so-and-so', giving my name. None of these answers, however, presents the *whole* of myself in its absolute 'such-ness'. And no matter how many times I may repeat the formula 'I am *X*', changing each time the semantic referent of the *X*, I shall never be able to present directly and immediately the 'whole man' that I am. All that is presented by this formula is nothing but a partial and relative aspect of my existence, an objectified qualification of the 'whole man'. Instead of presenting the pure subjectivity that I am as the 'whole man', the formula presents myself only as a relative object. But what Zen is exclusively concerned with is precisely the 'whole man'. And herewith begins the real Zen problem concerning the ego consciousness. Zen may be said to take its start by putting a huge question mark to the word 'I' as it appears as the subject-term of all sentences of the type: 'I am *X*' or 'I do *X*'. One enters into the world of Zen only when one realizes that his own I has itself turned into an existential question mark.

In the authentic tradition of Zen Buddhism in China it was customary for a master to ask a newcomer to his monastery questions in order to probe the spiritual depth of the man. The standard question, the most commonly used for this purpose, was: 'Who are you?' This simple, innocent-looking question was in reality one which the Zen disciples were most afraid of. We shall have later occasion to see how vitally important this question is in Zen. But it will already be clear enough that the question is of such grave importance because it demands of us that we reveal immediately and on the spot the reality of the I underlying the common usage of the first person pronoun, that is, the 'whole man' in its absolute subjectivity. Without going into theoretical details. I shall give here a classical example.³ Nan Yüeh Huai Jang (J.: Nangaku Ejō, 677-744) who was later to become the successor to the Sixth Patriarch of Zen Buddhism in China, the famous Hui Nêng (J.: Enō, 637-713), came to visit the latter. Quite abruptly Hui Nêng asked him: 'What is *this thing* that has come to me in this way?'. This put the young Nan Yüeh completely at a loss for a reply. He left the master. And it took him eight years to solve the problem. In other words, the question 'What are you?' functioned for the young Nan Yüeh as a *kōan*. And, let me add, it can be or is in fact a *kōan* for anyone who wants to have an insight into the spirit of Zen. The answer, by the way, which Nan Yüeh presented to the master after eight years' struggle was a very simple one: 'Whatever I say in the form of *I am X* will miss the point. That exactly is the real I'.

Making reference to this famous anecdote, Master Musō, an outstanding Zen master of fourteenth century Japan,⁴ makes the following remark. 'To me, too', he says, 'many men of inferior capacity come and ask various questions about the spirit of Buddhism. To these people I usually put the question: "Who is the one who is actually asking me such a question about the spirit of Buddhism?" To this there are some who answer: "I am so-and-so", or "I am such-and-such". There are some who answer: "Why is it necessary at all to ask such a question? It is too obvious." There are some who answer not by words but by gestures meant to symbolize the famous dictum: "My own Mind, that is the Buddha". There are still others who answer (by repeating or imitating like a parrot the sayings of ancient masters, like) "Looking above, there is nothing to be sought after. Looking below, there is nothing to be thrown away". All these people will never be able to attain enlightenment'.

This naturally reminds us of what is known in the history of Zen as the 'concluding words of Master Pai Chang'. Pai Chang Huai Hai (J.: Hyakujō Ekai, 720-814) was one of the greatest Zen masters of the T'ang dynasty. It is recorded that whenever he gave a public sermon to the monks of his temple, he brought it to an end by directly addressing the audience: 'You people!' And as all turned towards the master in a state of unusual spiritual tension, at that very moment he flung down upon them like a thunderbolt the shout: 'WHAT IS THAT?' Those among the audience who were mature enough to get enlightened were supposed to attain enlightenment on the spot.

'What is that?' 'Who are you?' 'What are you?' 'Where do you come from?' These and other similar questions addressed by an enlightened master to a newcomer all directly point to the real I of the latter which ordinarily lies hidden behind the veil of his empirical I. These questions are extremely difficult to answer in a Zen context. Let us recall that Nan Yüeh had to grapple with his *kōan* for eight years before he found his own solution for it – not, of course, a verbal solution, but an existential one. The difficulty consists in that a question of this sort in the Zen context of a dialogue between master and disciple demands of the latter an immediate realization of the I as pure and unconditioned subjectivity. This is difficult almost to the extent of being utterly impossible because at the very moment that the disciple turns his attention to his own self which under ordinary conditions he is wont to express quite naïvely and unreflectingly by the first person pronoun, the self becomes objectified, or we should say, petrified, and the sought-for pure subjectivity is lost. The pure Ego can be realized only through a total transformation of the empirical ego into something entirely different, functioning in an entirely different dimension of human existence.

II Zen Theory of Consciousness

In order to elucidate the nature of the problem, let me go back once again to the image of the circle with which I proposed to represent symbolically the world as experienced by man at the pre-enlightenment stage. The world in the view of the plain man, I said, may conveniently be represented as a vaguely illumined circle with the empirical ego at its center as the source of illumination. Around the empirical ego there spreads out a more or less narrowly limited circle of existence within which things are perceived and events take place. Such is the world-view of the plain man.

The circle of existence seen in this way would seem to have a peculiar structure. The center of the circle, the empirical ego, establishes itself as the 'subject' and, as such, cognitively opposes itself to the 'object' which is constituted by the world extending from and around it. Each of the things existing in the world and the world itself, indeed everything other than the 'subject', is regarded as an 'object'. Zen does not necessarily criticize this structure as something entirely false or baseless. Zen takes a definitely negative attitude toward such a view as a falsification of the reality only when the 'subject' becomes conscious of itself as the 'subject', that is to say, when the 'subjective' position of the center of the circle comes to produce the consciousness of the ego as an enduring individual entity. For in such a context, the 'subject' turns into an 'object'. The 'subject' may even then conceptually still remain 'subjective', but insofar as it is conscious of itself as a self-subsistent entity, it belongs to the sphere of the 'objective'. It is but another 'object' among myriads of other 'objects'. Viewed in such a light, the entire circle of the world of Being together with its center, the ego, proves to be an 'objective' order of things. That is to say, what is seemingly the center of the circle is not the real center; the 'subject' is not the real Subject.

In fact, it is characteristic of the psychological mechanism of man that no matter how far he may go in search of his real self in its pure and absolute subjectivity, it goes on escaping his grip. For the very act of turning attention to the 'subject' immediately turns it into an 'object'.

What Zen primarily aims at may be said to be the rein-statement of the 'subject' in its proper, original position, at the very center of the circle, not as an 'object' but in its absolute subjectivity, as the real Subject or pure Ego. But the essential nature of the 'subject' being such as has just been indicated, the task of reinstating it in this sense cannot possibly be accomplished unless the illuminated circle of existence sur-rounding the 'subject' be also completely transformed. We may perhaps describe the situation by saying that the primary aim of Zen consists in trying to broaden the 'circle' to infinity to the extent that we might actualize an infintely large circle with its circumference nowhere to be found, so that its center be found everywhere, always mobile and ubiquitous, fixed at no definite point. Only as the center of such a circle could the 'subject' be the pure Ego.

In ancient Indian Buddhism, the pure Ego thus actualized used to be designated by the word *prajñā* or Transcendental Wisdom. Zen, using the traditional, common terminology of Buddhism that has developed in China, often calls it the 'Buddha Nature', or simply 'Mind', But Zen possesses also its specific vocabulary which is more colorful and more charateristically Chinese, for designating the same thing, like 'No-Mind', the 'Master', the 'True-Man-without-any-rank', 'your-original-Face-which-you-possessed-prior-to-the-birth-of-your-own-father-and-mother', or more simply, 'This Thing', 'That' or still more simply 'It'. All these and other names are designed to point to the transfigured ego function-ing as the center of the transfigured 'circle'.

For a better understanding of the transfiguration of the ego here spoken of, we would do well to consider the Zen idea of the structure of consciousness. Buddhism, in conformity with the general trend of Indian philosophy and spirituality, was concerned from the earliest periods of its historical develop-ment in India, and later on in China, with a meticulous analysis of the psychological processes ranging from sensation, perception and imagination to logical thinking, translogical thinking and transcendental intuition. As a result, many different psychological and epistemological theories have been proposed. And this has been done in terms of the structure of consciousness. Characteristic of these theories of consciousness is that consciousness is represented as something of a multilayer structure. Consciousness, in this view, consists of a number of layers or different dimensions organically related to each other but each functioning in its own way.

The most typical of all theories of consciousness that have developed in Mahayana Buddhism is that of the Yogācāra School (otherwise called the Vijñaptimātratā School, i.e., Consciousness-Only School). The philosophers of this school recognize in human consciousness three distinctively different levels. The first or 'surface' level is the ordinary psychological dimension in which the sense-organs play the preponderant role producing sensory and perceptual images of the external things. Under this uppermost layer comes the *mano-vijñāna* or Manas-Consciousness. This is the dimension of the ego-consciousness.

According to the Yogācāra School, the consciousness of ego which we ordinarily have is but an infinitesimal part of the Manas-Consciousness. It is only the tip of a huge iceberg that shows above the surface. The greater part of the iceberg is submerged beneath the water. The submerged part of the iceberg consists of the so-called 'egotistic attachments' which have been accumulated there since time immemorial and which are intensely alive and active in the invisible depths of the psyche, sustaining, as it were, from below what we are ordinarily conscious of as our 'I'.

The Manas-Consciousness itself is sustained from below by the *ālaya-vijñāna*, the Storehouse-Consciousness which constitutes the deepest layer of human consciousness. Unlike the Manas-Consciousness of which at least the smallest part is illumined in the form of the empirical ego-consciousness, the Storehouse-Consciousness lies entirely in darkness. It is a 'storehouse' or repository of all the karmic effects of our past actions, mental and bodily. They are 'stored' there under the form of primordial Images which constantly come up to the above-mentioned surface level of consciousness arousing there the sensory and perceptual images of the phenomenal things and producing at the second level of consciousness i.e., the level of *mano-vijñāna*, the consciousness of the ego. What is remarkable about the nature of the Storehouse-Consciousness is that, in the view of the Yogācāra School, it is not confined to the individual person. It exceeds the boundaries of an individual mind extending even beyond the personal unconscious that belongs to the individual, for it is the 'storehouse' of all the karmic vestiges that have been left by the experiences of mankind since the beginning of time. As such the concept of the Storehouse-Consciousness may be said to be the closest equivalent in Buddhism to the Collective Unconscious.

However, the philosophers of the Yogācāra School speak of transcending the Storehouse-Consciousness by the force of a spiritual illumination that issues forth from the World of Purest Reality as they call it, which they say could be opened up by man's going through the arduous process of the spiritual discipline of meditation.

As a branch of Mahayana Buddhism closely connected with the Yogācāra School, Zen bases itself philosophically on a similar conception of the structure of consciousness. However, being by nature averse to all theorizing, let alone philosophizing, Zen has elaborated no special doctrine concerning this problem, at least in an explicit form. But under the innumerable anecdotes, *kōans*, poems, and popular sermons which constitute the main body of Zen literature, a group of major ideas about the structure of consciousness is clearly discernible. And it is not so hard for us to bring them out in a theoretic form and develop them into a Zen doctrine of consciousness.

It immediately becomes clear that Zen also holds a multilayer theory of consciousness. Here, however, as in all other cases, Zen greatly simplifies the matter. It regards consciousness as consisting of two entirely different, though intimately related, layers which we may distinguish as (1) the intentional and (2) the non-intentional dimension of consciousness, the word 'intentional' being used in the original sense as exemplified by the use of the Latin word *intentio* in Medieval philosophy.

In the intentional dimension, the I as the 'subject' is empirically given as a correlate of the 'object'. There is an essential correlation between the 'subject' and 'object'. All noetic experience in this dimension is necessarily of dualistic structure. I regard myself as 'I' only insofar as I am aware of external things and events as 'objects' of cognition. There would be no ego-consciosuness if there were absolutely no 'object' to be cognized. More generally, it is characteristic of this dimension that our consciousness is always and necessarily a 'consciousness-of'. It is an awareness *intending* something i.e., directed toward something; it is an awareness with an objective reference.

It is, in other words, of the very nature of consciousness in this dimension that it cannot but objectify whatever appears before it. And paradoxically or ironically enough, this holds true even of the 'subject'. The very moment I become aware of myself, my I turns into an objectified I, an 'object' among all other 'objects'. This is the main reason, as I said earlier, why it is so difficult to realize the 'subject' in its pure subjectivity. One can never hope to actualize the pure Ego as long as one remains in the intentional dimension of consciousness.

Zen, however, recognizes – and knows through experience – another dimension of consciousness which is what I have called above the 'non-intentional' dimension, and in which consciousness functions without being divided into the subjective and objective. It is a noetic dimension which is to be cultivated through the yogic, introspective techniques of *zazen*, a special dimension in which consciousness is activated not as 'consciousness-of' but as Consciousness pure and simple. This would exactly correspond to what Vasubandhu, a representative philosopher of the Yogācāra School, once said[5]: 'As the mind perceives no object, it remains as pure Awareness'.

The non-intentional awareness is found to be at work, albeit usually in vague and indistinct form, even in our day-to-day experience. Already the Sautrāntika School of Hinayana Buddhism[6] noticed the existence of the non-

intentional aspect in the mind of the plain man. The proposition, for example, 'I feel happy' in contradistinction to a
proposition like 'I see a mountain', expresses a kind of non-
intentional awareness. For being-happy is an awareness of a
pleasurable mode of being, an elation which is vaguely diffused in the whole of my mind-body complex, with no
definite, particular 'object' of which I can say I am conscious,
unless I become by *intentio secunda* conscious of my being-
happy. The proposition 'I see a mountain', on the contrary, is
clearly a description of a perceptual event taking place between the 'subject' and the 'object'.

What Zen is interested in, however, is not a non-intentional
awareness such as is expressed by propositions of the type: 'I
am happy'. Rather Zen is interested in opening up a special
dimension of consciousness which is, we might say, systematically non-intentional. It is a dimension in which even a proposition like 'I see the mountain' for example will be found to
signify a peculiar state of awareness of such a nature that
exactly the same propositional content may be expressed
interchangeably by four linguistically different sentences: (1)
'I see the mountain', (2) 'The mountain sees me', (3) 'The
mountain sees the mountain', (4) 'I see myself'. The non-
intentional dimension of consciousness in which Zen is
interested is such that these four sentences are exactly
synonymous with each other. Until these four sentences are
realized to be exactly synonymous with each other, you are
still in the intentional dimension of consciousness. Furthermore, in the non-intentional dimension of consciousness
these four synonymous sentences can very well be reduced to
a one word sentence: 'Mountain!', and this word again can-
freely be reduced to one single word 'I'.

Here we observe how the original sentence: 'I see the
mountain' from which we started has ultimately been con-
densed into one single point of 'I'. The 'I' thus actualized
conceals within itself all the sentential variants that have been
passed through, so that it can at any moment reveal itself as
the 'Mountain!' or expand into any of the four full sentences.
In whichever form it may appear, it is a pure non-intentional
awareness, a pure consciousness instead of 'consciousness-
of'. Nothing is here objectified. What Zen considers to be the
true Self or absolute Ego is precisely the I actualized in such a

dimension of consciousness as an immediate self-expression of this very dimension.

Zen has a special technical term for the non-intentional dimension of consciousness: *fei-ssŭ-liang* (J.: *hi-shiryō*) literally meaning 'non-thinking'. This phrase may perhaps better be translated as the 'a-thinking mode of thinking'.[7] For, despite its purely negative form, this expression does not mean a passive void of consciousness or absence of consciousness. Quite the contrary; in the 'a-thinking' state the consciousness is activated and heightened to the extreme limit of its power of concentration without, however, 'intending' anything.

This particular expression, *fei-ssŭ-liang*, 'a-thinking thinking', was first introduced into Zen at a very early period of its history, by the third Patriarch, Sêng Ts'an (J.: Sōsan, ?-606) in his famous philosophical poem *Hsin Hsin Ming* (J.: *Shinjin Mei*). Later, in the T'ang dynasty, the same word was used by one of the greatest Zen masters of the age, Yao Shan Wei Yen (J.: Yakusan Igen, 751-834) in a very significant way, as recorded in the following famous *mondo*.

> Once Master Yao Shan was sitting in deep meditation when a monk came up to him and asked: 'Solidly seated as a rock, what are you thinking?'
> Master answered: 'Thinking of something which is absolutely unthinkable'.
> The monk: 'How can one think of anything which is absolutely unthinkable?'
> Master: 'By the a-thinking thinking, *fei-ssŭ-liang!*'

Since then the word has become an important technical term in Zen Buddhism. The *mondo* just quoted clearly shows that the *zazen* praxis is a spiritual discipline whose primary aim is to explore the non-intentional dimension of consciousness, in which the 'subject' is active as pure Awareness without 'intending' anything, instead of acting as 'subject' as opposed to 'object'.

III The Ego-less Ego

But how, in practical terms, could we hope to bring about such a situation? More concretely put, how could we realize the I in its pure and absolute subjectivity as the pure Ego in the sense I have just indicated?

To repeat what I have said earlier, the pure Ego is usually unrealizable because in the intentional dimension of consciousness everything is an 'object' of consciousness. Even the I, the 'subject of cognition, turns into an 'object' as soon as I turn my attention to myself by reflection or introspection. Hence the very first step in the praxis of Zen discipline is – to use the celebrated words of the aforementioned Japanese Zen master, Dōgen – one's 'forgetting one's own I'.[8]

'Forgetting one's own I' – this characteristic phrase carries in Zen a very important positive meaning. It must not be taken in the negative sense of simply losing consciousness, be it in a state of ecstasy, let alone blank stupefaction. Instead of being a state of 'mindlessness' in any sense, it is 'mindfulness', an extreme intensification of consciousness, except that the 'mindfulness' is to be maintained not in the dimension of ordinary noetic experience in which the ego stands as the 'subject' opposed to other things or other egos as its 'objects', but in a totally different dimension in which the very opposition of 'subject' and 'object' becomes meaningless.

> To get disciplined in the Way of Buddha means getting disciplined in dealing properly with your own I. To get disciplined in dealing properly with your I means nothing other than forgetting your I. To forget your I means that you become illumined by the 'external' things. To be illumined by the things means that you obliterate the distinction between your (so-called) ego and the (so-called) egos of other things.

It will easily be seen that the discipline of 'forgetting one's I' is immediately backed by another, more positive discipline of becoming 'illumined by the things'. Losing the consciousness of the I as the 'subject' standing in opposition to other things as its 'objects', one is to get entirely and totally absorbed into the things themselves in such a way that the things 'illumine' or resuscitate the I that has once disappeared from the 'subject'-'object' dimension in another form in another dimension, the non-intentional dimension of consciousness.

This positive aspect of the Zen discipline is known in the traditional terminology of Far Eastern spirituality as 'one's *becoming* the thing'.[9] The idea of man's becoming things has played in the Far East an exceedingly important role in various fields of culture such as religion, philosophy, and fine arts.[10] It is indeed no exaggeration to say that the spirit of Far Eastern culture can never be understood without a full understanding of this principle.

A few years ago, as I well remember, participating in a conference I had a chance to read a paper on the art of black-and-white ink painting in China and Japan. In the course of the lecture, I mentioned as the highest principle of this kind of art the idea that the painter should *become* the thing which he wants to paint. The painter who is going to paint a bamboo must, before taking up his brush, sit in contemplation until he feels himself completely identified with the bamboo. So I said.

After the lecture a man came to me – it was a famous authority on mysticism – and said that in his view it was utterly impossible for a man to *become* a bamboo. It is, he said, not only scientifically absurd, but it is, as a matter of practical experience, an impossibility.

The truth is that the pros and cons of the matter depend solely upon how one understands the meaning of this peculiar expression: 'Man becomes a bamboo'. It is obvious that my critic understood it in a purely ontological sense instead of taking it in the sense in which it is customarily understood by Far Easterners.

From the point of view of a Far Eastern painter, as he understands the expression in the traditional way, it *is* possible for him to become a bamboo. Or rather, he *must* become a bamboo. Otherwise, the bamboo he paints would be but a lifeless bamboo, a dead object having only a formal similarity to a real bamboo.

What is meant by this expression in the view of a Far Eastern painter may somehow become understandable to you if you imagine what actually takes place in the following way. The painter sits in quiet contemplation, intensely concentrating his mind upon the ideal image of the bamboo. He begins to feel in himself the rhythmic pulsebeat of the life-energy which keeps the bamboo alive and which makes the bamboo a bamboo, becoming gradually concordant with the pulsebeat of the life-energy which is running through his mind-body complex. And finally there comes a moment of complete unification, at which there remains no distinction whatsoever between the life-energy of the painter and the life-energy of the bamboo. Then there is no longer any trace in the consciousness of the painter of himself as an individual self-subsistent person. There is actualized only the Bamboo. Where is it actualized? Internally? Or externally? No one knows. It does not matter. For the word 'becoming' in the particular context here at issue concerns a state of contemplative awareness having in itself no ontological implication.

There is absolutely no 'consciousness of' anything whatsoever. The sole fact is that the Bamboo is there, actualized with an unusual vivacity and freshness, pulsating with a mysterious life-energy pervading the whole universe. At that very moment the painter takes up the brush. The brush moves, as it were, of its own accord, in conformity with the pulsation of the life-rhythm which is actualized in the bamboo. In terms of the traditional Far Eastern theory of the pictorial art, it is then not the man who draws the picture of the bamboo; rather, the bamboo draws its own picture on the paper. The movement of the brush is the movement of the inner life of the bamboo.

It is important to remark that according to Zen such an experience is by no means confined to the pictorial art, or, for that matter, to any particular domain of human life. From the point of view of Zen, existence itself in its entirety is to be an experience of this nature. No matter what man may hear, he *is* the thing in the sense I have just explained. He sees for instance a flowing river. He *is* the water flowing in the form of a river. A man is a man; he can never become water; he can never *be* water, you may say. But if such a thing were absolutely impossible in any sense, Zen would be sheer nonsense.

Zen argues as follows. One cannot *become* water because one is observing it from outside, that is to say, because the ego is, as an outsider, looking at water as an 'object'. Instead of doing so, Zen continues to argue, one must first learn to 'forget one's ego-subject' and let oneself be completely absorbed into the water. One would then be flowing *as* the flowing river. No more would there be any consciousness of the ego. Nor would there be any 'consciousness of' the water. Strictly speaking, it is not even the case that one *becomes* the water and flows on as the water. For in such a dimension there would be no ego existent to *become* anything. Simply: The water flows on. No more, no less.

Often when we are absorbed in listening to an enchanting piece of music, a state of artistic *samādhi* is actualized. In such a state there is Music pure and simple. The Music fills up the whole field of existence. It is only after the music has come to an end and when we 'come back' to ourselves that we realize with a feeling of surprise that we have been completely 'identified with' music. But when we actually realize it, the I and the music are already split apart into two different things.

The experience of musical *samādhi* is for most of us a particular experience occurring only from time to time, on rare occasions or intermittently. For a man of Zen, experiences of this nature must be just ordinary, day-to-day events. Thus to come back to the example of the flowing water, Zen demands that man be such that he be the flowing water from eternity to eternity. The water flows on eternally, cosmically, in the eternal Now. The water here is not an 'object' of cognition. Nor is there consciousness of the I as the noetic 'subject'. From no one knows where there emerges the flowing water. It does not involve the awareness of my 'I', nor does it involve the awareness *of* the 'water'. But it is a pure Awareness. And that Awareness *is* the flowing water.

What generally looks like an objective description of Nature in Zen poetry and Zen painting is in the majority of cases a presentation, pictorial or poetic, of such an experience. By depicting a flower, tree, or bird, the poet or painter expresses the cosmic illumination of the pure Awareness. A flower depicted in this manner is not an objective flower. It is Something else. It is Something which at this moment is being actualized as a Flower, but which could very well be actualized as the 'I'. Such is the nature of the pure Ego as understood by Zen, the 'True-man-without-any-rank'. Dynamic, functional, and mobile it is constantly changing. Now it expresses itself verbally or visually as a Flower. At the very next moment it may express itself as 'I'. Since in either case the life-energy of the whole spiritual universe is poured into the expression, the Flower and the I are one and the same thing, for they are but two different crystallizations of exactly the same amount of the universal life-energy. And since, further, it makes absolutely no difference whether the life-energy of the whole universe expresses itself as Flower or I, or indeed, for that matter, as anything whatsoever, it could also express itself as Nothing. This is what is generally known as the 'Oriental Nothingness'.

The Oriental Nothingness is not a purely negative ontological state of there being nothing. On the contrary, it is a plenitude of Being. It is so full that it cannot as such be identified as anything determined, anything special. But it is, on the other hand, so full that it can manifest itself as anything in the empirical dimension of our experience, as a crystallization of the whole spiritual energy contained therein. The Oriental Nothingness thus understood *is* the true, absolute Ego as Zen Buddhism understands it.

Notes

1. On Dōgen (1200-1253), see Essay I, Note 3.

2. Master Ikkyū (1394-1481). The quotation is from his *Mizukagami*.

3. *Wu Têng Hui Yüan*, III.

4. The National Teacher, Musō (1275-1351), particularly famous for initiating the tradition of landscape gardening in Japanese culture. The following passage is found in his work *Muchū Mondō Shū*, II.

5. In his *Triṃshika-Vijñaptimātratā-Siddhi*.

6. See an excellent exposition of the matter by H. Guenther: *Buddhist Philosophy,* Harmondsworth-Baltimore, 1972, pp. 68-70.

7. The 'a-thinking' thinking will be dealt with in Essay V (particularly sec. III). The *kōan* which we are going to quote will also be fully explained there.

8. The phrase is found in the *Shōbōgenzō* (Chapter '*Genjō Kōan*'). It will be more fully discussed in Essay V.

9. This problem will be discussed in Essays V and VI.

10. *Ibid.*

Essay III

SENSE AND NONSENSE IN ZEN BUDDHISM

Note: The Essay was originally an Eranos lecture for the year 1970, subsequently published in Eranos-Jahrbuch XXXIX, 1973, Leiden.

I Zen Nonsense

The main topic of the present Essay is the problem of meaning and meaningfulness in Zen. This topic and the one which
we discussed in the preceding Essay, namely, the basic structure of Selfhood are, as we shall see, closely and inseparably
connected with each other. Or, rather we should say that the
problem of language and meaning is essentially related to and
ultimately reducible to the problem of Selfhood. Indeed,
whichever aspect of Zen one may take up, and from
whichever angle one may approach it, one is sure to be
brought back ultimately to the problem of Selfhood.

With this basic understanding, I shall turn immediately to
the discussion of meaningfulness about which Zen raises a
number of interesting problems. As one could imagine, the
problems are raised in a very peculiar context, for language in
Zen tends to be used in quite an unnatural way. In the context
of Zen, language usually does not remain in its natural state.
It is often distorted to the degree of becoming almost meaningless and nonsensical.

The problem of meaning in Zen Buddhism is thus interesting in rather a paradoxical sense because most of the typical
Zen sayings are obviously devoid of meaning and nonsensical
if we observe them from the point of view of our ordinary
understanding of language. Language exists for the purpose
of communication between men. Where there is no need for
communication, there is no need of saying anything. This
basic principle applies to Zen as well. When we observe two
persons engaged in talking with each other in a Zen context,
we naturally get the impression that communication of some
sort is taking place between them. But we observe at the same
time a very strange fact, namely, that the words that are
exchanged do not make sense, that they are mostly meaning-

less or nonsensical to us, outside observers. How could there be communication at all when the words used do not make sense? What kind of communication will it be, when it is made through nonsensical utterances? Such indeed is the most important question that confronts us at the outset as soon as we approach Zen from the point of view of meaningful communication.

In order to bring into focus the very core of the whole question, let us begin by giving a typical example of nonsensical communication at the pre-linguistic level of behavior, that is, communication through gesture. Let us remark that in Zen Buddhism, gesture plays practically the same role as language, except that language presents a far more complicated structure, because, as we shall see later, language involves the very important factor of articulation, i.e,, the semantic articulation of reality, which is foreign to the use of gestures. But precisely because of this simplicity and non-complexity, gesture is perhaps more appropriate than language in giving us a preliminary idea as to where the central problem lies.

The example I am going to give is a very famous one. It is found in the *kōan* collection *Wu Mên Kuan* (J.: *Mu Mon Kan*), No. 3; it is also found in another celebrated *kōan* collection, *Pi Yen Lu* (J.: *Hekigan Roku*), No. 19. It is an anecdote known as the one-finger-Zen of Master Chü Chih (J.: Gu Tei).

The hero of the anecdote is Chü Chih (J.: Gu Tei), a famous Zen Master of the ninth century. This Master, whenever and whatever he was asked about Zen, used to stick up one finger. Raising one finger without saying anything was his invariable answer to any question whatsoever he was asked concerning Zen. 'What is the supreme and absolute Truth?' – answer: the silent raising of one finger. 'What is the essence of Buddhism?' – answer: again the selfsame silent raising of one finger.

It will be evident that in the normal circumstances of life, this action does not make sense, for the simple raising of one finger in no way constitutes a reasonable answer to any of the questions asked, except perhaps when the question runs: 'Where is your finger?' The answer is not understandable, and since it is not understandable, it is no answer; and being no answer, it is nonsensical. Yet on the other hand, we feel in our perplexed mind something which persistently tells us that there must be some hidden meaning in Master Chü Chih's raising one finger, that it cannot be total nonsense. What then is this hidden meaning which Master Chü Chih supposedly wanted to convey by silently sticking up one finger? That precisely is the problem. I shall explain the meaning of Chü Chih's one-finger-Zen later on. At this stage there are many other things to be clarified in a preliminary way in order that we might grasp the core of the whole question.

The anecdote, by the way, has not come to an end. It has a very important sequel. Master Chü Chih had a young disciple, a boy apprentice, who followed the Master, serving him at home and out of doors. Having observed his Master's pattern of behavior this boy himself began to raise one finger whenever people asked him questions about Zen in the absence of the Master. At first, the Master did not notice it, and everything went well for some time. But the fatal moment came at last. The Master came to hear about what the boy had been doing behind his back.

One day, the Master hid a knife in the sleeve, summoned the boy to his presence, and said, 'I hear that you have understood the essence of Buddhism. Is it true?' The boy replied 'Yes it is'. Thereupon the Master asked, 'What is the Buddha?' The boy in answer stuck up one finger. Master Chü Chih suddenly took hold of the boy and cut off with the knife the finger which the boy had just raised. As the boy was running out of the room screaming with pain, the Master called to him. The boy turned round. At that very moment, quick as lightning came the Master's question: 'What is the Buddha?' Almost by conditioned reflex, we might say, the boy held up his hand to raise his finger. There was no finger there. The boy on the spot attained enlightenment.

The anecdote may very well be a fiction. But, fictitious or real, it is indeed a very interesting and significant anecdote. It is interesting and significant not only because the story is narrated in an atmosphere of high dramatic tension, but also, and mainly, because the whole anecdote is an admirable dramatization of what we might call Zen experience. Zen experience is embodied not solely in the last crucial stage at which the boy attains enlightenment. The whole story from the very beginning till the end is alive with the spirit of Zen. Each single event in the story represents in a dramatic way a particular state in the evolvement of Zen consciousness. For the moment, however, we shall refrain from going further into the analytic elucidation of the actual content of this anecdote. Our immediate concern is with a more formal aspect of the story.

It is important to remark that the anecdote is interesting as a dramatization of the evolvement of Zen consciousness only in an authentically Zen context. In other words, the anecdote tells something positive, it makes sense, it is meaningful, only to those who are already familiar with Zen or something similar to it in another religious tradition. Otherwise the whole anecdote would naturally remain nonsensical in the sense that no stage in the evolvement of the story will really be understandable. To begin with, why did Master Chü Chih stick up one finger whenever he was asked any question about Buddhism? Why did he cut off the finger of the boy who imitated him? How did the boy attain enlightenment when he wanted to raise his finger which was no longer there? Nothing is understandable except to those who have an inside knowledge of the Zen theory and practice.

What is so meaningful to a Zen Buddhist may thus be completely meaningless to an outsider. Moreover, even within the narrowly limited context of this anecdote, the act of raising one finger was meaningful in the case of the Master while exactly the same act was judged to be meaningless and nonsensical when it occurred as an imitation by the disciple. Again the selfsame act of raising one finger by the disciple suddenly assumed a decisive importance and turned meaningful at the moment when it came in the form of the raising of a non-finger. All these observations would seem to lead us toward thinking that Zen must have a definite standard by which it can judge anything, whether verbal or non-verbal, to be meaningful or meaningless as the case may be, and that, further, it must be quite an original standard, totally different from the standard of meaningfulness which is normally applied in ordinary situations, so much so that a judgement passed by the Zen standard could be – and very often is – diametrically opposed to the judgement given in accordance with the ordinary standard.

Indeed I may as well have entitled this Essay 'The Problem of the Criterion for Meaningfulness in Zen Buddhism'. For such in fact is the matter which I want to discuss here. In other words, the main problem that will concern us is whether there is such a thing as the criterion for meaningfulness in Zen, and if there *is* one, whether there is any reliable means by which we can come to know the inner make-up of that criterion.

II Meaningful or Meaningless?

Meaningfulness is evidently a matter of primary concern for contemporary intellectuals. In the field of philosophy, as the result of the development of British empiricism and American positivism with their extraordinary emphasis upon the problems of meaning, the concept of meaningfulness (and meaninglessness) of what we say has become one of the major intellectual problems.

Even in ordinary non-philosophic situations, we are often reminded of the importance of 'making sense'. We often find ourselves saying, 'It makes sense', 'It makes no sense', and the like. And the kind of judgement is always accompanied by valuation, positive or negative; or it is itself a value judgement. Not-making-sense is nothing other than talking nonsense, saying something absurd and ridiculous. Talking nonsense is felt to be something we should be ashamed of. Thus we naturally try to avoid talking nonsense.

A number of popular books have been written in recent years, which purport to teach us how we could avoid falling into the pitfalls of nonsensical talk or nonsensical thinking. Thus, to give a few examples, the general semanticist, Mr. Irving J. Lee has written a book entitled: *How to Talk with People* carrying a significant subtitle which reads: *A program for preventing troubles that come when people talk together.* Another book of a more serious nature by Professor Lionel Ruby is entitled: *The Art of Making Sense*, with the subtitle: *A guide to logical thinking*. These and other similar works analyze in great detail the pitfalls of nonsense and try to guide the reader toward what is called 'straight' thinking. Otherwise expressed, the authors of these books are concerned with how we can use language meaningfully. Making-sense is now an art. It is a special technique considered to be indispensable in modern life.

It is very interesting to remark that, from such a point of view almost all the famous Zen sayings typify sheer nonsense. That is to say, Zen sayings do not in the majority of cases satisfy the criterion for meaningfulness that is proposed in these books. What is still more remarkable is the fact that, from the viewpoint of Zen, those ordinary words and propositions that fully satisfy the normal criterion for meaningfulness can very well be meaningless, even nonsensical. So-called 'straight' thinking and so-called 'meaningful' talk may from the Zen point of view be judged to be 'crooked' and meaningless because they tend to distort and deform what Zen regards as the reality of things. Zen says for example[1]:

> Empty-handed, I hold a spade in my hands,
> I am walking on foot, but on the back of an ox I
>   ride,
> As I pass over the bridge, lo,
> The water does not flow, it is the bridge that flows.

This saying which, as everybody sees, consists entirely of glaring contradictions does make good sense in Zen. Indeed, in a Zen context, to say: 'I am empty-handed and I have a spade in the hands; I walk on foot and I ride on the back of an ox; The water stands still while the bridge flows', makes even better sense than saying: 'I am not empty-handed because I have a spade in my hands: I am walking on foot, therefore I am not riding on the back of an ox; The river flows and the bridge stands still'. How and on what basis can this kind of nonsensical saying be said to make good sense in Zen?

Before answering this crucial question, I shall give here one more example of Zen nonsense of a somewhat different nature. It is an extremely short *kōan* recorded in the above-mentioned *Wu Mên Kuan* (J.: *Mu Mon Kan*), No. 18. It reads:

> A monk asked Master Tung Shan: 'What is the
>   Buddha?'
> Tung Shan replied: 'Three pounds of flax!'

Tung Shan (J.: Tō Zan, 910-990) is a disciple of the celebrated Master Yün Mên (J.: Ummon) of the tenth century (?-949), himself being also an outstanding Zen Master. One day he was weighing flax. Just at that moment a monk came up to him and suddenly flung this question at him: 'What is the Buddha?', a question which in the Western world would be equivalent to 'What is God?' or 'What is absolute Reality?' Instantaneously came Tung Shan's answer: 'Three pounds of flax!' The Zen documents abound in examples of this type. Thus, to give one more example, Yün Mên, the teacher of Tung Shan, when asked exactly the same question by a monk, answered by simply saying: 'A dried-up dirt-scraper!'

> Once a monk asked Yün Mên, 'What is the
> Buddha?'
> Mên replied: 'A dried-up dirt-scraper!'

That is all. To an outsider, these short dialogues would be nothing more than sheer nonsense. But at least one may notice the existence of a definite pattern underlying these two instances of Zen dialogue. As an answer to the metaphysical question concerning the Absolute, both Tung Shang and Yün Mên just thrust under the interlocutor's nose a concrete object in a verbal form: 'three pounds of flax' in the case of Tung Shan, and a dried-up, i.e., useless 'dirt-scraper' in the case of Yün Mên. Tung Shan was most probably weighing the flax when he was asked the metaphysical question. He answered on the spot by the most concrete thing that happened to be there in his hands.

Zen likes the most concrete. It is one of its characteristics. Examples can be given indefinitely from the old Zen records. In terms of the problem of meaningfulness, one might naturally be reminded of the principle of verification as it has been developed by the contemporary positivist philosophers. Verifiability is for them the ultimate criterion for meaningfulness. Only what is verifiable by experience is acceptable as real; accordingly a word or proposition is meaningful if and only if there are possible sense-perceptions which verify the presence of the object or the event indicated. 'God' or the 'Absolute' is a typical example of those words that are considered meaningless because there is no possible sense-perception that would verify the existence of such an entity.

On the face of it, Zen which evinces special liking for concrete things would seem to behave in conformity with the rule of verification set up by the positivists. Zen daringly commands its students to 'kill the Buddha', 'kill the Patriarchs', in short, to kill God! Instead of talking about God and the Absolute, Zen Masters talk about 'three pounds of flax', 'a dried-up dirt-scraper', 'the cypress tree in the courtyard of the temple', and the like. These words and phrases are perfectly meaningful by the positivist criterion for meaningfulness, because they are all verifiable, particularly because they are usually uttered in the very presence of the sensible objects.

Yet all these words turn completely meaningless and nonsensical as soon as we place them in their original contexts. That is to say, none of these expressions makes sense as a constituent part of a whole dialogue. 'What is the true significance of Bodhidharma's coming from the West (i.e., from India to China)?', a monk asks (*A*). Chao Chou (J.: Jō Shū, 778-897) answers: 'The cypress tree in the courtyard of the temple (*B*)'.[2] The dialogue is nonsensical because there can apparently be no communication between the monk who asks the question and the Master who answers, because there is no reasonable connection between *A* and *B*.

III   Speech and Language in a Zen Context

In the course of its historical development, Zen has produced a huge amount of documentary records. The earliest form of them is represented by what is known as the 'records of sayings' (*yü lu*, J.: *go roku*), i.e., the collections of the Sayings of great Masters, which began to enjoy remarkable popularity in the eighth and ninth centuries. Unlike the Mahayana Sutras which had been predominant up to those ages and in which all the cardinal teachings were put into the mouth of the Buddha himself, the Records of Sayings were all records of what individual Zen Masters said and how they behaved. Moreover, a Record of Saying does not purport to present a continuous and coherent description of the life of a Zen Master in the form of a biography; it consists merely of a series of fragmentary records of sayings and doings of a Master in daily circumstances.

The core of the Records of Sayings is constituted by *mondōs* each of which is a personal dialogue that takes place in a very concrete situation between the Master and a disciple or a visiting monk. It is typical of the *mondō* that it consists in most cases of one single question and one single answer. The dialogue is therefore mostly of extreme concision and brevity. It is a real verbal fight. And the fight is over almost instantaneously, just like a contest fought with real swords by two masters of Japanese swordsmanship. There is no room here for a *dialektiké*. The Zen dialogue does not last long like a Platonic dialogue which can last interminably to the utmost limit of the logical development and intellectual elaboration of a given theme.

Rather, the Zen dialogue aims at grasping the ultimate and eternal Truth in a momentary flash of words that are exchanged between two living persons at the extreme point of spiritual tension, and in a concrete and unique situation of life. The momentary dialogue may result in producing what would strike the outsiders as sheer nonsense. No matter. For in the view of the two participants the fight has been fought. The eternal Truth may or may not have been glimpsed. No matter, the Truth has flashed for a moment.

The nature of the Zen dialogue discloses in an extraordinary, or we would perhaps say, shocking form, the typically Chinese way of thinking which consists in aiming at grasping immediately and on the spot this or that aspect of the eternal Truth in a real, concrete situation which is never to be repeated. This feature of the Chinese way of thinking is observable, albeit in a far less tense form, in the *Analects of Confucius* (*Lun Yü*; J.: *Ron Go*). It is a mode of thinking which is essentially different from those forms of thinking that are developed on the abstract and theoretical level of the intellect and reason. It is, on the contrary, a peculiar mode of thinking that evolves in the midst of concrete life prompted by some concrete event or concrete thing. This typically Chinese form of thought was once overwhelmed by the development in China of logical discursive ways of thinking under the influence of Mahayana Buddhism which had preceded the rise of Zen Buddhism. With Zen it came back again to life in the periods extending from the T'ang dynasty down to the Sung dynasty. Many of the representative dialogues that we find in the Records of Sayings were codified in the Sung dynasty between the tenth and the thirteenth century in the form of *kōans* as effective means of educating and training Zen students.

It will have been understood that the words used in a way peculiar to Zen are all words uttered, as it were in limit-situations. Hence the characteristic distortion or deformation of ordinary language as we observe it in the *mondōs*. Zen does not shun or despise langauge. It only requires that language be used in a very peculiar way, not indiscriminately. It requires that the words should come out of one specific source which we may call 'the primary dimension of Reality'. The structure of this dimension of Reality will be analyzed later on. For the moment let us be content with remarking that what is of decisive importance for Zen, in this respect, is the source from which words issue forth. The kind of language that has its source and basis in the ordinary level of consciousness is for Zen meaningless. Perfect silence is far better than meaningless talk. The famous watchword of Zen: 'No use of words and letters' refers to this aspect of the Zen attitude toward language.

In a passage of his *Structural Anthropology*, M. Lévi-Strauss mentions two different attitudes toward the use of language and distinguishes between them in terms of cultural patterns. He says: 'Among us [i.e., in European culture], language is used in a rather reckless way – we talk all the time, we ask questions about many things. This is not at all a universal situation. There are cultures . . . which are rather thrifty in relation to language. They don't believe that language should be used indiscriminately but only in certain specific frames of reference and somewhat sparingly.[3]

I do not know whether or not M. Lévi-Strauss was actually thinking of Oriental cultures when he wrote these lines. In any case the description he gives of the second of the two cultural patterns applies to the linguistic aspect of Zen.

The word 'Zen' naturally reminds us of the practice of *zazen*, i.e., sitting cross-legged in meditation. In the state of *zazen* language is to stop functioning, even the inner or mental speech, not to speak of external speech. Language is simply an impediment in the way of the concentration of the mind. It must be completely done away with. But once out of the state of meditation, the Zen student may at any moment be asked by the Master to 'say something, say something', to use language – not indiscriminately, of course, but in a very specific frame of reference. In fact, in a certain sense no living religion attaches greater importance to speaking and talking than Zen Buddhism. The Master constantly urges the student to open the mouth and say something. He commands him: 'Bring me a phrase!', i.e., a decisive phrase. Asking the student to say something constitutes an integral part of the educational process of Zen. For, the moment he opens the mouth and 'brings a decisive phrase', the student discloses to the eyes of the Master the exact degree of his spiritual maturity.

It is important to remark, however, that the linguistic behaviour which is asked of the student here is of an extremely specific nature. it consists neither in speaking in an ordinary way nor in keeping silent. What is required is that words should gush out from a certain dimension of consciousness which is totally different from the dimension of speaking and not speaking.

One of the celebrated 'Three Key Phrases' (*san chuan yü*)[4] of Master Sung Yüan (J.: Shō Gen, 1132-1202) was: 'Speaking is not a matter of moving the tongue'. That is to say, in the view of Zen, it is not with the tongue that man speaks. Another famous Master, Pai Chang (J. Hyakujō, 720-814) is related to have once asked his disciples: 'How will it be possible for you to speak in a state in which your throat, lips and mouth have been snatched away?'[5] He is here urging his disciples to say something without using the throat, lips and mouth. This seemingly unreasonable request simply indicates that language as understood in an authentic Zen context consists in the act of speaking in which the vocal organs, though actually activated, remain inactivated as if they were not used.

In order to understand this point we must remember that as a branch of Mahayana Buddhism, Zen upholds – at least at the initial stage of theorizing[6] – a fundamental distinction between two levels of Reality. One is what is called the 'sacred truth' *shêng ti* (J.: *shō tai*) corresponding to the Sanscrit *paramârtha-satya*: and the other is the 'customary or worldly truth' *su ti* (J.: *zoku tai*) corresponding to the *saṃvṛtti-satya*. The former which is also called in Zen Buddhism the 'primary truth', refers to a very specific view of Reality which is disclosed to man only through the actual experience of enlightenment. The inner structure of the primary level of Reality will be elucidated in what follows. The 'customary truth' which is also called the 'secondary truth' refers, on the contrary, to the common-sense view of Reality as it appears to the eyes of ordinary people.

From the standpoint of Zen, the normal exchange of words as we usually understand it by such words as 'speech', 'speaking', 'language', and 'dialogue', belongs to the level of the 'secondary truth', while what is understood by these words in a Zen context belongs to the level of the 'primary truth'. When words are uttered or exchanged in this latter dimension of Reality, they give rise to a very strange and unusual situation.

(1)   The fundamental structure of speech or *parole* as defined by Ferdinand de Saussure is no longer observable in this dimension, for there is no distinction here between the speaker and the hearer. What is actually seen is a spectacle of words flowing out from no one knows where, glittering for a moment in the air like a flash of lightning, and immediately disappearing into the eternal darkness. Speech does occur, but it is a speech that occurs in a void space where the existence of the speaker and the hearer has completely lost its significance. Since there is neither speaker nor hearer, the act of speech is no speech. It does not constitute *parole* in the proper sense of the word.

(2)   Another characteristic of speech in a Zen context is that language is deprived of its most basic function, i.e., the semantic articulation of reality. Of course, as long as a word is actually used, semantic articulation is still clearly and undeniably there – particularly when viewed with the eye of a man who has no idea at all of what Zen considers the primary level of Reality. But from the Zen point of view, it is as though the semantic articulation became transparent, permeable, flexible and non-resistant to such a degree that it is almost non-existent. One of the reasons why Zen sayings look completely nonsensical to the outsider – take for example the above-cited *kōan* which asserts that the river stands still while the bridge flows – lies in the fact that the outsider does not properly understand this peculiar transformation which the function of semantic articulation undergoes when a word is uttered in a Zen context. Let me explain this point a little further.

When, for instance, we say 'table', the word naturally exercises its normal function for articulation. That is to say, the word cuts out a certain portion of reality and presents it to our mind as a specific thing called by that name, distinguishing it from all other things. The 'table' is 'table' just because it is different from all non-tables. And as uttered in a definite actual context, the word refers to a particular table which is concretely existent there. The same holds true from the Zen point of view, too. To that extent Zen is still in the secondary or worldly dimension of Reality. As I have said before, however, semantic articulation in a Zen context is infinitely flexible. The articulated picture of reality is here permeable; it offers no resistance. That is to say, a product of articulation does not obstruct our view; it does not force our view to stop at that point. The 'table', for instance, which is a product of articulation, does not obtrude itself in a Zen context as a solid semantic mass as it does in ordinary speech. Rather, it makes itself transparent so that it allows our view to go direct to the very source from which the form of the table has emerged. Through the articulated form of the 'table' the primary level of Reality reveals itself in its original inarticulate state. This situation is what is usually referred to in Mahayana Buddhism as seeing a thing in its *tathatā* or Suchness. It is not the case, be it remarked, that the word 'table' works as a symbol indicating Something-beyond. Rather, the 'table' in its verbal form is itself the most immediate presentation of the primary level of Reality.

(3) I would point out as the third characteristic of the use of language in Zen the fact that the content of whatever is said in a Zen context in the form of a proposition does not constitute an independent semantic (or representational) entity. This is but a direct sequence of the second characteristic which has just been explained.

When we say for example, 'The table is square' or 'The sky is blue' in the secondary or customary dimension of Reality, the proposition produces in the mind of the hearer a kind of semantic entity standing out against the background of silence. In the primary dimension of Reality, on the contrary, no such independent mental unit is produced. For no sooner is the proposition uttered than it becomes totally dissolved into its original source which is nothing other than the primary dimension of Reality. We can also express the same idea from its reverse side by saying that whatever is said is in itself a total and integral presentation of the primary dimension of Reality. The proposition: 'The sky is blue' is not an objective description of Nature. Nor is it a subjective expression of the speaker's psychological state. It is a momentary self-presentation of the absolute Reality itself. And as such, the proposition does not *mean* anything: it does not indicate or point to anything other than itself.

In a far more poetic way, Master Tung Shan (Tōzan, 807-869)[7] in his celebrated Zen poem *Pao Ching San Mei* (J.: *Hō Kyō San Mai*) expressed this state of affairs as follows:

Snow heaped up in a silver bowl,
A white heron hidden in the light of the full moon,
The two are alike, yet not the same,
Interfused, yet each having its own place.

The 'silver bowl' symbolizes the primary, non-articulated Reality while 'snow' symbolizes a piece of articulated Reality. Likewise the 'light of the full moon' and the 'white heron'. 'The two are alike', i.e., the two things, being of the same color, are not clearly distinguishable from one another. Yet they are not the same, i.e., the 'snow' *is* 'snow' and the 'bird' *is* 'bird'.

The absolute Reality or the primary level of Reality as understood by Zen has no real name; it is impossible to present it verbally in its absoluteness. But when a Zen Master in a moment of extreme spiritual tension says: 'The sky is blue', the unnamable Reality becomes named and presented in this particular form. The timeless Reality glitters and flashes for a moment in a time-space dimension. In so far as it appears in the articulate form of the-sky-being-blue, it is distinguishable; it is distinguished from the original non-articulation as well as from what is expressed by all other propositions. Yet insofar as it is an immediate and naked presentation of the non-articulated Reality, it is not to be distinguished from the latter.

Following in Tō Zan's footsteps, a Zen Master of the tenth century, Pa Ling (J.: Ha Ryō, exact dates unknown), when asked: 'What kind of thing is the Deva sect?', answered: 'It is snow piled up in a silver bowl'.[8] 'Deva' refers to Kāna-Deva, a disciple of Nāgârjuna (J.: Ryūju, *ca.* 150-250). Kāna-Deva was noted for his philosophic capability. The 'Deva sect' therefore refers to the philosophy of Nothingness (*śūnyatā*) which characterizes Nāgârjuna's Middle-Path position. Thus this anecdote shows that this peculiar view of the relation between the non-articulated Reality and its articulated forms is precisely what constitutes the core of Mahayana philosophy.

IV The Ontology of Meaning in Mahayana Buddhism

The anecdote which has just been mentioned is interesting in that it incidentally brings to our attention the fact that the Zen approach to language has a historical background in the *Mādhyamika* or Middle-Path school of Mahayana Buddhism. But it must be noted that the philosophy of language of Zen is also related with *Vijñaptimātratā* or Ideation-Only school going back to Vasubandhu (*ca.* 400-480).

In the history of Indian philosophy in general, the Mahayana philosophy of language stands diametrically opposed to the semantic theory upheld by the Vaiśeṣika and Nyāya schools. What characterizes the latter theory is the view that a word is a symbol for something existent in the external world. To every single word there corresponds something that really exists. Whenever there is a word, one can be sure of the existence of a corresponding object in the world; and conversely, whatever is knowable in the world is namable. This view is so predominant in the Vaiśeṣika school that in its ontology 'existent' is called *padârtha*, i.e., the meaning of a word, or what is meant by a word.

Thus in the thought of this school, the very fact that we have the word 'ox', for example, is by itself a definite proof that there *is* in the external world a particular substance designated by that name. Since, further, we predicate of this substance various properties, saying: 'The ox is white', 'The ox walks' etc., we can be sure that properties like 'whiteness', and 'walking', etc. are also existent in the real world. And since the word 'ox' applies universally to various kinds of ox (*e.g.,* walking, running, reposing, etc.), the ox as a universal must also exist in reality. Likewise the various properties that distinguish the universal-ox from other species of animal like horse, sheep, dog, etc..[9]

The ontology of Vaiśeṣika is an outspoken atomism in which all existents are considered ultimately reducible to atoms (*paramâṇu* meaning 'extremely fine or small'). The atoms are the basic substances that are themselves invisible. An ox, for example, is a composite substance which is an aggregate of such atoms. A composite substance is a visible body; it is a new independent entity which is different from the atoms that are its constituent parts, just as a piece of cloth which is made of threads is in itself a different substance from the threads.

Both the Middle-Path school and the Ideation-Only school of Mahayana Buddhism take the position of radical opposition to such a view concerning the relation between language and reality. Language, Buddhism asserts, has no ontological significance. A word does not correspond to a piece of Reality. Words are merely signs established for the convenience of daily life. They have nothing to do with the structure of Reality. The Vaiśeṣika school takes the position that to a world like 'pot' or 'table' there corresponds in the external world a real object, a substance. According to Buddhism this is merely a view proper to the secondary, i.e., worldly, level of Reality. The common people always think this way and their whole scheme of life and behavior is formed on this very basis. From the point of view of the primary level of Reality, however, all this is false and even sheer nonsense. A 'table', for example, is not a substance endowed with an unchanging, eternally self-identical nature. In other words, it is in reality 'nothing', for in itself it is provided with no permanent ontological solidity. But as a phenomenal existent, the table *appears* as if it really existed, just as a phantom or the moon reflected in the water appears as if it existed. According to the doctrine upheld by the Ideation-Only school, it is language that induces such a false view of Reality.

Language is inseparably connected with conceptualization. The meaning of the word is universalized into a concept, and the seeming solidity and permanence of the concept is readily projected onto the structure of the world. Thus 'table' comes to appear as a self-subsistent entity having real solidity and permanence. The same is true of the properties of the table such as its colors and forms.

In *Trimśikā Vijñaptimātratāsiddhih* (XX) Vasubandhu declares that all those 'things' that are produced by this natural tendency of the human mind are nothing but so many falsely imagined forms of being and that they are really non-existent. Man is accustomed, Vasubandhu argues, to imagine the existence of an external object corresponding to a word – the object-table, for example, corresponding to the word-'table'. He imagines in addition that the eye exists as the organ of perceiving the object-table. In truth what really deserves to be said to 'exist' is only the act of perception as a continuous stream of consciousness (*citta-saṃtāna*) which goes on changing its actual content from moment to moment. Both the object-table and the eye which perceives it are products of the discriminating function of the mind which takes out these subjective and objective entities by analysis from the stream of consciousness. Man simply ignores thereby the fact that the content of consciousness differs from moment to moment. Thus man falsely posits 'table' as a universal which remains the same in spite of all the differences in time and space. Strictly speaking, however, even this particular table which I am perceiving at this present moment is different from the so-called same table which I perceived one moment ago as it will be different from the table which I shall be perceiving after a moment. And as the object-table changes from moment to moment, the eye that perceives it is also different from moment to moment. Needless to say, the eye that perceives a round table is not the same as the eye that perceives a square table. Thus the eye, no less than the object, is something falsely posited by imagination under the influence of the articulating function of language. And these false entities are phenomenal forms that spring forth interminably from the deep potential powers which remain stored in the Subconscious known in this school as the *ālaya*-consciousness.

In a similar way Nāgârjuna, founder of the Middle-path school and the representative of the philosophy of Nothingness, asserts that the so-called essence is nothing but a hypostatization of word-meaning. The word, he says, is not of such a nature that it indicates a real object. Instead of being a sure guarantee of the existence of an ontological essence, every word is itself a mere baseless mental construct whose meaning is determined by the relation in which it stands to other words. Thus the meaning of a word immediately changes as soon as the whole network of which it is but a member changes even slightly.

Ordinary people, living as they do in accordance with the 'worldly view' (*lokavyavahāra*) which is based on linguistic convention, cannot but exist in a world composed of an infinite number of different things that are nothing but hypo-statized word-meanings. This linguistically articulated view of the world is superimposed upon Reality as it really is in its original pure non-articulation, in its limitless openness as Zen calls it. But ordinary people are not aware of this latter stratum of Reality.

Nāgārjuna argues that the first of these two dimensions, i.e., the linguistically articulated world, is sheer imagination. What really *is* is the dimension of Reality before it is analyti-cally grasped through the network of articulating words. That pre-linguistic Reality is the Reality, i.e., Nothingness (*śūnya-tā*). The word *śūnyatā* refers to the original metaphysical state of absolute Reality where there are no falsely posited, fixed things. The simple fact that there are absolutely no fixed essences behind the ever-changing forms of phenomena, when subjectively realized by man, constitutes the highest Truth. When man attains to this highest stage and looks back from this vantage point, he discovers that the very distinction which he initially made between the primary or 'sacred' level of Reality and the secondary or 'vulgar' level of Reality was but sheer imagination. Even the 'sacred' is an articulated piece of Reality, which distinguishes itself from what is not 'sacred'.

The *kōan* No. 1 of the *Pi Yen Lu* describes this situation in a very brisk and concise way which is typical of Zen thinking. The Emperor Wu of Liang asks Bodhidharma: 'What is the primary meaning of the sacred Truth?' To this Bodhidharma answers: 'Limitlessly open! Nothing sacred!'

A limitlessly open circle that has its center everywhere and nowhere, defying all attempts at fixation – nothing here is fixed, nothing has essential boundaries. There is nothing to be permanently fixed as the 'sacred'. In this laconic answer the semi-legendary first Patriarch of Zen Buddhism epitomizes the central teaching of Nāgārjuna.[10]

V   The Problem of Semantic Articulation

It would be natural that language in such a special context should raise grave semantic problems. It is, as we have remarked above, of the very nature of language to articulate Reality into fixed entities. Yet Zen demands that language be used without articulating a single thing.

> Master Shou Shan (J.: Shu Zan, 926-993) held up his bamboo staff.
> Showing it to his disciples he said: 'If you, monks, call this a bamboo staff, you fix it. If you don't call it a bamboo staff, you go against the fact. Tell me, you monks, right now: What will you call it?'

Against the philosophical background which has just been given, it will be easy to understand Master Shou Shan's intention. If you call a bamboo staff a 'bamboo staff', you are simply hypostatizing the meaning of the word into a separate, self-subsistent substance, falsely articulating Reality as it really is in its limitless openness. If, on the contrary, you refuse to admit that it is a bamboo staff, if you say that it is *not* a bamboo staff, then you are going against the fact that Reality here and now is appearing in the phenomenal form of a bamboo staff.

Commenting upon this anecdote Master Wu Mên (J.: Mumon, 1183-1260), author of the *Wu Mên Kuan* says:

> If you call it a bamboo staff, you fix it. If you don't call it a bamboo staff, you go against the fact. Thus you can neither say something nor not say anything. (What is it then?) Tell me on the spot! Tell me on the spot![11]

'Tell me on the spot!' or 'Say something at once!' is very significant in a Zen context of this nature. It means: 'Say something decisive without reflection, without thinking!' For even the slightest reflection will immediately lead man away from the primary level of Reality. Rather, the primary level of Reality must be actualized on the spot in the form of a word or gesture gushing forth from a dimension of consciousness which is over and above articulation.

This *kōan* does not tell us whether or not there was among the disciples anybody who could give a proper response to Master Shou Shan's challenging question. There is, however, another *kōan* in the same book in which a disciple gives an appropriate answer to his Master's question in a similar situation.[12]

> Master Pai Chang (J.: Hyakujō, 720-814)[13] brought out a water-bottle, put it on the floor, and asked a question: 'If you are not to call it a water-bottle, what would you call it?'
> The head monk of the monastery answered by saying: 'It cannot possibly be called a piece of wood!'
> Thereupon the Master turned to Wei Shan (J.: Isan, 771-853) and asked him to give his answer.
> On the spot, Wei Shan tipped over the water-bottle with his foot. The Master laughed and remarked: 'The head monk has been beaten by this monk in the contest'.

Wei Shan who was then in the position of *tien tsuo* (J.: *tenzo*) – one who looks after the food of the monks in the monastery – was as the result of this victory chosen as the director of a newly-opened monastery. Later he became a first rate Master and opened a brilliant chapter in the history of Zen in China.

Let us now examine the meaning of this seemingly nonsensical behaviour of Master Wei Shan. The answer given by the head monk is perfectly in accord with common sense. 'It cannot possibly be called a piece of wood' – that is to say, 'a bottle is a bottle, it can never be wood'. The statement does make sense from the viewpoint of the secondary level of Reality. Philosophically it is essentialism which goes back to the central thesis of realism upheld by the Hinayâna *Sarvâstivâdin*. The thesis may be briefly summarized by the formula: A is A; it is not, it cannot be, anything other than A, because it is fixed to itself by its own permanent essence. As is easy to see, this ontological position collides head-on with the thesis of *niḥsvabhāva* or 'non-essentialism' that has been advanced by Nāgârjuna.

It is to be remarked that as long as one remains attached to the secondary level of Reality, one can never go out of the boundaries of this kind of simple realism. One may, while remaining on this level, become aware of the untenability of essentialism, and in order to break the magic spell of such a position call the water-bottle for example God or Buddha or even Nothing. One will still be within the domain of hypo-statized word-meanings. For in the secondary dimension of Reality no sooner is a word like 'God' or 'Nothing' uttered than its semantic content becomes fixed and crystallized into a fixed entity having an essence of its own. Zen demands that one should rather jump into an entirely different dimension of Reality – the primary dimension – where *A* is neither *A* nor non-*A*, and yet, or just because of this, *A* is undeniably *A*. The water-bottle in this new dimension of Reality is neither a water-bottle nor a non-water-bottle, being over and above such a distinction, because this dimension is that of *śūnyatā* where no fixed essence is established. But just because of this absolute non-distinction and non-articulation, everything, anything can be a total manifestation of the whole Reality. A water-bottle *is* a water-bottle in this particular sense. In a water-bottle the whole *śūnyatā* is actualized. The water-bottle is not sustained by its own essence. It is sustained and backed by *śūnyatā*. Otherwise expressed, in a single water-bottle is contained the whole universe. It *is* the whole universe. Is the water-bottle in such a situation still a water-bottle? Yes and No. The young monk Wei Shan in the above-quoted *kōan* gave expression to this view by his seem-ingly irrational behavior.

It is against the background of such a view of Reality that the one-finger Zen of Master Chü Chih is to be understood. Mention was made at the outset of Master Chü Chih who had a strange habit of sticking up one finger in answer to whatever question he was asked about Zen. In the dimension of Reality in which the Master was living, the finger he raised was a no-finger, that is to say, it was an immediate and naked manifestation of that dimension itself in the form of a finger. In other words, when Chü Chih raised his finger, the whole universe was raised with it. The raising of one finger in this dimension is nothing other than the instantaneous raising of the whole phenomenal world.

The fundamental structure of the phenomenal world from such a point of view has been elucidated in the most magnificent way by the Hua Yen (J.: Kegon) school of Mahayana philosophy which flourished in China. Everything in the universe, this philosophy teaches, is a unique embodiment of the absolute Reality; everything is a mirror reflecting the supreme Light. And all the mirrors, each reflecting in itself the same supreme Light, reflect each other in such a way that each one of the mirrors reflects all the rest of the mirrors. The whole universe is represented as a limitless number of luminous mirrors facing one another so that the world is made to appear as an infinite mass of light with an unfathomable depth. In such a situation, the slightest movement of even one single mirror cannot but affect the whole world of light. And since in the phenomenal dimension all things are moving from moment to moment, and since each single movement of every single thing brings into being a new order of things, a new world is born afresh at every moment.

Referring to this Hua Yen view, Master Yüan Wu (J.: Engo, 1063-1135), the celebrated compiler of the *Pi Yen Lu*, says in his Introductory Remark to the above-mentioned *kōan* in which the one-finger Zen of Chü Chih is narrated:

> As a mote of dust flies up, the whole earth is said to rise therein; when a flower comes into bloom, its movement is said to vibrate the whole universe.
> Well then, what is the state in which no dust yet rises, no flower yet blooms?

It goes without saying that the first two sentences refer to the phenomenal structure of Reality, while the third sentence is a reference to *śūnyatā*, the original, non-articulated oneness of Reality which may be compared to the supreme Light in the above-mentioned metaphor, that remains eternally unmoved and changeless through all the phenomenal forms in which it actualizes itself. Master Chü Chih who raised one finger was simply reproducing by his whole person this metaphysical process by which the world of phenomenal things arises out of the depth of the eternal stillness and quietude.

Master Chü Chih could perform such a feat, because the finger he raised was the no-finger, that is, *śūnyatā* itself. The disciple who imitated his Master also raised one finger. Outwardly the boy did exactly the same thing as the Master. But the finger which he stuck up was not more than a 'finger', for while raising it, he was conscious that he was raising his 'finger'. Since the boy lived exclusively in the secondary dimension of Reality, the finger he raised was an essentially limited phenomenal object. The finger as a phenomenal object was raised, but the universe did not arise with it.

When, his finger having been cut off and he himself having been called to by the Master, he turned round and wanted to raise his finger in answer to his Master's question: 'What is the Buddha?', he noticed that the finger did not rise. At that very precise instant he realized like a flash the non-existence of his finger in the most profound sense. That is to say, instead of a phenomenal finger he saw there the no-finger. He could not raise his phenomenal finger, but he could raise the non-phenomenal, invisible and non-existent finger. By raising this no-finger, he raised the whole universe. At that moment he saw the whole universe arising out of an invisible dimension of Reality. Thus the boy attained enlightenment. The no-finger which he raised there and then was exactly of the same nature as the 'three pounds of flax' of Master Tung Shan and the 'cypress tree in the courtyard' of Master Chao Chou.

Silent, wordless gesture is not the only means by which the primary level of Reality becomes actualized. Recourse is often had to language, full-fledged speech, in order to actualize here and now the eternal Truth. Thus, to give a typical example:

> Once a monk asked Master Fêng Hsüeh (J.: Fūketsu, 896-973) saying: 'Speech spoils the transcendence (of Reality), while silence spoils the manifestation. How could one combine speech and silence without spoiling Reality?'
> The Master replied: 'I always remember the spring scenery I saw once in Chiang Nan. Partridges were chirping there among fragrant flowers in full bloom!'[14]

The monk says, if we use words in order to describe the primary level of Reality, its original non-articulation inevitably gets articulated into limited entities. If, on the other hand, we keep silent, everything becomes submerged into the eternal Nothingness and the phenomenal aspect of Reality is thereby lost. Hence the question: How can we combine speech and silence so that we might present the absolute Reality in both of its aspects?

Instead of answering by telling the monk *how* one could combine speech and silence, Master Fêng Hsüeh directly presents to the monk's eyes the primary level of Reality as a combination of silence and speech. In order to clarify the structure of his presentation, we must keep in mind that the exquisite spring scenery here described in words is a landscape evoked out of the depth of memory. It is a landscape that lies both temporally and spatially far away from the actual point at which the poet stands. It is, in other words, non-existent. Yet as being actually evoked in memory, the landscape is there, vividly alive. The chirpings of the partridges are not being heard at the present spatio-temporal point of the external reality. But in a different dimension the partridges are undeniably chirping among fragrant flowers. All the elements of the poem, including the subject-I, are in this way both absent and present at one and the same time. It is a peculiar combination of silence and speech.

From the semantic point of view we must remark that the articulating function of language is no less at work here than in the normal cases of language use. Since words are actually uttered, a number of definite semantic entities are produced – 'I', 'partridge', 'chirping', 'flower', 'fragrance'. But all these things, being in reality non-existent, do not present themselves as solid self-subsistent entities. They are transparent and permeable. Reflecting each other, interpenetrating each other, and dissolving themselves into each other, they form an integral whole which is nothing other than the direct appearance of the primary level of Reality. In this sense, the semantic function of articulation is in such a context reduced almost to nullity. For articulation loses its functional basis, it does not work properly, in the presence of the trans-subjective and trans-objective awareness of the interfusion of all things, where, for example, the word 'partridge', instead of establishing an independent external substance, means rather its identification with the 'flower' and all other things, so that they all end up by being fused into one. The majority of authentic Zen sayings are ultimately of this nature.[15]

To illustrate this point, I shall give here an example which is

far more typically Zen than the preceding one. It is the *kōan*
No. IV of the *Wu Mên Kuan*, entitled 'The Barbarian Has No
Beard'. The word 'barbarian' or 'the barbarian of the West'
refers to Bodhidharma who, having come from the West, i.e.,
India, allegedly started the movement of Zen Buddhism in
China. This strange appellation for the venerated first Patriarch of Zen is purposely used in order to shock the common
people out of their belief that Bodhidharma was an extraordinary, sacred or divine person. It is intended to suggest that
he was just an ordinary man like anybody else. The *kōan* itself
consists in an extremely short interrogatory sentence which is
attributed to Master Huo An (J.: Waku-An, 1108-1179). It
reads:

That Western barbarian – why has he no beard?

An excellent example of Zen nonsense, one might say. Why
and with what intention did Master Huo An ask such a
nonsensical question? The very picture of Bodhidharma
without a beard goes against the prevalent image of this grave
and stern Master of meditation. In fact in the traditional
Chinese and Japanese drawings we find him almost invariably
appearing with a dark shaggy beard.

In the verbal picture by Huo An, however, Bodhidharma is
presented beardless, for in truth he appears here as an
immediate actualization of the primary level of Reality. It is
highly interesting to observe that Reality is presented as a
combination of silence and speech just as it was in the spring
scenery of Master Fêng Hsüeh, but in an incomparably more
concise and straightforward way. The aspect of silence is
represented in this verbal picture by the beardless
Bodhidharma. There is not even a single hair visible on his
face. It refers to the aspect of Nothingness of Reality, the
śūnyatā, which is absolutely inarticulate, 'limitlessly open'
with no distinction whatsoever. The aspect of speech is represented by his being 'beard-less'. The word 'beard' is actually used. The word, as soon as it is uttered, inevitably produces a semantic entity by its intrinsic faculty of articulation.
Something becomes articulated into an entity, the object-
'beard'. But it is immediately negated – 'beard-less'.

The combination of these two aspects verbally presents the
primary level of Reality in its two essential forms. The abso-

lute Nothingness discloses itself in a flash in the form of a beard, then it disappears into its original darkness. The semantic articulation is made, but it is immediately nullified. It is as though no articulation were ever made. Master Huo An is demanding his students to grasp instantaneously, at this precise fleeting moment, the structure of the integral whole of Reality.

This, however, is by no means an easy task to accomplish. For the effect of articulation is persistent. Once the 'beard' is articulated out of Nothingness, it tends to remain as a semantic entity, even if the word is immediately negated. For the 'beard' continues to subsist in a negative form. The 'beardless' is posited as a negative entity. The negation then comes to stand on a par with affirmation on the same level of discourse, and the original Negation, i.e., the *śūnyatā* is forever lost. Master Wu Mên referring to this danger says in his poem on this *kōan*:

> Do not talk about your dream
> In the presence of fools.
> The barbarian has no beard, you say.
> You simply add obscurity to what is clear in itself.

By trying to show the primary level of Reality in the twinkling of an eye in the form of 'no-beard', Huo An simply leads ordinary men into an unnecessary intellectual entanglement, for it is so difficult for ordinary men to obliterate and nullify the effect of articulation immediately after it has occurred. But unless such a nullification of the articulated entity be effected, one can never hope to jump into an entirely different dimension of Reality and grasp the *śūnyatā* that has just manifested itself momentarily in the form of a 'beard' which is in reality a 'no-beard'.

In India a philosopher of the Middle-Path school of the sixth century, Candrakīrti has admirably elucidated this point through a metaphor in his *Prasannapadā* (XVIII).[16]

Suppose, so he says, a man afflicted with an eye disease sees flickering before his eyes a hair floating in the air. A trustworthy friend of his assures him that the hair which he is perceiving now is unreal. The man then may believe that the hair which is actually visible to him is not really existent. But he has not yet grasped the truth that there is absolutely no hair there, because he *is* actually perceiving the hair. It is only when he gets completely cured of his eye disease that he understands the non-existence of the hair – this time by not perceiving it at all. As the hallucination disappears his consciousness goes beyond the stage at which the question is raised as to whether the hair exists or does not exist. As there is no longer any hallucination, the question itself of the existence or non-existence of the hair loses its meaning. The problem simply does not exist. Affirmation and negation are equally invalidated. This is the state of real Negation in the sense that it is beyond both affirmation and negation which are valid only at the stage of hallucination. The Nothingness or *śūnyatā* which is taught in Mahayana Buddhism – Candra-kīrti thus concludes – is of such a structure.

To this we may add that the 'no-beard' of Master Huo An is also exactly of this nature. It is comparable with the falsely perceived hair in the air at the very moment when the hallucination disappears – the 'hair' which is 'no-hair'. The positing of the beard on the smooth face of Bodhidharma through semantic articulation is, as Master Wu Mên rightly remarks, putting a spot of obscurity on the face of clarity. Yet Huo An had to do so, for otherwise the original universal 'clarity' would not have been grasped as such. Only through the process of activating the linguistic function of articulation which then immediately turns into non-articulation, can a passing glimpse be afforded into the real structure of Reality.

But Zen Masters are not always so kind to their disciples as Master Huo An. In the majority of cases, they simply show the aspect of articulation without then nullifying it. Thus Tung Shan just thrust the 'three pounds of flax' before the visiting monk, and Chao Chou the 'cypress tree in the court-yard'. It is left to the disciples themselves to turn the articulation into non-articulation.

Sometimes, again, the articulation is made by the visiting monk and the Master answers by abruptly presenting to him the non-articulation. This is best exemplified by the most celebrated of all Zen *kōans*, the *kōan* No. 1 of the *Wu Mên Kuan* which is entitled 'Chao Chou's Dog', but which is better known as the '*Wu*-Word of Chao Cou'. The word *wu* (J.: *mu*) simply means No!

A monk once asked Master Chao Chou: 'Has the dog the Buddha-nature?'
The Master replied: 'No!'

Innumerable commentaries have been written on this *kōan* concerning the word 'No!' So many divergent opinions have been advanced. Particularly interesting is the way it was handled by Master Ta Hui (J.: Daie, 1089-1163) of the Lin Chi (J.: Rinzai) school. He established in this school the tradition of utilizing this particular *kōan* as a most effective means by which to attain enlightenment. The tradition is still alive in Japan. There the word *wu!* or *mu!* is made to function almost magically, somewhat like the sound *aum* in Indian mysticism. The very sound of *wu!*, not its meaning, is thought to be psychologically effective in inducing the student's mind to go beyond the opposition of affirmation and negation in such a way that his subjectivity might be ultimately transformed into *Wu!* (Nothingness) itself.

Linguistically, however, it is far more simple to interpret Chao Chou's *wu!* as a direct presentation of the dimension of non-articulation which has just been explained. Chao Chou, in other words, nullifies on the spot the effect of the articulation made by the monk, by which the non-articulated Reality has been split into two entities, the dog and the Buddha-nature, and brings them back to the original Nothingness in which there is nothing to be distinguished as a dog or the Buddha-nature.

I shall bring this paper to an end by quoting another *kōan*[17] from the same *Wu Mên Kuan*, in which we see a perfect dramatization of the process by which articulation turns into non-articulation. The anecdote describes vividly how the monk Tê Shan (J.: Tokusan, *ca*. 782-865) who was to become later a famous Master, attained for the first time enlightenment.

> Once Tê Shan came to visit Master Lung T'an (J.: Ryūtan, *ca*. 850) asking for instruction, and stayed there till the night settled in.
> T'an said: 'The night has advanced. Why don't you retire and repose?'
> Shan made a deep bow, lifted the blind, and went out. But it

was thick darkness outside. He came back and told the Master
that it was utterly dark out there.
T'an lit a candle and handed it to him. Shan was about to take
it, when all of a sudden T'an blew the light out.
On the spot, Shan attained enlightenment.

After what has been said in the preceding, this anecdote will
need no detailed elucidation. It is a silent drama. No words
are used at the last critical moment. It goes without saying
that the candle light which illumines the world of darkness
and divides it up into visible things is here playing the role of
language with its essential function of articulation. When the
Master blew the light out, the once illumined world sank
again into the original darkness where nothing could be distinguished. The articulation became nullified and turned into
non-articulation. It is important to remark, however, that
since Tê Shan had seen the illumined world (i.e., the articulated world) a moment ago, the darkness now was not sheer
darkness; it was rather a darkness into which all the articulated things had been engulfed; it was non-existence as the
plenitude of existence.

It will be but natural that words uttered in contexts of this
kind should often look completely non-sensical to those who
remain entangled in the meshes of semantic articulation.

Notes

1. In the *kōan* system of Master Hakuin – a celebrated Japanese Zen Master
of the Lin Chi (J.: Rinzai) school, 1685-1768, who was the first to sys-
tematize *kōan* into several fundamental categories in terms of the grades of
perfection to be actualized in the Zen student – this saying is classified as
belonging in the second category called *kikan*, i.e. free and flexible machinery. The *kōans* in this category are those that are used by the Master for the
purpose of training the students who have already passed the first stage of
englightenment so that they might develop a capability of infinitely free,
flexible, and unobstructed actions in whatever situations they may find
themselves. Most of the *kōans* of this category are of glaring irrationality
and illogicality.

2. *Wu Mên Kuan*, No. 37. This *kōan* has been discussed in Essay I (Sec. VI)
from a somewhat different angle.

3. Claude Lévi-Strauss: *Structural Anthropology*, Eng. tr., Doubleday
Anchor Book, New York, 1967, p. 67.

4. *Chuan yü* (J.: *ten go*) literally means 'turning (*chuan*) word'. It means (1) a word (or series of words) that naturally springs forth from the 'turning-point' of consciousness, as well as (2) a word that could cause a 'turning-point' in the consciousness of one who listens to it. To be able to utter such a 'turning' word is considered an indubitable sign of the subject's having attained enlightenment. The *kōan* here in question is found in the *Wu Mên Kuan*, No. XX.

5. *Pi Yen Lu* (J.: *Hekigan Roku*) No. 70, 71, 72.

6. At the more advanced stages subsequent to the attainment of enlightenment, the distinction itself becomes obliterated because at such stages Zen makes no distinction between the 'sacred' and the 'vulgar'. The famous dictum of Master Nan Ch'üan (J.: Nan Sen, 748-834): 'The ordinary common mind – that *is* the Way' is a direct expression of such an attitude. (See *Wu Mên Kuan*, No. 19).

7. Tung Shan Liang Chieh (J.: Tōzan Ryōkai), founder of the Ts'ao Tung (J.: Sō Tō) sect in Zen Buddhism, to be distinguished from Tung Shan to whom reference has earlier been made (Section II). Concerning the following poem see Essay I (V).

8. *Pi Yen Lu*, No. 13.

9. On the universals as the referents of words according to Vaiśeṣika, Mimānsā, Nyāya, see R.C. Pandeya: *The Problem of Meaning in Indian Philosophy*, Motilal Banarsidass, Delhi, 1963, pp. 193-199.

10. Friedrich Georg Jünger in his *Sprache und Denken*, Vittorio Klostermann, Frankfurt am Main 1962, p. 218 (Chapter on *Bi-Yän-Lu*) shows a remarkably exact understanding of this *kōan*. He writes: . . . Bodhidharma antwortet: 'Offene Weite – nichts von heilig'. Heiligkeit und offene Weite werden gegenübergestellt, und in dieser Weite verschwindet auch die Heiligkeit als eine das Bewusstsein einengende, starr machende Grenze. In die offene Weite dringt – sie ist kein Vakuum – alles ein, dringt so ein, dass es kommt und geht, durchgeht, vorübergeht. Der Standort, jeder Standort muss aufgegeben werden, muss verlassen werden. Die Leere hat keinen Punkt, in dem sie befestigt werden könnte; die offene Weite ist ohne Mittelpunkt und Peripherie.

11. *Wu Mên Kuan*, No. 43.

12. *Ibid.*, No. 40.

13. Mentioned above, Section III.

14. *Wu Mên Kuan*, No. 24. Fêng Hsüeh's answer is a quotation from Tu Fu (J.: To Ho, 712-770), one of the most outstanding poets of the T'ang dynasty.

15. Cf. Chang Chung-yuan: *Creativity and Taoism*, the Julian Press, New York, 1963, pp. 20-21.

16. *Prasannapadā* is a celebrated commentary by Candrakīrti on the *Madhyamakakārikā* 'The Theory of the Middle Path' by Nāgârjuna.

17. No. XXVIII.

Essay IV

THE PHILOSOPHICAL
PROBLEM OF ARTICULATION

Note: First published in *Revue Internationale de Philosophie* (107-108), 1974–fasc. 1-2. as 'The Philosophical Problem of Articulation in Zen Buddhism'.

As we have observed in the preceding Essay (sec. V), 'articulation' is philosophically one of the most interesting questions raised by Zen Buddhism. For Zen itself it is a problem of vital importance because it directly concerns the structure of Zen experience known as *satori* or enlightenment. The present Essay purports to elucidate the nature of the 'articulation' of reality by discussing it specifically as a semantic and metaphysical-ontological problem.

I The Problem of Articulation

Zen centers round an experience which one often lightly disposes of by referring to it as something 'ineffable', 'inexpressible', 'not to be described by words', 'not to be grasped through rational thinking', etc.. And Zen at the first glance seems fully to corroborate this view. In fact the Zen documents which have come down to us are filled with admonitions by famous masters against trying to conceive of the Zen experience (*satori*) in any form whatsoever, to say nothing of talking about it.

The curious fact, however, is that Zen throughout its long history has constantly articulated itself in various verbal forms: primarily and most pre-eminently in the form of Zen dialogue (which has come to be known as *mondō*), and secondarily in poetry and philosophy. Otherwise we would not now be in possession of the enormous amount of Zen writings, both prose and poetry. It is particularly noteworthy that the philosophization of Zen (together with the philosophical presentation of the Zen world-view) which would seem to be the remotest thing imaginable from the very spirit of Zen, has actually had illustrious representatives in the course of the historical development of Zen Buddhism, and that even in the earliest phase, notably in the third Patriarch in China, Sōsan,[1] whose *Shinjin Mei* (Ch. *Hsin Hsin Ming*) is generally considered to be the first comprehensive philosophical account of Zen, and Master Sekito[2] whose *Sandōkai* (Ch. *Tsan T'ung Chi*) is by common consent a very unique treatise dealing philosophically with the doctrine of the unity of the absolute and relative in terms of light and darkness. We may mention in this connection also the name of a Japanese Zen master of a much later period, Dōgen, whose voluminous work *Shōbōgenzō* is regarded now by many as a work of an unusual philosophical profundity.[3]

But what is perhaps even more curious and interesting about the self-articulation of Zen is the fact that what constitutes the very core of Zen experience, when analyzed in a theoretic way, may most appropriately be described as a peculiar sort of articulation (psychological and ontological) of reality itself. What is meant here by the 'psychological and ontological articulation of reality' is a process by which what Zen regards as the ultimate reality – which can be presented as a kind of metaphysical 'field'[4] to be actualized in a dimension beyond the subject-object bifurcation – articulates itself into a certain number of distinct stages through a gradual transformation of human consciousness in the state of deep meditation on the one hand, and through a natural articulation of the *Urgrund* of existence on the other. It is to be noted that, according to Zen, the stages of human awareness and the stages of the ontological unfolding of reality which are at issue here, exactly correspond to one another, stage by stage, and that the two ultimately constitute one and the same process of the self-articulation of the ultimate reality itself.

This process of the self-articulation of reality, although it is essentially of a non-verbal nature in its original form, has thus an inner structure which is fully entitled to be analyzed and rearticulated in a verbal and conceptual form. When this is done, Zen experience will most naturally be presented as a 'Zen philosophy' or at least as the initial step toward the formation of a thought-system (or a number of thought-systems) typical of the Zen world-view. It goes without saying that such an analysis on our part must strictly be phenomenological in the sense that it should follow and represent as closely as possible what is originally experienced in the course of the *dhyāna* discipline (known as *zazen*) leading up to the enlightenment and leading further on to the post-enlightenment vision of the world of being. The present Essay is mainly concerned with this aspect of the problem of articulation in Zen Buddhism.

II Articulation as a Dynamic Process

As we have briefly indicated above, Zen experience in its
fundamental structure is in itself an articulation-experience,
or at least there is a certain respect in which it can justly be
regarded as an articulation-experience, i.e., an experience of
the articulation of both human awareness and metaphysical
reality.

Zen experience, in spite of its seeming simplicity, is in truth
of a fairly complicated nature. It is therefore no easy task to
formulate it in a concise form. The late Thomas Merton,[5] for
instance, who was one of those Westerners having a penetrating insight into the spirit of Zen, once defined Zen as 'the
ontological awareness of pure being beyond subject and
object, an immediate grasp of being in its suchness and this-
ness'. This definition is undeniably quite correct in the sense
that it correctly expresses the most important metaphysical
aspect of Zen. It has, however, the weakness of being too
static; that is to say, the definition, if taken as it stands, would
make one lose sight of the dynamic aspect of Zen experience.
The latter must rather be grasped as something essentially
more dynamic, as a spiritual event or process of an epistemological and ontological nature.

The dynamic structure of Zen experience here in question
may best be represented as a process comprising three major
stages:

$$(1)\ \text{articulation} \nearrow \quad (2)\ \text{non-articulation} \searrow \quad (3)\ \text{articulation}$$

These three stages may variously be indicated as: (1) differentiation → (2) non-differentiation → (3) differentiation; (1)
multiplicity → (2) unity → (3) multiplicity; (1) the phenomenal → (2) the noumenal → (3) the phenomenal, etc.

What is important to remark in this connection is that whichever formulation we may choose, the whole thing must strictly be understood as an objective-ontological as well as subjective-cognitive process. Otherwise expressed, the transition from (1) to (2) and from (2) to (3) is, in the view of Zen, an event that occurs to human consciousness just as it is an ontological event taking place in the 'external' world.

Viewed as a cognitive process, the first half (1 → 2) of the diagram represents the subjective process by which the mind in ever deeper meditation goes on losing the consciousness of the difference between the various things existing in the world (including the total obliteration of ego-consciousness) until finally it reaches the state of 'pure consciousness' as distinguished from the 'consciousness-of' which is the normal state of mind at the stage of the initial articulation. Here there is no trace left of the ego as the subject of cognition. Nor are there any more articulated things as objects of cognition. Just awareness – the pure awareness illuminating itself without there being either subject or object in a spiritual dimension of being beyond time and space. In the technical terminology of Zen Buddhism this state of pure awareness is often called the Mind (or No-Mind). And it is to this state that Master Banzan Hōshaku[6] refers to in his celebrated stanza on the Mind, which reads:

> The Mind-moon shines, solitary and perfectly round.
> Its light has engulfed all things in the world.
> Not that the light illumines the things.
> Not that the world subsists in the light.
> For the light and the world are both non-existent.
> What kind of a Thing is IT then?

The transition from stage (2) to stage (3) – the actual personal realization of which constitutes what is commonly known as *satori* – is a process by which the mind, leaving behind the stage of pure consciousness, goes back again to the stage of consciousness-of. The subject-object division of reality that has been totally obliterated at stage (2), becomes reinstated, and the subject of cognition again begins to perceive around itself a world of swarming forms and colors. However, the subject that has once gone through the stage of absolute non-articulation (2) cannot but be an internally transformed consciousness. The subject (3) is now a subject totally different from what it was at the initial stage (1) in that it now sees all things in the world as so many articulated forms of the non-articulated. Paradoxical though this may sound, the subject (3) is in reality a non-subject in the sense that it has completely identified itself with the non-articulated (2). It is a subject of cognition which is not a 'subject' (standing against 'the objects'), looking as it does at all things and every thing from the vantage point of the non-articulated itself. In other words, there is always a most lucid awareness of the non-articulated at the back of every individual thing. And this infinite lucidity of the awareness of the non-articulated is the subject at stage (3). To this refers the famous saying of Master Chōsha:[7] 'The whole universe is but the light of the Self ', the word 'self ' here meaning, as Dōgen[8] observes, 'your original face which you had even before your parents were born', i.e., the subject that is aware of its being completely at one with the non-articulated.

Viewed as a metaphysical process, the first half of the above-given diagram represents a process by which the world of multiplicity with its infinitely divergent things and events is seen to be ultimately reduced to the state of unity, in which things lose their ontological differences and become submerged in an absolute undifferentiation. This state of undifferentiation is technically designated by the term 'Nothing' or 'Nothingness'. It will be obvious that the Nothing thus understood is the plenitude of being, for it is the *Urgrund* of all existential forms.

The second half of the diagram represents (again metaphysically) a process by which all existents emerge out of the Nothing which is their ultimate source, constituting the world of phenomena. It is important to remark that the phenomena thus restituted after having been once lost in the undifferentiation of the noumenal, are the same phenomena as those of the initial stage (1). Yet, on the other hand, the phenomena at stage (3) are significantly different from what they were before in that they are now all 'open' entities instead of being 'closed' ones. Otherwise expressed, all things at this stage are ontologically transparent, a situation which we might describe equally well by saying that all things are articulated and non-articulated at the same time. Certainly, the things are here articulated – 'a mountain is a mountain and a river is a river'. But they are articulated in such a subtle way that each one of them is not caught in its own form of articulation. There is as it were a peculiar kind of ontological fluidity reigning over all things. The result is that they interpenetrate each other and fuse into one another. Every single thing, while being a limited, particular thing, can be and *is* any of the rest of the things: indeed it is all other things.

III Language and Articulation

The problem of articulation – at least implicitly, if not explicitly formulated as such – has always been a problem of
central importance in Zen Buddhism throughout its history.
The problem has repeatedly been raised and discussed in a
variety of forms from divergent points of view. Here I shall
first take up two typical cases in which articulation forms the
focal point of discussion, and then turn to what I consider to
be the most important of all the problems relating to articulation, namely, the problem of the absolute freedom of articulation in Zen.
  The first of the two cases is that which is concerned with the
problem of naming. Naming is precisely articulating. A name
is the result of man's having articulated through language a
given portion of reality. One of its most important functions
consists in articulating reality into a certain number of units
and crystallizing them into so many discrete entities which
then form among themselves a complicated network of
closely or remotely related things, qualities, actions and
relations.
  Language being semantically of such a nature, the central
problem for Zen is naturally: How can language with its
naming (i.e., articulating) function cope with the peculiar
relationship we have observed above between the non-
articulated and the articulated? In dealing with this problem
we must keep in mind that from the Zen point of view, neither
the non-articulated alone (be it called the Absolute, the One,
the All, or the Noumenal) nor the articulated alone (the
relative, phenomenal things, or Many) is the ultimate reality,
i.e., reality in its 'suchness'. Rather reality in its suchness is the
non-articulated as articulated into myriad things in the
phenomenal order of being, and the articulated things as

embodying each in itself the non-articulated. The non-articulated and articulated are to be envisaged as two aspects of the ultimate reality, each of the two aspects being always – except in abstraction – at the back of the other, from whichever side one may approach the reality. Now the question is: Is language capable of representing these two aspects of the suchness of reality by means of words? The answer must evidently be negative. For, as we have just seen, the semantic function of words consists in articulating; they can never 'non-articulate'. This intrinsic difficulty of language with regard to the problem of representing reality simultaneously in its two aspects of articulation and non-articulation is the subject-matter of the following famous *kōan*.[9]

> Once a monk asked Master Fūketsu:[10] 'Speech spoils the transcendence (of Reality), while silence spoils the manifestation. How could one combine speech and silence without spoiling Reality?'
> The Master replied:
> I always remember the spring scenery I once saw in Kōnan. Partridges were chirping there among fragrant flowers in full bloom.

Here the problem raised by the monk is implicitly quite a philosophical one. In asking this question he stands in the domain of reasoning. It is evident that he knows at least theoretically the peculiar relation between the non-articulated and the articulated, which we have just pointed out. The gist of his argument may be formulated in the following manner. Whether we speak or remain silent, the ultimate reality in its suchness can never be indicated. For if we use language in trying to re-present the reality, the latter will necessarily become articulated on the spot, and consequently only the phenomena will be apparent and the *Urgrund* lost, while if we keep silent, the non-articulated may very well be symbolically presented, but the aspect of articulation will be left in the dark.

As we have remarked above, language is semantically an instrument of articulation. Words articulate reality into rigidly fixed entities. Thus on the level of linguistic representation there could not possibly be any free communion between the bird, for instance, and the flower. Linguistically articulated, every thing is just itself, nothing else. Ironically enough, even the word 'non-articulated' does articulate the original undifferentiation of reality into something clearly differentiated from the 'articulated' things, and the non-articulated thereby becomes an articulated thing. Similarly, by calling the metaphysical *Urgrund* the 'Absolute', we determine it (i.e., we deprive it of its 'absolute' nature) and thereby bring it down to the level of the 'relative'.

If, on the other hand, we refrain from using language in order to avoid this difficulty, we fall into another pitfall. Certainly, by not using language we could make silence function as a symbol of the non-articulated; but, then, the articulated aspect of that non-articulated will totally be lost sight of. In other words, the non-articulated will be presented as sheer 'nothing' in the negative sense of the word, which is exactly the contrary of what Zen holds to be true. For from the Zen point of view, what we have *provisionally* articulated as the 'non-articulated' can never subsist apart from the infinitely variegated forms of its own articulation. If we look at the matter from the side of the human act of cognition, we may adequately describe it by saying that the phenomenal world is constantly and uninterruptedly emerging out of, and sinking instantaneously back into, the metaphysical depths of the Nothing, and that as each of the phenomena thus makes itself manifest for an instant, the non-articulated discloses itself like a flash. The non-articulated is nowhere to be found except in such metaphysical 'flashes'.

Thus, the monk concludes, neither speech nor silence will be able to do full justice to the reality in its original wholeness. What can we do, then?

It is interesting to observe that in reply to this intellectual question, Master Fūketsu directly presents the reality as articulated *and* non-articulated by utilizing a very special function of human language. He uses language poetically.

Surely, poetry is a linguistic art, and as such it does and must use language. And since it uses language it also articulates. But the articulating function exercised by poetic language – at least in the hands of real poets – is of a completely different nature from the articulating function exercised by prosaic language. In the non-poetic use of language, articulation means determination, discrimination or delimitation; it is always the act of pointing specifically to X. Every word is a closed semantic unit. Consequently the X which is indicated by the word is of necessity a closed entity. The word 'flower', for example, cuts off a certain portion of reality, distinguishes it from the rest, and crystallizes it into an independent entity. The flower thus articulated is something distinctly separated from the stem, the leaf, the root. It is not the earth; it is not the sun; it is not the air. Much less is it the same as partridges chirping among fragrant flowers. What semantically characterizes words in the non-poetic use of language is in this way their closedness. The flower tightly closes itself up into being-flower.

In poetry, on the contrary, words are essentially open or, we might say, transparent. Here the 'flower' *is* the leaf, the stem, the root. It *is* the sun, the earth, the spring breeze, the birds. Poetic language does not primarily discriminate. Its primary function consists rather in fusing things one into another. The flower in poetry opens itself up to all other things in the world. One single flower contains in itself the whole universe.

Thus the poem quoted by Fūketsu conjures up the beautiful scenery of the spring in Kōnan (which is at the same time an eternal or timeless,[11] metaphysical scenery) by virtue of the 'fusing' function of poetic language, that is, through the very special use of language by which articulation turns immediately into non-articulation. The fragrant flowers bloom and the partridges are merrily chirping among the flowers. The flowers and birds are in this dimension open to one another; they interpenetrate each other and fuse into one. Since, however, each of these words, 'flower' and 'bird', contains all other words by dint of a semantic network of suggestive associations, what is depicted turns out ultimately to be the interpenetration of all things. The interpenetration of all things through the 'flower' and 'bird' *is* the emergence of the spring. And the emergence of the spring is nothing other than the very emergence of reality in its suchness, articulating itself into this particular form, yet eternally remaining in the state of non-articulation. In terms of the initial question raised by the monk it is to be noticed that speech and silence are here combined with each other, and through this combination the intrinsic limitations of each have been overcome.

The second case which we are now going to examine deals with the same problem (namely, the relation between the articulated and the non-articulated) in a more philosophical way. As often happens, however, the philosophical thought is here developed in the form of a dialogue, between a master and a visiting monk.[12] I shall first translate into English the whole *mondō*, and then briefly explicate the main points of the argument from the particular point of view of articulation and non-articulation.

(1) Monk: Is the dog possessed of the Buddha-nature or not?
(2) Master: It certainly is.
(3) Monk: Are you possessed of it or not, Master?
(4) Master: I am not.
(5) Monk: (According to some Sutras) all sentient beings are possessed of the Buddha-nature. Why are you alone not possessed of it?
(6) Master: That is because I am not all-sentient-beings.
(7) Monk: You are not a sentient being! Does that mean that you are a Buddha?
(9) Master: Not a Buddha.
(9) Monk: What kind of a thing is it, then?
(10) Master: Not a thing.
(11) Monk: Is it visible or conceivable at all?
(12) Master: Thinking cannot grasp it. Arguing cannot reach it. Therfore it is said to be unthinkable and inconceivable.

(1) – (2): The monk, referring to the celebrated *kōan*[13] of Jōshū begins by asking whether the dog possesses the inborn capability of becoming a Buddha, i.e., becoming enlightened. The Buddha-nature (one would rather say in the West: the divine nature, the Truth, the Absolute, and the like) is nothing other than the 'non-articulated' as the *Urgrund* of being. Note that the primordial non-articulation is here explicitly contrasted with one of its own articulated forms, namely, the dog. The Buddha-nature and dog (or the non-articulated and the articulated) are represented as two separate entities clearly distinguished from one another. In other words, the primordial non-articulation is represented not in its suchness, but as something articulated. Under such an understanding, the master finds himself almost forced to describe the ontological relation between the non-articulated and the articulated as the latter being-in-possession-of the former. That is to say,

the dog's being an articulated (or manifested) form of the Absolute must linguistically be described as the Absolute being inherent in the dog. Hence the master's answer: 'Yes, the dog is possessed of the Buddha-nature'.

(3) – (4): Yet Master Ikan himself is aware of his being in the position of the non-articulated, his being completely identical with it. Thus it is impossible for him to say that he *has* (or is possessed of) the Buddha-nature. Rather, he *is* the Buddha-nature. So quite naturally he says: 'I am not possessed of the Buddha-nature'.

(5) – (6): The monk completely misses the point. Hence his question (5). The master answers saying that in the spiritual dimension in which he now stands, he – perhaps it will be better to write: He – is not yet articulated as a sentient being.

(7): If the master is not any of the sentient beings, he must be a Buddha.

(8) The master says that he (or He) is beyond even the articulation of being-a-Buddha. The implication is that it is precisely because he (He) is beyond being-a-Buddha that he is the Buddha in its deepest and most real sense. The non-articulated necessarily loses it absoluteness and becomes something relative as soon as it gets articulated into a particular thing (even a Buddha) and crystallized in the form of that particular thing. As we have observed earlier, the 'absolute' as conceived as something absolute is but a 'relative' thing.

(9) – (10): The monk again misses the point. The master repeats that the non-articulated in its absolute non-articulation is 'not a thing', i.e., not an articulated thing.

(11) – 12: The non-articulated can never be an object of thought or conceptualization. By its very nature it forever evades being conceived of in whatever form it may be. The moment man thinks of it as something – even as the Buddha – it falls into the state of an 'unnatural' articulation. It goes without saying that the latter must strictly be distinguished from the natural articulation of reality, which is, as we have seen above, involved in the very structure of the ultimate reality in its suchness.

IV Absolute Freedom of Articulation

The *kōan* which we have just analyzed presents in a very terse
form one of the cardinal tenets of Zen Buddhism; namely,
that the non-articulated viewed in its aspect of absolute non-
articulation, should not be confused with any of its articulated
forms, be it even the so-called Absolute. What is perhaps
even more important from the Zen point of view, however, is
what is directly implied by this latter statement, namely, that
the non-articulated, precisely because it is not essentially
bound to any particular articulation-form, is capable of being
articulated into anything whatsoever. Zen in fact is characterized by its assertion of an absolute, unlimited freedom in
the articulation of reality on the part of man – the word 'man'
being understood here in the sense of an enlightened man. It
is noteworthy that this freedom of articulation is manifested
in Zen everywhere and in various dimensions. Historically it
has created a peculiar Weltanschauung. Thus to give a typical
example:

> A monk once asked Ummon:[14] 'Where do Buddhas come
> from?' Ummon answered: 'Lo! The East Mountain goes
> flowing over the water'.

A mountain, observed exclusively in its being-a-mountain, is
something solidly immovable – at least so it appears. In such a
vision, the non-articulated is not observable; it is completely
hidden behind the articulated form of a mountain. What is
outwardly visible is only the articulation-aspect of reality
which has crystallized itself into a particular individuum called 'mountain'. And as such it differs essentially from all other
things. In reference to the ontological zero-point of non-
articulation, however, the mountain is by no means *essentially*
different from other things. It can, for instance, turn into

something 'watery' at any moment and begin to flow like the flowing water. Rather, it is (while it is 'mountain') already 'water'; it *is* actually flowing. The zero-point of non-articulation thus dissolves, as it were, all the essential fixities of individual things, and thereby re-creates a totally new vision of the world in which all things interpenetrate each other. It is in such a world that the absolute freedom of articulation is exercised by those men who actually see with their own eyes the mutual interpenetration of all things.

The freedom of articulation here at issue has naturally been often discussed in a peculiarly Zen fashion by many a Zen master. Examples abound in Zen literature. The most celebrated of all is Master Isan's 'tipping over a water-bottle'[15] One day Master Hyakujō, (Ch.: Pai Chang) in order to test his disciples, took out a water-bottle, put it on the floor, and asked the following question. 'If you are not to call this a water-bottle, tell me, what would you call it?' The head monk of the monastery, who was the first to answer, said: 'It cannot possibly be called a piece of wood!' This answer did not give satisfaction to Hyakujō. There upon Isan (Ch.: Wei Shan) stood up and kicked over the water-bottle, which fully satisfied the master. It will be obvious that this non-verbal answer by Isan satisfied Hyakujō because the action was a direct presentation of the above-mentioned zero-point of non-articulation which allows of being articulated into a water-bottle as well as into any other thing.

The following *kōan*[16] approaches exactly the same problem, namely, the problem of the articulation and non-articulation, in a somewhat different form.

> Bashō once said to the assembled monks: 'If you happen to have a staff, I will give you one. If, on the contrary, you have no staff, I will snatch it away from you'.

'If you happen to have a staff', that is to say, if you are immovably tied up by the articulated appearances of reality by regarding your staff, for example, as a self-subsistent substance, then 'I will give you one', that is to say, I will make you aware of the real (i.e., absolute) Staff (which is nothing other than the non-articulated itself hidden behind the articulated form of the staff). 'If, on the contrary, you have no staff ', that is to say, if you have *no-staff*, or if you are satisfied with only the intellectual understanding that your staff is in reality a no-staff, being as it is an articulated form of the non-articulated, then 'I will snatch it away from you', that is to say, I will shatter that conviction of yours by the solid fact that a staff is really a staff in the phenomenal dimension of reality (precisely because it is an articulated form of the non-articulated), for, otherwise, the staff would be nothing other than an insubstantial dream.

It is evident that what is pointed to by this famous *kōan* is again an absolute freedom of articulation on the part of those who have seen the structure of reality in its immediate suchness.

Many more examples of this sort could be given. But enough, I think, has already been given for our specific purposes. Instead, therefore, of going further in this direction, let us turn our attention to Dōgen,[17] by common consent perhaps the most original thinker Zen Buddhism has produced, and who is known for the philosophical breadth and depth of his thought. Let us see how this 'Zen philosopher' deals with the problem of the absolute freedom of articulation. The starting point of his argument[18] is the observation he makes of the fact that man by his nature tends to articulate reality as he sees it around himself in quite an arbitrary way in accordance with the basic patterns of cognition that are furnished and determined primarily by his sense organs and secondarily by his reason. Thus it comes about that a mountain, for example, is articulated into the fixed form of 'mountain', while water is articulated into an eternally unchangeable thing called 'water', these two never being confused with one another. All things become in this manner established as rigidly determined things according to the 'natural' articulation of reality – 'natural' because it conforms to the natural functions of man's sense organs. Thus for an ordinary man it is an impossibility even to imagine that a mountain could be a non-mountain or water non-water. In other words, man is unaware of the fact that his 'natural' articulation of reality is in truth, i.e., from the Zen point of view, of quite an arbitrary nature.

Thus Dōgen (although he does not explicitly use a word signifying 'articulation') begins by pointing out with great emphasis the arbitrariness of man's articulation of reality.

Man articulates reality – which is ultimately the primordial non-articulation whose structure has just been discussed – naturally (that is, arbitrarily!) into a number of more or less clearly demarcated segments. Even within the boundaries of each segment, Dōgen observes, man's nature is such that he tends to see (and in many cases obstinately refuses to see anything other than) an *essentially* fixed entity characterized by an *essentially* determined property or properties, ignoring thereby hundreds of other ontological possibilities that remain always open to that particular thing. Water, for example, is usually conceived as a liquid substance which always 'flows downwards', while in reality it is of an infinitely flexible nature, existing as it does in many different forms in many different places, and flowing as it does in every direction.

> The way man ordinarily looks at water is narrowly limited; he knows water only as something flowing downwards without stopping. This, however, is nothing but one out of many varied ways of looking at water that are humanly possible. In reality, even the 'flowing' of water is of many kinds. That is to say, even within the boundaries of the articulation of water as 'something flowing', water still manifests an almost illimitable flexibility. Thus it flows in the earth. It flows through the sky. It flows upwards. It flows downwards. Sometimes it flows into a village; sometimes it flows into a bottomless abyss. It goes up to form clouds. It comes down to form deep pools.

In this way, water as it comes into the sensory experience of man manifests an amazing variety of forms and functions. But, according to Dōgen, the sensible water with all its ontological possibilities is in truth but one single aspect of the reality which may provisionally be represented as reality-Water. What is ordinarily regarded as 'water' by man is only a small portion of the reality-Water, for it is but a sensible aspect of the latter. The latter comprises in itself also a vast domain of super-sensory articulations. It is upon such an understanding that Dōgen asserts the ubiquitous presence of water. Water, in his view, exists everywhere in every form because it is no other than the non-articulated. If the latter is here called 'water', it is simply because it is being observed in the particular status of its being ready to articulate itself (or manifest itself) as reality-Water. And thus understood, everything that exists in the world is a special form assumed by the

reality-Water. There is nothing in the world except Water.
Indeed, the whole universe is Water as it goes on transform-
ing itself moment by moment into myriads of different forms,
sensible and non-sensible. Says Dōgen:

> The view that there are places where water does not exist is a
> view peculiar to the Hinayanists or a doctrine of the heretics.
> In reality, water does exist in the burning fire. It exists in the
> human act of thinking, cogitation, and reasoning. It exists in
> the higest wisdom of enlightenment. It exists even in the
> Buddha-nature.

Thus 'water' as ordinarily understood by man is the result of
man's having arbitrarily articulated the originally inarticulate
reality into a narrowly limited entity. The original reality,
even in its 'water'-aspect (i.e., even as the reality-Water) goes
far beyond the sensory experience of man. The man of
enlightenment, in the view of Dōgen, is one who has overcome and transcended the limitations of such an arbitrarily
articulated world and who has attained to the stage of absolute freedom in articulating the non-articulated.

As a first step toward transcending this arbitrariness which
is observable in our inborn tendency to articulate reality in
rigidly determined directions, Dōgen proposes that we should
in imagination get rid of the 'natural' framework of sensory
experience provided by our sense organs, and picture to
ourselves how water, for instance, would look to non-human
beings. The imagery used by Dōgen in the following passage
is that of old, traditional Buddhism, but the philosophical
import of his argument will easily be seen through it.

> Water is seen differently by different kinds of beings. There
> are beings (i.e., celestial beings) who, looking at what we,
> human beings, see as 'water', see gorgeous necklaces adorned
> with jewels. This, however, does imply that they regard as
> 'water' what we, human beings, usually call 'necklaces'. What
> they regard as 'water' may be completely different from what
> we understand by the word 'water'. What will it be? We are
> not sure about that point. What is certain (on the authority of
> the Sutras) is that what for them is a necklace is for us 'water'.
> There are some beings who regard our 'water' as beautiful
> flowers. This, however, does not necessarily imply that they
> regard what we call 'flower' as 'water'.
> The hungry ghosts are said to regard our 'water' as burning

flames or bloody pus. (They cannot drink it, no matter·how thirsty they might be).
It may be that to the fishes our 'water' is a palace or belvedere.
Some beings there may be who regard our 'water' as precious stones.
There may be some others to whom our 'water appears as trees, walls or enclosures.
. . . . . .
We, human beings, regard it as 'water'.
In attentively considering the fact here described lies indeed a clue to the solution of a problem of life-and-death importance. Different kinds of beings have different views! Ponder upon this fact. Is it the case that one and the same aspect of reality is seen in a number of different ways? Or is it rather the case that a number of different aspects of reality are mistakenly considered one? Concentrate upon this question and pursue it further and further.

The Non-Articulated is capable of being articulated in infinitely different ways. The gist of Dōgen's argument is that we should not remain attached to the false view that the way we, human beings, see 'water' is the *only* way in which it could be seen. Indeed, 'water' must be observed from an open viewpoint transcending the narrow vista which is rigidly determined by the structure of our sense organs. We must learn to see 'water' with the eyes of fishes, heavenly beings, hungry ghosts, etc., thus broadening our vista indefinitely. For the *human* way of seeing 'water' is but one out of many possible ways of seeing the reality.

But, Dōgen goes on to say, all these possible ways of seeing 'water' themselves must ultimately be transcended. We must transcend the stage of man (or any other being)-seeing-water until we attain to the stage of water-seeing-water.

Try to learn to see the 'water' existing in all dimensions of being, from the different viewpoints of all these dimensions of being. You should not restrict yourselves to learning to see 'water' from the viewpoints of the human and heavenly beings alone. Know that you must learn to see 'water' in the way 'water' sees 'water'. Since, at such a stage, it is 'water' that sees 'water', necessarily 'water' comes to illumine and express 'water' itself. You must learn to see 'water' precisely in that way.

'Water-seeing-water' means for Dōgen 'water' illuminating itself and disclosing itself as the primordial Non-Articulated. Certainly insofar as there is 'water' clearly expressing itself as 'water' in no matter which dimension of being it may be, the non-articulated reality is here evidently articulated. Since, however, the 'water' at this stage of spiritual experience is no longer seen as an object of sight by a seeing subject, whether human, heavenly, or otherwise, and since it is 'water' itself that is seeing 'water', the ontological articulation of reality nullifies, as it were, its own act of articulation. The result is a seeming contradiction: the reality *is* and *is not* articulated into 'water'. Otherwise expressed, the reality articulates itself before the eyes of an enlightened man like a flash into 'water' and then it goes back instantaneously into the original state of non-articulation.

This is, in the understanding of Dōgen, the deepest mystery of ontological articulation. Reality in all its dimensions is constantly and unceasingly articulating itself into myriads of concrete forms. But these concrete forms are not necessarily confined to those which we, human beings, recognize as such. Quite the contrary, there are an infinity of forms that are alien and inaccessible to the human power of cognition. Furthermore, even with regard to those forms which are familiar to human beings, there is no rigidly fixed correspondence between them and the portions of reality with which they are customarily associated by man.

The articulation of reality with such a metaphysical freedom, Dōgen observes, is taking place everywhere at every moment. The universe is dynamically alive in this sense. But he observes at the same time how the reality, by articulating itself into myriads of forms, is actually articulating itself into itself, so that, in his view, the universal act of articulation goes on nullifying its own articulation moment by moment in such a way that the All remains in this sense eternally still and quiet in its original non-articulation. Articulation is non-articulation. It is this ontological paradox which is referred to by Dōgen's peculiar expression: 'water sees water' (i.e., the reality articulates itself into itself), for where there is absolutely nothing observable except water, the reality-articulating-itself-into-water necessarily nullifies its own meaning.

In the light of such an observation, Dōgen urges us to go beyond the narrow confines that are imposed upon us by the 'natural' function of our mind, and attain to the spiritual stage of an infinite freedom in the act of articulating reality. In accordance with the absolute metaphysical freedom exercised by reality in its self-articulation, the enlightened mind must also exercise an infinite freedom in articulating reality. That is to say, we must, Dōgen emphasizes, develop the spiritual ability to look at things not in terms of a culturally conditioned pattern of looking at things, not even in terms of the humanly predetermined categories of cognition, but in terms of the limitless ontological possibilities of the Non-Articulated itself. Only at such a stage of the freedom of articulation could Master Unmon unhesitatingly say in answer to the monk's question regarding the very source and foundation of Buddhism: 'Lo! The East Mountain goes flowing over the water'.

Notes

1. Sōsan (Ch. Sêng Ts'an, d. 606).

2. Sekitō (Ch. Shih T'ou, 700-790).

3. Reference has earlier been made (Essay I, Note 3) to Dōgen Kigen (1200-1253). Dōgen was not a philosopher; nor did he evidently have any awareness of writing something philosophical in writing his *Shōbōgenzō*. And the majority of Zen masters today would doubtless strongly object to our considering him a philosopher. It remains true, however, that the thought and ideas he developed in this work are for us of a great philosophical significance. His view on the 'articulation' of reality will be discussed in detail toward the end of the present Essay.

4. For an elucidation of the 'field'-structure of Zen experience, see my *Philosophy of Zen* (in 'Contemporary Philosophy' ed. Raymond Klibansky, vol. IV, Florence, 1971). See also Essay III.

5. Thomas Merton: *Mystics and Zen Masters* (New York, 1967), p. 16.

6. A disciple of Baso and an outstanding master of the 8th century.

7. Chōsha Keishin (dates unknown) was a great Zen master of the T'ang dynasty.

8. *Shōbōgenzō* (*op. cit.*), LV.

9. *Mu Mon Kan*, No. XXIV.

10. Fūketsu (Ch.: Fêng Hsüeh 896-973), a Chinese Zen master in the T'ang dynasty. 'Kōnan' is the Japanese pronunciation of Chiang Nan, a province of South China. I have discussed this *kōan* in a different context (Essay II, sec. V).

11. Note that the poet says: I *always* remember.

12. The principal *dramatis persona* is Master Ikan (755-817), an outstanding pupil of Master Baso in the T'ang dynasty. The dialogue is found in the *Keitoku Dentōroku* (Ch.: *Ching Tê Ch'üan Têng Lu*, 'Transmission of the Lamp') vol. VII.

13. It is a *kōan* enjoying tremendous popularity as 'the *Mu*-Word *kōan* of Master Jōshū'. A much shorter version of this *kōan* has been given before (see Essay III, sec. V). The Chinese pronunciation of Jōshū is Chao Chou.

14. Ummon (Ch.: Yün Mên 864-949), one of the greatest Zen masters of China (T'ang dynasty), known for his mysteriously cryptic utterances.

15. Isan (771-819) a disciple of Hyakujō. The incident is narrated in the *Mu Mon Kan*, Case XL. This anecdote had been analyzed before (see Essay III, sec. V.)

16. *Mu Mon Kan*, XLIV. Bashō was a Korean Zen master of the 9th century.

17. On Dōgen and *Shōbōgenzō*, see above, Essay I, Note 3.

18. What follows is based on an important chapter entitled *Sansui Kyō* ('Mountain and Water Sutra') of his *Shōbōgenzō*.

Essay V

THINKING AND A-THINKING THROUGH KŌAN

Note: This Essay has concurrently been published as a separate paper under the title of 'Meditation and Intellection in Japanese Zen Buddhism', by the Imperial Iranian Academy of Philosophy in *Traditional Modes of Contemplation and Action*, ed. Yusuf Ibish and Peter L. Wilson.

I Mistrust in Thinking

Mention has frequently been made of '*kōan*' in the preceding pages, but no systematic explanation of the word has yet been given. In view of the fact that the reality of Zen cannot be understood without an exact knowledge as to what kind of thing *kōan* is and how it is to be properly handled, I shall in this Essay attempt to elucidate the essential structure of *kōan* and its actual use in authentically Zen contexts. The problem will be dealt with in special reference to the relation between intellection and meditation as Zen has traditionally understood them. The word 'intellection', be it remarked at the outset, is here taken in the sense of the act of cogitation or discriminating function of the discursive intellect. Thus understood, no sooner is the problem posed than the answer – apparently the only right answer to be given – would seem to be found at hand. For all those who have some knowledge of Zen, whether practical or theoretical, will no doubt agree that these two terms, meditation and intellection, are absolutely incompatible with each other.

In fact Zen abhors all forms of intellectualism, verbalism and conceptualism, not to speak of those random thoughts and ideas that constantly arise and dart about in the mind to perturb its serenity. Not that the 'masters', i.e., those who have already attained enlightenment, remain permanently in a state of mental void and silence. Quite the contrary; they are in complete possession of their thinking faculty, which they exercise freely and spontaneously. In other words, they do think, too, in a certain sense. The point to note, however, is that their thinking unfolds itself in a totally different form and at quite a different level of consciousness from that with which we are familiar in ordinary circumstances. We shall deal with this aspect of the matter later on. As for the 'disciples', i.e., those who have not yet attained enlightenment, they are strictly forbidden by their masters to think. They are told that the more seriously one thinks the more hopeless will it become for one to experience the final 'break-through.' The very first step in the Zen practice of meditation consists in the disciple's wiping out of his mind all the habitual patterns of thinking which are deep-rooted in his mind.

Thus the Cartesian *cogito* which may very well be fully effective and valid in its proper field, is, from the viewpoint of Zen, far from being something that leads us directly to the awareness of the reality of human existence; on the contrary, *cogito* is considered the very source of all delusions about existence; *cogito* is a distraction that leads us away from an immediate grasp of reality as it really is.

There is inherent in Zen a deep, ineradicable mistrust in ratiocination or thinking in general. Zen regards philosophy with a suspicious eye, philosophy being a typical example of the discriminating function of the intellect. This negative attitude toward intellection would seem to be easily accounted for by the fact that what matters for Zen primarily or exclusively is a direct experience of reality in its primordial non-differentiation, which in Zen terminology is often called 'your original Face even before your parents were born.' The purity of 'original Face' is contaminated by the differentiating, discriminating activity of the discursive intellect. Hence the natural abhorrence of all kinds of abstract and theoretical thinking.

Furthermore the mistrust of Zen in abstract thinking, particularly in philosophy, has a historical basis. Historically Zen arose in China as a vigorous reaction against the multitudinous systems of Mahayana philosophy that had developed in India and China, in which Buddhist thinkers indulged themselves in extremely complicated, and often hairsplitting, abstract arguments. Regarding these arguments simply as nothing but futile entanglements of discursive intellect, Zen started by shattering the grandiose systems of philosophical thinking and trying to bring Buddhism back to its simplest and most original form, that is to say, to what in the view of Zen was the fundamental personal experience of the historical Buddha himself. This attitude has been kept intact throughout the ages, and anti-intellectualism has always been the very core of all Zen teaching, whether in China or Japan. The man of Zen aims at reducing all the historical forms of Buddhism to the enlightenment-experience of the Buddha himself, re-experiencing it in its original form, and plumbing the depths of spiritual life in a realm of the psyche which lies beyond the limits of intellect. It would be but natural that the man of Zen should in practice and on principle oppose any use of intellect in the understanding of the central part of Zen teaching. In the 'Lotus Sutra' we read: 'This Dharma is not to be comprehended through thinking and intellection'. For a man of Zen this is still an understatement. More positively, one must methodically and systematically eliminate all intellection. For as long as the intellect remains activated in no matter how subtle a form, one could never hope to re-experience the original enlightenment-experience of the Buddha. This cannot be otherwise because what Zen considers to be the original experience of the Buddha is primarily an awakening to a dimension of supra-consciousness or an ontological awareness of Being in its pure 'suchness' prior to its being articulated into myriads of things and events through the discriminating activity of the intellect.

In fact, ever since Zen arose in China, all the masters have unremittingly demanded of their disciples a drastic abandonment of thought. Absolutely no thinking! Do not try to comprehend anything, for there is properly nothing to be comprehended. Instead of thinking, what should the disciple do then, in order to attain enlightenment? He is to muster his entire inner force of concentration in order to fight against the ever-surging waves of thought and finally to sweep out of his consciousness all images, ideas, and concepts. Only then, he is told, will he be able to witness an entirely new realm of his psyche opening up in the deepest recesses of his mind.

The semi-legendary first Patriarch of Zen in China, Bodhidharma, is said to have remarked to his Chinese successor, E-Ka (Ch.: Hui K'o) when he was asked by the latter as to how one could enter into the realm of absolute Reality (Tao):

> No more agitations in the external world,
> No more panting of the mind inwardly,
> When your mind is like a perpendicular wall,
> Then only can you enter into the realm of Reality.

This is nothing other than a strong exhortation to the practice of meditation. Bodhidharma is here urging upon his future successor the absolute necessity of disciplining the psyche through imperturbable meditation in which the mind becomes transformed into something like a straight-standing wall of rock.

Incidentally, Bodhidharma, so the legend goes, having retired to the Shōrin (Ch.: Shao Lin) Temple in the province of Honan, sat in meditation there in a cave for nine consecutive years facing a tall rock-wall. Be this as it may, it is clear that Zen was from the beginning, and has always been, a religion – if we are entitled to call such a thing 'religion' – based on meditation and nothing but meditation. Meditational discipline in Zen is called *zazen* (Ch.: *tso ch'an*), i.e., sitting in *dhyāna* or meditation. More concretely, *zazen* means one's sitting in the full-lotus or half-lotus posture in a state of profound one-pointed concentration of the mind.

It is to be remarked that meditation itself is a common phenomenon observable in almost all religions to a certain extent at least. And no branch of Buddhism dispenses with meditational practices. What characterizes the Zen branch of Buddhism, however, is the fact that in both its historical origin and its fundamental structure it is a religion wholly based on meditation. As we have just observed in the words of Bodhidharma, the primary, or shall we say exclusive, concern of the man of Zen is to 'enter into the realm of absolute Reality', and entering into the realm of absolute Reality is actualizable only through sitting in meditation. From the point of view of Zen we must go a step further and say that sitting in meditation *is* entering into the realm of absolute Reality. The meaning of this will be clarified later when we shall discuss the position of Sōtō Zen in Japan as represented by its founder, Dōgen of the thirteenth century. A question will naturally be raised at this point: What, then, distinguishes Zen from the various systems of yoga in India? This will be clarified later on when we shall explain the characteristic features of the Zen meditation techniques that have been developed in the course of history in China and Japan. Let us for the time being continue to devote our attention to the anti-intellectualist aspect of Zen.

II Elimination of Discursive Thinking

It will be interesting to notice that at the back of this anti-intellectualism of Zen there is a clearly delineated philosophy, although the Zen people themselves would be loath to recognize it as 'philosophy' of any kind. In any case it is a fundamental idea which is both metaphysical and psychological, and which, though it is not in itself a 'philosophy' in the ordinary understanding of the term, could very well be developed and elaborated into a grand-scale system of metaphysics and depth-psychology. This fundamental idea or vision which, as we shall see, underlies the whole structure of Zen practice and thought, was given its earliest explicit formulation in the celebrated stanza ascribed to the first Patriarch, Bodhidharma, who is said to have made in this verse the first proclamation of the foundation of the school of Zen in China. The second half of this stanza runs:

> Directly pointing to one's Mind.
> Attainment of Buddhahood by seeing into one's Self-nature.

These two lines indicate the idea that in the existential depths of every human being there lies hidden a noumenon which is technically known as the Self-nature – also called Buddha-nature – and the sudden realization of which is nothing other than the attainment of Buddhahood, that is to say, *satori* or enlightenment in the Buddhist sense. The Self-nature is the noumenon as the ultimate ground of all phenomena. It is the metaphysical depth of Being itself, the Unity of all things, the word 'unity' being here taken not in the sense of the 'unification' of many things in one place but in the sense of the primordial non-differentiation, i.e., the metaphysical Ground of all things before it is bifurcated into the ego-entity and the objective world – your 'original Face before your parents were born.'

Such being the case it is only in metaphorical language that we can speak of the Self-nature lying hidden in the existential depths of each of us. In reality, the Self-nature cannot be confined in any individual being; it permeates and runs through the entire world of Being; it is supra-individual. But the curious thing about this noumenon is that it can 'exist' (or 'ex-ist') only in concrete individual things, and that it can be realized only in the consciousness of a concrete individual person. Each individual man is in this sense a double person-ality: he is individual and supra-individual at one and the same time; that is to say, he exists as an individual point into which is concentrated the universal existential energy infinitely surpassing its narrow personal confines. Ordinarily, however, man is not aware of this; that is, there is no aware-ness in him of the supra-individual noumenon in this very body of his, here and now. This realization is impeded by thinking. Even the slightest activation of the discursive intel-lect renders the immediate grasp of the primordially Undif-ferentiated utterly impossible, because at the very moment the discursive intellect begins to function, the Undifferen-tiated necessarily becomes differentiated; the noumenon turns into a phenomenon; the 'I', the empirical ego, becomes conscious of itself as a discrete entity standing against an external world, and the resulting dualism of 'myself' and 'not-myself' intrudes itself contaminating the original non-differentiation.

Nothing illustrates this subtle transition from the original non-differentiation to differentiation through thinking better than a celebrated passage in the 'Rinzai Record' (*Lin Chi Lu*)[1] in which Rinzai, the outstanding Zen Master of the T'ang dynasty describes what he calls the 'True Man without any rank'. Without any rank – that is to say, without any delimitations. This is a typically Chinese expression for what Bodhidharma designated in the above-quoted stanza as Self-nature and Mind. It is interesting to observe that what appeared in the Bodhidharma's verse in the form of abstract concepts is presented by Rinzai in a human form, full of vigor, strikingly alive: the True Man who is not restricted to the empirical self but who manifests himself in and through the empirical self. The passage reads:

> One day the Master took his seat in the lecture hall and said: 'Over the bulky mass of your reddish flesh there is a True Man without any rank. He is constantly coming in and going out through the gates of your face (i.e., your sense-organs). If you have not yet encountered him, catch him, catch him here and now!' At that moment a monk came out and asked, 'What kind of a fellow is this True Man?'
> The Master suddenly came down from the platform, grabbed at the monk, and urged him, 'Tell me, tell me!'
> The monk shrank for an instant.
> The Master on the spot thrust him away, saying 'Ah, what a useless dirt-scraper this True-Man-without-any-rank of yours is!' And immediately he retired to his private quarters.

The monk shrank or hesitated for an instant; he reflected a moment in order to give an appropriate response to the violent urging of the Master. This was the moment when discursive thinking became activated. Note that at that very moment the True-Man-without-any-rank turned into a useless dirt-scraper.[2]

Reasoning or thinking, in whatever form it may appear, always involves the 'I' (the ego-entity) becoming conscious of something. It is in its basic structure 'consciousness-of '. The thinking ego and the object of thinking are separated from one another; they stand against one another. The 'consciousness-of ' is dualism. But what Zen is concerned with above everything else is the actualization of 'consciousness' pure and simple, not 'consciousness-of.' Though similar in verbal form, 'consciousness-pure-and-simple' and 'consciousness-of ' are worlds apart. For the former is an absolute, metaphysical Awareness without the thinking subject and without the object thought of. It is not *our* awareness of the external world. Rather, it is the whole world of Being becoming aware of itself in us and through us. And it is to this metaphysical awareness of Being that Bodhidharma refers with the word Mind or Self-nature and Rinzai with his peculiar expression; the True-Man-without-Rank. The metaphysical state here in question may be interpreted as pure subjectivity. It may also be interpreted as pure objectivity. In truth it is above and beyond both subjectivity and objectivity. But it is a state which is ready to realize itself at any moment in the form of an absolute Subject and in that of the phenomenal things. It will be quite understandable now why Zen considers all forms of thinking as a deadly hindrance to the attainment of enlightenment. Discursive thinking must be arrested at all costs. Even cherishing the idea of enlightenment in the mind works as a formidable obstacle in the way of the disciple. As Daie (Ch.: Ta Hui)[3] remarks in one of his *Epistles*: 'If you are to make the slightest effort to attain enlightenment, you will never be able to get it. Such an effort is comparable to your trying to grasp limitless space with your hands – sheer waste of time.'

Shōsan Suzuki, one of the famous Zen men of Japan in the seventeenth century,[4] when asked about the attainment of Buddhahood, made the following remark:

Attainment of Buddhahood properly means to 'become empty.' It means that you return to the primordial state (of non-differentiation) in which there is not a speck of 'I', 'the other', the Truth, and the Buddha. It means that you thrust away everything, wash your hands of everything, and produce for yourself an infinite space of freedom. This cannot be actualized as long as there remains in your mind anything at all, even the thought of enlightenment.

This kind of emptying the mind is not an easy and simple task to accomplish, because it is not a mere matter of suppressing arising thoughts. For trying consciously to prevent thoughts from arising is itself a thought; the very idea of abstaining from giving rise to a delusory thought is also a delusory thought. Another famous Zen man of Japan, Master Bankei[5] explains this point as follows:

If, desiring to attain to the Unborn state, you try to suppress the rising of anger, indignation, regret, craving and the like, your very intention to suppress these emotions changes the original one mind into two minds. It is just like someone chasing another man running at the same speed. As long as you consciously go on trying to abstain from giving rise to wild thoughts, they will never be stopped, because the rising thoughts and the thought that you should stop them will endlessly be engaged in a desperate fight against each other

. . . The only important thing for you to do is to keep the one
mind from being divided into two minds.

It will be evident that such a thoroughgoing sweeping-away of
thoughts and ideas can be accomplished only through a rigorous, methodical training of the mind. For what is required is
not only the purification of the mind from all distracting
thoughts, but the purification of the mind for its own self. The
mind, if left untrained, cannot hope to go to that extent. As
the most effective method for accomplishing such a
purification of the mind, Zen, in the course of its historical
development, has devised two different forms of meditational
discipline, one of them being the 'silent-illumination' method
of meditation peculiar to the Sōtō school and the other the
kōan-exercise peculiar to the Rinzai school. But before we
proceed to examine the inner structure of these two forms of
zazen, or 'sitting cross-legged in meditation,' we must devote
some more time to a discussion of the positive aspect of the
mental purification in Zen. For the training method here in
question is in reality far from aiming at inducing in the disciple
a purely negative state of quietistic inaction or a total blankness of consciousness. Quite the contrary; what it aims at
primarily is the cultivation of mindfulness, a dynamic intensification of awareness, which allows – or forces – the mind to
sustain itself taut and concentrated. There is thus a definitely
positive aspect to the meditational discipline of Zen. And the
realization of this fact brings us immediately to the most
crucial point in the understanding of Zen.

III The A-thinking Thinking

Up till now we have been devoting our attention exclusively
to the negative aspects of Zen, and in particular to the negative attitude Zen takes toward intellection. This negation is an
established fact. There is no denying that anti-intellectualism
is one of the most salient features of Zen practice and Zen
thought.

Yet we must remember that the elimination of discursive
thinking (which by itself could lead to a negative state, i.e., a
total stopping of consciousness) is in the actual practice of
Zen meditation so designed that it should go hand in hand
with the process of a gradual unification of the mind, making
the mind intensely one-pointed. And this latter process cannot but lead to 'mindfulness' instead of 'mindlessness' in a
purely negative sense. During meditation exercise the disciple is to preserve his mindfulness, keeping his mind in a state
of clear awareness, never allowing it to become slack and
inactive. To do so the dynamic power of concentration must
be mobilized. And this fact distinguishes *zazen* from a technique of passive introversion (exemplified in the West by the
'prayer of quiet') by which one learns to sit in mental stillness,
emptying the mind of all stirring thoughts and images, and
gradually falling into a blank state of mindlessness. The difference between the two techniques of meditation will spring
to the eye if we but observe the so-called 'life-and-death
struggle' involved in the traditional *kōan* exercise in Zen. All
kōans are precisely so devised as to keep the mind of the
disciple unusually alert and active; in grappling with a given
kōan, the disciple is necessarily prevented from resting calm
and peaceful in the lucid serenity of a thoughtless vacuity. If
he does experience such serenity, he must further brace himself up and break through that serene state of mind itself.

Zen likes to use words and expressions of a negative nature. Many of the key-terms of Zen thought are in fact linguistically negative – 'nothingness,' 'void', 'emptiness', 'no-mind', 'from-the-beginning-nothing-was', etc. These negative expressions, if taken psychologically, are liable to suggest trance, unconsciousness and the like, if not apathy and torpor. Rendering the mind thus passively inactive, however, is exactly the contrary of what Zen intends to achieve. What is meant by no-mindness is not a purely negative state in which the mind has ceased to function. As we have indicated above, no-mindness is mindfulness; it is a peculiar state to be reached at the extreme limit of mindfulness, a state of apparent inaction brought about by an unusually intensified activity of the mind. Paradoxical though it may sound, we might say that the complete cessation of thinking does activate THINKING. That is to say, the cessation of thinking at the level of images and concepts activates another kind of 'thinking' in the subliminal regions of mind. Zen meditation in this sense is definitely of a noetic nature. It has a noetic quality in that it involves an active awareness, a peculiar type of 'thinking' (or THINKING) by which one achieves a metaphysical knowledge of Being in the supra-conceptual dimension of consciousness.

It is highly important and interesting to observe that in the midst of the notoriously anti-intellectualist context of Zen there is still a possibility of our talking about a peculiar kind of thinking, though, to be sure, it is of such a peculiar nature that it would not ordinarily be recognized as thinking, because 'thinking' – at least in the Cartesian tradition of the West – is a conscious manipulation of clear and distinct ideas.

Let us now turn to the inner structure of THINKING. I would first draw attention to the fact that what we are now indicating as THINKING is not a newly invented concept of ours. It is, on the contrary, a concept which we find well-established in the history of Zen Buddhism, although here again Zen has preferred to use a negative expression: 'not-thinking' (*hi-shiryô*), or rather 'a-thinking' instead of 'thinking'. The locus classicus concerning this problem is the famous *mondō* (or Zen dialogue) between Yakusan (Ch.: Yao Shan),[6] an outstanding Zen Master of the T'ang dynasty, and a visiting monk.

Once Master Yakusan was sitting in deep meditation, when a monk came up to him and asked: 'Solidly seated as a rock, what are you thinking?'
Master answered: 'Thinking of something which is absolutely unthinkable (*fu-shiryô*), 'not-to-be-thought-of').'
The monk: 'How can one think of anything which is absolutely unthinkable?'
Master: 'By the a-thinking thinking (*hi-shiryô*), 'thinking-which-is-non-thinking').'

Commenting upon the *mondō*, Dōgen[7] observes that in the case of Master Yakusan there is no contradiction, as the monk thought there was, between 'thinking' and 'something absolutely unthinkable,' for he says, 'thinking' here does not mean ordinary thinking at the level of ideas and concepts, but a depth-thinking, a 'depth-thinking going down to the very marrow of reality.' Likewise, the 'unthinkable' here in question is not to be taken as an ordinary mental object eluding the grasp of thinking; rather it is an 'unthinkable' pertaining to the very marrow or reality. The depth-thinking by which one thinks of the unthinkable in such a sense by no means conforms to the usual pattern of thinking in which a thinking subject thinks of something as an object of thought, both the subject and the object remaining at the same level of consciousness. The depth-thinking in this sense is not thinking; it is an 'a-thinking'. We might as well say that it is a thinking which is not thinking, because it is not an act of thinking-about-something as its object.

In its normal form, our thinking cannot function without having an object to think about. The mind in this sense cannot work in the void. Thinking is always thinking-about or thinking-of; it needs something to hold on to. In the *mondō* which has just been quoted, too, the first statement of Yakusan *verbally* presents THINKING as a thinking-of, that is, as if he meant the ordinary pattern of thinking having a definite object to which it is directed. Since, however, that 'object' happens to be of such a nature that it is not-to-be-thought-of, the thinking in this case is left in the void, without any definitely delimited object. THINKING, as Yakusan understands it, is an objectless thinking.

But a thinking which has no object is at the same time a thinking without a subject, i.e. thinking subject. An absolutely 'object'-less thinking is, according to Zen, impossible to be actualized as long as there remains in the thinking subject the 'subject'-consciousness, i.e., ego-consciousness. THINKING is objectless and subjectless, which is exactly what is meant by Yakusan by the term 'a-thinking,' that is, a thinking-which-is-non-thinking.

It is very important to remark that from the viewpoint of Zen, 'THINKING which is objectless and subjectless' does not mean an act of thinking from which the consciousness of both the object and subject has been eliminated. If such were the case, THINKING would simply be a peculiar psychological event. What Zen means is rather a dynamic metaphysical awareness of Being-itself, or pure Existence, *before* it bifurcates itself into the subject and object, the knower and the known – or we might also say, the 'I' and the world. This point is best shown in another, equally famous *mondō* in which a Zen Master answers to one of his disciples who has asked him how enlightenment could be attained. 'Enlightenment can be attained,' he says, 'only by seeing into Nothingness.'

> Disciple goes on to ask the Master: 'You say: Nothingness. But is it not already "something" to be seen (i.e. object of thought)?'
> Master: 'There certainly is "seeing", but its object does not constitute "something"!'
> Disciple: 'If it does not constitute "something", what is the "seeing"?'
> Master: 'Seeing where there is absolutely no object, that is true "seeing"'

The reference is to the apparent thoughtlessness of *samādhi*. On the surface of consciousness there is no longer any thought-in-motion, because the bifurcating intellect has completely ceased to function. But the mind in such a state is no longer 'mind' in the ordinary sense of the word; rather, it is the plenitude of Being spontaneously disclosing itself as an illuminated Awareness which is here designated as 'seeing where there is no object' – to which we must add 'and no subject'. 'Where there is neither subject nor object' can be nothing other than an absolute 'emptiness'. But the important point to note is that the 'emptiness' here in question is not a psychological state of there being nothing in the consciousness. It is rather a metaphysical state of emptiness which, because it is not limited to any definite thing, whether subjective or objective, is the very plenitude of Being.

Thus THINKING (or the a-thinking-form of thinking) which constitutes the crux of the meditational discipline in Zen consists in man's plunging right into the existential depths of himself beyond even the subliminal regions of the so-called unconscious. But by doing so man is no longer probing the depths of *his* being; he is in reality probing the depths of the metaphysical ground of Being itself which remains eternally untouched by the stream of images and concepts that pass across the empirical plane of consciousness. What is actualized here is neither I-and-Thou nor I-and-it. For there is no longer I as a subjective entity nor Thou or It as an objective entity. There remains only IS, a self-illuminating 'is', which is precisely the THINKING.

IV   Sōtō Zen and Rinzai Zen

In the earlier phases of Zen history, there was no systematic method of meditational discipline, although from the very beginning meditation itself had always been practiced. Up until the end of the T'ang dynasty, each individual Zen man trained himself in his own way. In the course of history, however, a special training method was worked out for helping the disciple-aspirant activate in himself THINKING, or the thinking which is a-thinking, as we have explained in the preceding section. The training method comprised two major varieties known respectively as 'zazen-only' method and kōan method, the former characterizing the Sōtō (Ch.: Ts'ao Tung) school and the latter the Rinzai (Ch.: Lin Chi) school. Zen was introduced into Japan from China in the Kamakura period (12th-13th centuries) through the channel of these two rival sects that were flourishing in China at that time, each providing a different method of spiritual discipline. These two schools have survived in Japan up to the present time, and the two training methods are still being practiced in thousands of places.

The Sōtō (Ts'ao Tung) school which was established in Japan by Dōgen (1200-1253) goes back to two great Masters of the T'ang dynasty in China, Tōzan Ryōkai (Ch.: Tung Shan Liang Chieh, 807-869) and his disciple-successor Sōzan Honjaku (Ch.: Ts'ao Shan Pên Chi, 840-901). As is clearly indicated by the popular title 'silent illumination (moku shō, Ch.: mo chao) Zen' under which this school has come to be known, the Sōtō emphasizes above everything else the importance of sitting in meditation. The underlying idea is that enlightenment can be achieved only through total participation and transformation of the whole personality of the disciple. The attainment of enlightenment cannot and should not be a sudden happening; it must be a gradual process of spiritual maturing. Only by sitting in meditation over a long period of time can the total transformation of personality be carried out. Only at the end of, and as the result of, such a gradual process of quiet mind-illumination can the real nature of Self, i.e. the real nature of Being, be realized. Because of this position the Sōtō school is known as the school of 'gradual enlightenment' in contradistinction from the Rinzai which is known as the school of 'sudden enlightenment.'

The Rinzai (Ch.: Lin Chi) school, as this very appellation indicates, goes back to the famous Zen Master of the T'ang dynasty, Rinzai Gegen (Ch.: Lin Chi I Hsüan, ?-866) known for his violent method of training the disciples through the use of blows and yells. But the Rinzai Zen as we know it at present with its characteristic *kōan* exercise goes back rather to an outstanding Master of this school in the Sung dynasty, Daie (Ch.: Ta Hui)[8] who collected and arranged representative *kōans* so that they might be used in a systematic way in the training process. And it was in this particular form that the Sōtō Zen was introduced into Japan by Eisai (1141-1215).

The Rinzai school advocates 'sudden enlightenment' in opposition to the 'gradual enlightenment' of the Sōtō. The Rinzai is vigorously dynamic in nature while the Sōtō is static. Emphasizing action and dynamism above all things, the Rinzai school rejects and condemns sitting in serene meditation. Not that it rejects meditational practice altogether. Quite the contrary. But the practice by which it disciplines the disciple is not the 'silent illumination' type of static meditation. From the Rinzai point of view, just sitting in serenity and tranquility with a mind emptied of all images and thoughts is nothing other than 'falling into the devil's pit' of blank emptiness.

Against the static meditation of the Sōtō school, the Rinzai advocates dynamic meditation, that is, a particular type of meditation in which one observes a vigorous, dynamic activity of the mind. The *kōan* is used for this particular purpose. The disciple is sternly ordered by his Master to solve a given *kōan* through meditation; he is ordered to grapple with the problem 'with body-and-mind' while sitting in meditation. Of necessity the meditation becomes a kind of spiritual battle-field. The *kōan* grows into an 'iron ball of doubt' and exhausts all the mental resources of the disciple. Suddenly the ball of doubt is broken to pieces, and the Self-nature is realized. The Rinzai school thus holds that enlightenment cannot come gradually, by degrees, but that it can come only as an abrupt and sudden spiritual event.

Now we turn to a more detailed examination of the inner structure of meditational practice as it is conceived by the Sōtō and Rinzai schools. Let us take up first the Sōtō position.

As we have noted above, the Sōtō position concerning meditation is generally known as '*zazen*-only' or 'silent-illumination.' The Sōtō position which can historically be traced back to Jinshū (Ch.: Shên Hsin, ?-706), the founder of the so-called Northern school of Zen, is markedly colored with quietism. It emphasizes the importance of a serene, quietistic contemplation of the 'original purity of the Mind.' This position stands on a basic theoretic assumption that the consciousness is broadly of a two level structure, consisting as it does of a 'surface level' and a 'depth level.' It goes without saying that it is in truth nothing but a figurative manner of speech, for in the authentic view of Zen there are properly no real 'layers' to be distinguished in the consciousness; the consciousness as Zen understands it is not an entity having a structure of any kind. But for the sake of practical explanation the two-level-structure theory is very convenient.

What is meant by the 'surface level' is our ordinary waking consciousness characterized by incessant agitation which is brought about by an uncontrollable proliferation of images, concepts, and thought-forms, particularly by the activity of the discursive thinking which never ceases to chase after objects in the external world. The 'depth level' refers to the same consciousness as it remains serene and undisturbed in spite of the constant turmoil observable at the 'surface level.' Zen likes to represent this structure of consciousness by the image of an ocean whose surface is agitated with waves but in whose depths there is a zone of eternal calmness.

With such an image in mind it will be easy to understand that the primary aim of *zazen* as understood in the Sōtō school is to bring the whole of the psychic energy into an intensely concentrated state of unity, so that the mind, now absolutely one-pointed, might immediately witness its own 'depth level' which under ordinary conditions remains invisible, being submerged under the 'waves' of thought-forms.

The *zazen*-only' type of meditation consists physically in one's sitting with stability and equanimity, 'solidly immovable like a rock' in the full-lotus or half-lotus posture, cross-legged, keeping the back erect and straight, with rhythmically regulated breathing into and out of the depths of the lower region of the abdomen.

With the body thus massively planted, one must go on intensifying one-pointed inner concentration, the mind being kept alert and attentive. Yet curiously enough, this one-pointed awareness is to have nothing definite on which to be focussed. This is to say, no tangible object of concentration is actually provided. Having nothing to hold onto, the mind as it were is left in the void. The concentration is not to be supported, as it is in the Rinzai type of *zazen*, by an all-absorbing attention to the solving of a *kōan* problem. Nor is it supported by the continued visualization of some shape or pattern, or by the act of holding some definite idea before the mental eye. Recourse is not had even to the most elementary yogic technique of counting the breath or pursuing the in-coming out-going breaths. Only a heightened state of concentration is to be sustained, the mind, as it were, sinking deeper, ever deeper beyond the realm of ideas and concepts, then beyond the subliminal realm of visions into a purely one-pointed-awareness of Being.

Such in brief is the fundamental idea underlying the meditational practice of the Sōtō school, the '*zazen*-only' school. And such an understanding of *zazen* reached its culmination in the view of Dōgen, the Japanese founder of the Sōtō Zen, who saw in the practice of sitting in meditation the very actualization of the Buddha-nature itself, that is, the intrinsically undifferentiated oneness of Being. For Dōgen *zazen* is not an artificially devised technique for achieving enlightenment. In fact the highest principle of Zen established by Dōgen is that enlightenment and practice are exactly one and the same thing. A man is enlightened by sitting in meditation, whether he be aware of it or not. For sitting in such a situation is not merely a bodily posture. Rather it is the most limpid awareness of the highest degree of existential plenitude. 'He' is the sitting itself. And 'he' is the awareness of Being. 'He' is a living crystallization point of universal Life. Dōgen says:[9]

> *Zazen* consists solely in sitting in tranquility. It is not a means by which to seek something. Sitting itself is enlightenment. If, as ordinary people think, practice were different from enlightenment, the two would become conscious of one another (i.e. one would become conscious of enlightenment while engaged in *zazen*, and one would remain conscious of the process of self-discipline after one has attained the state of enlightenment). Such an enlightenment contaminated by this kind of consciousness is not a genuine enlightenment.

Evidently the 'silent illumination' type of meditation is essentially of a static nature and is liable to lead to pure quietism. The Rinzai school vigorously protests against this tendency saying that quietism goes against the spirit of Zen. In so doing the Rinzai school upholds the dynamism of the sixth Patriarch Enō (Hui Nêng).

Master Nangaku (Ch.: Nan Yüeh)[10] who succeeded Enō in the transmission of the teachings of the Southern school is said to have admonished one of his disciples in the following way:

> Do you want to be master of *zazen*, or do you intend to attain Buddhahood! If your intention is to study Zen itself, (you must know that) Zen does not consist in sitting or in lying. Do you want to attain Buddhahood by the cross-legged sitting posture? But the Buddha has no specific form. . . . Trying to attain Buddhahood by merely sitting cross-legged in meditation is nothing other than murdering the Buddha. As long as you remain attached to such a sitting posture you will never be able to reach the Mind.

The Rinzai school which faithfully follows the teaching of the sixth Patriarch in this respect takes a very strong stand against the meditational method of the Sōtō school. Thus Daie (Ch.: Ta Hui), the above-mentioned Master of the Rinzai school, says:[11]

> When you are talking with your guest, just concentrate your energies on talking with him. When you feel like sitting quietly in meditation, go and sit concentrating your energies on the act of sitting quietly. But never, while sitting, regard sitting as something supreme. In these days there are a number of false

Zen Masters who are leading their disciples astray by teaching that quiet sitting in 'silent illumination' is the ultimate thing in Zen.

It is quite clear that by the expression 'false Zen Masters' Daie is referring to the Masters of the Sōtō school.

Nevertheless, the Rinzai school does not dispense with meditation. Quite the contrary; for the Rinzai people, too, sitting in meditation is the pivotal point of the whole process by which one advances toward enlightenment. However the inner structure of Rinzai meditation is totally different from that of the Sōtō variety. For *zazen* as understood by the Rinzai school does not consist in sitting in the tranquil serenity of meditation with a mind emptied of all thoughts; rather *zazen* consists in making the consciousness concerned exclusively with a vital, existential Problem or Thought so much so that the mind wholly becomes the Problem, the Thought; that is to say, the 'I', losing itself, becomes, so to speak, totally transformed into the Thought. This is in short the Rinzai understanding of THINKING, 'the thinking which is a-thinking.' And this existential transformation is effectuated by means of *kōans*.

V Kōan

The *kōan* (Ch.: kung an) which originally, i.e. in the T'ang dynasty, had been a legal term denoting a legal case establishing a precedent to be relied upon in making decisions in cases of a similar nature, came to be used as a Zen technical term in the later Sung dynasty, meaning a special problem or theme for meditation. The *kōan* exercise was standardized by Daie in the eleventh century and has since then remained popular in the Rinzai school in China and Japan throughout the past eight centuries. Many *kōan* collections have been compiled, the *Hekigan Roku* (Ch.: *Pi Yen Lu*, compiled in 1125) and the *Mu Mon Kan* (Ch.: *Wu Mên Kuan*, compiled in 1228) being among the most celebrated of all.

These *kōans* are all intended to be meditation themes artificially constructed from (1) some of the famous old *mondōs*, i.e. questions-and-answers, between disciples and Masters of the T'ang and early Sung periods, (2) fragments of some of the Buddhist Sutras, (3) significant portions of the Masters' discourses, and (4) anecdotes relating to various aspects of the Masters.

The *kōans*, no matter how variegated their contents may be, are all of one and the same structure insofar as they are considered meditation themes. Each of them is an expression in paradoxical, shocking or baffling language, of ultimate Reality as Zen understands it. It is meant to be a direct, vigorous presentation, in a verbal form, of Being, as we have explained in the preceding section – a naked, individual crystallization of the originally Undifferentiated. As a problem to be given by the Master to his disciples it is, in the majority of cases, deliberately meaningless;[12] it is designed in such a way that it might confound at the very outset the discursive thinking with a view to awakening in the disciple a special level of existential understanding involving the whole of his personality, body and mind, far beyond the reach of the intellect.

However, it is a mistake to think that a *kōan* is only disconcertingly irrational or meaningless. Keeping in mind the way the *kōans* were originally constructed from earlier *mondōs*, anecdotes, etc., it is easy to see that each *kōan* yields a certain meaning in the realm of intellectual understanding as well, if only we can return it to its historical context, whether fictitious or real, and approach it from that angle. In other words, there is a particular sense in which each *kōan* can be regarded as an epitome of Zen philosophy.

Thus it comes about that the *kōan* is in principle a two-dimensional construct. There are two entirely different dimensions to it, in which it can be handled differently. And the observation of this fact is very important because the two dimensions are liable to be confused and in fact have often been confused with one another, and the confusion turns out to be fatal for a right understanding of the Rinzai Zen.

In one of the two dimensions (which we would call 'first dimension'), a *kōan* is to be treated as a meaningful utterance or anecdote, no matter how nonsensical it might look at first sight. In this dimension the *kōan* does have a solid philosophical meaning perfectly graspable by the intellect. Every *kōan* in this sense is a kind of 'historical' document allowing for an intellectual interpretation. At first it may seem to offer an insurmountable barrier to any intellectual approach, but the barrier is such that it could ultimately be broken down.

In the second of the two dimensions as distinguished above, on the contrary, the *kōan* is not a meaningful utterance or anecdote in any sense; at least it is not supposed to be taken as such. In this dimension the *kōan* is a totally irrational problem so calculated from the beginning to bring the mind to a dead-end closing off one after another all possible avenues to the habitual pattern of thinking in order to make the mind go through a state of formidable inner tension verging on the state of psychosis and thus to lead it to a final 'break-through'. Each *kōan* in this aspect is a kind of artificially devised means for giving a psychological shock to the disciple. But the remarkable thing about this is that our mind is so firmly habituated to work on the level of intellectual understanding and never to stand still until it finds a 'mear ng' in any verbal utterance or statement, that it seems to be almost an impossibility for it to begin to grapple with a *kōan* as a violent, drastic psychological shock. Hence the stringent admonition of all Zen Masters against 'thinking', against any attempt on the part of the disciple to 'understand' the meaning of *kōans*.

Now to illustrate the two different dimensions of the *kōan*, which have just been outlined. Take for example the following famous *kōan*, the 'cypress tree in the courtyard' of Jōshū (Ch.: Chao Chou).[13]

> Once a monk asked Jōshū, 'Tell me what is the significance of the First Patriarch's coming from the West (i.e. What is the ultimate truth of Zen Buddhism)?'
> Jōshū replied, 'The cypress tree in the courtyard!'

What relation is there between a cypress tree in the courtyard and the real, living essence of Buddhism that was brought to China from India by Bodhidharma? In ordinary circumstances Jōshū's answer would sound nonsensical, completely devoid of meaning. However, from the point of view of Zen philosophy (i.e. in the 'first dimension') Jōshū's words do make sense as an answer to the monk's question. Briefly stated, the Cypress Tree of Jōshū points to exactly the same thing as the above-mentioned True-Man-without-any-rank. The only difference between the two is that in the latter the primordially Undifferentiated is presented as pure subjectivity while in the former the same Undifferentiated manifests itself as pure objectivity. As we have observed earlier, the primordially Undifferentiated as envisioned by Zen is in itself beyond subjectivity and objectivity, but it is at the same time of such a nature that it can freely manifest itself as the absolute Subject or as the absolute Object – or even both, i.e. Subject-Object – as the case may be.

The important point to note is that the Undifferentiated cannot *ex-ist* in its original non-differentiation; that in order to *ex-ist* it must necessarily differentiate itself, i.e. concretely crystallize itself as something, whether subjective or objective. And since the Undifferentiated differentiates itself wholly, i.e. without any residue, into every one of the myriads of things, each of these things does not differ from

the Undifferentiated except in terms of non-articulation
and articulation.

The cypress tree in the courtyard! As by a magical invoca-
tion the whole world emerges out of its metaphysical ground,
the Emptiness (*sūnyatā*).

The whole world is the Cypress Tree. Jōshū is the Cypress
Tree. The monk also is the Cypress Tree. There is in short
nothing other than the Awareness of the Cypress Tree,
because at this metaphysical zero-point, Being itself in its
very non-differentiation is illuminating itself as the Cypress
Tree, unique and universal at the same time.

Let us try to interpret (of course in the 'first dimension' again)
another *kōan* illustrating in a somewhat different form the
same aspect of Zen metaphysics. The *kōan* consists of a single
and very simple imperative sentence.

Listen to the sound of one hand clapping!

Unlike the majority of *kōans* ordinarily mentioned in Zen
textbooks, which are of Chinese origin and which relate to the
sayings and doings of the T'ang dynasty Masters, this short
kōan is an original meditation theme newly devised by
Hakuin[14] in the eighteenth century, who was by far the
greatest of all Rinzai Masters in Japan. The *kōan*, widely
known as *Sekishu* (One Hand) of the Master Hakuin, proved
to be so effective in actual Zen training that it has come to
acquire in Japan a popularity nearly as great as Jōshū's *Mu*
(No!').

Now Hakuin demands of his disciple to listen to the sound
of one hand clapping. If we clap both hands a sound is naturally produced. What is the sound of the clap of one hand? In
ordinary circumstances this would simply be a nonsensical
question. As in the case of the Cypress Tree, however, the
kōan conceals a hidden metaphysical meaning which will be
disclosed to the intellect in the 'first dimension.'

In order to better grasp this philosophical meaning, I would
suggest that we read first a well-known Zen anecdote concerning the omnipresence of the wind in the world. The
dramatis personae are Master Mayoku (Ch.: Ma Ku) of the
T'ang dynasty and a monk.

Once Master Mayoku Hōtetsu was using a fan, when a monk
came up to him and said: 'The wind-nature (i.e. wind-in-itself
or the noumenal reality of wind) is permanently ubiquitous so
that there is in the whole world no place which is not pervaded
by it. If so, why are you using the fan?'
Mayoku: 'What you know is only (the theory) that the wind is
diffused throughout the world.'
The monk: 'What is, then, the real meaning of the wind being
diffused throughout the world?'
The Master just went on fanning himself.
The monk made a reverential bow.

The 'wind-nature' is in fact not essentially different from what
we know under more usual appellations like 'Buddha-
nature,' 'Self-nature,' 'Mind,' etc., all of which point to the
'Absolute' as Zen understands it, that is, Reality as it really is
before the subject-object bifurcation, the primordially Undifferentiated which is still undifferentiated but which is at the
same time ready to differentiate itself as the phenomenal
wind.

The 'wind-nature' pervades all corners of the world; there
is not a single place which is not filled up with it. And according to the typically Zen way of thinking, this is precisely the
reason why there is actually cool 'wind' wherever a man uses a
fan. Yet the most important point is that this permanently
ubiquitous 'wind-nature' is not actualized here and now
unless a man fans himself; that the universal Wind can *ex-ist*
only through the unique act of the man's using the fan. Thus
we are again brought back to our old, familiar metaphysical
thesis, namely that the Undifferentiated *ex-ists* only through
its own differentiations.

Now to hark back to the 'one Hand' *kōan* of Hakuin. After
having understood the 'Wind' *kōan* of Mayoku, it will be
quite easy to grasp the inner structure of the one-hand-
clapping. Just as the 'wind-nature' is ubiquitous, the sound of
one hand – the 'sound-nature' so to speak – is permanently
ubiquitous. The 'sound-nature' which is in this case presented
as the 'sound of one hand clapping,' is everywhere present,
ready to actualize itself at any moment as an empirically
audible sound, whenever and wherever one chooses to strike
both hands together. Zen goes further and says that the Mind
is hearing the sound even before it is empirically actualized,

even at the stage of one-hand-clapping. Thus in the 'sound of one hand clapping' or 'sound-nature,' we encounter again the Undifferentiated in its particular ontological proclivity toward articulating itself as a physically audible sound. Zen in this case consists in 'seeing into' the 'sound-nature' at the precise moment when the latter begins to stir and disclose its intrinsic proclivity toward articulation. This is what is meant by the sound of one hand clapping. Note that when the two hands are actually clapped, the articulation has already taken place, and the 'sound-nature' conceals itself behind the physically audible sound.

It is in reference to this situation that another eminent Japanese Master, Bankei[15] makes the following remark about hearing the sound of a temple bell before it is heard:

> Listen, a bell is now ringing; you hear the sound.
> (Properly speaking) you are all permanently and unceasingly aware of the sound of the bell even before the bell is struck and before the sound is actually heard. The transparent awareness of the sound of the bell before the tolling of the bell – that awareness is what I call the unborn Buddha Mind. Becoming aware of the bell only after it has rung is merely following up a trace left by something that has actually taken place. There you have already fallen into the secondary position, tertiary position (i.e. you are no longer in the primary position of the Undifferentiated).

The pure, absolute Subject – the 'unborn Buddha Mind' of Bankei – remains always awake and is incessantly hearing the sound of the bell. This is why, when a bell is struck, we become immediately, i.e. without an instant's delay, aware of the sound *as* the sound of a bell. There is no room here for reflection. And in the view of Zen, the absolute Subject in such a context is totally identified with the sound (or 'sound-nature'); the absolute Subject *is* the sound.

These and all other similar interpretations, however, are after all matters pertaining to the 'first dimension' of *kōan*. That is to say, they are, from a strict Zen point of view, secondary matters. True, we cannot simply deny the existence of such a dimension of intellectual understanding. Yet, from the methodological viewpoint of the Zen Masters, i.e. in terms of the above-mentioned 'second dimension' of the *kōan*, all intellectual interpretations must categorically be rejected as something essentially unnecessary, futile, and noxious.

In fact, by obtaining a perfect intellectual understanding of a *kōan*, one achieves nothing significant. On the contrary, *kōan* is of such a nature that the more one deepens the intellectual understanding of it the farther removed one will necessarily be from its spirit, the immediate grasp of which is the sole objective of Zen training. Thus, from the Zen point of view, *any* understanding of any *kōan* by the intellect, no matter how profound and exact it may be, creates but hindrances in the way of one who is undergoing Zen discipline.

It is to be noted that the rejection of all intellectual understanding of *kōan* in Zen is absolute and thoroughgoing. The very mental attitude to try to understand a *kōan* is *the* thing which must be rejected from the outset. For the level of consciousness at which the intellect functions is exactly the kind of thing that must be overcome at all costs. This is the main reason why Zen so categorically rejects all *Philosophieren*. One may succeed in elaborating a system of profound philosophy on the basis of an intellectual interpretation of *kōans*; one still remains on the plane of the discriminating intellect; nothing has been achieved by way of total transformation of man toward an *immediate* grasp of the Undifferentiated, which is what Zen is exclusively interested in.

Kōan in its 'second dimension,' i.e. *kōan* as a practical means of discipline, as a 'method,' is not something to be understood by the intellect. It is, on the contrary, to be treated as a technique specially devised for the purpose of pushing the Zen student almost by force into an existential situation in which he has absolutely no way to allow his thoughts to function. In accordance with the principle, the student is told to sit in meditation, concentrating his mind day and night on a given *kōan*, not to think about it or try to understand its meaning, but simply to *solve* it totally and completely. But how can he hope to solve a problem which is calculated from the beginning to be unsolvable? That is the question he must confront at the very outset. The only authentic way to solve a *kōan*, in the traditional view of the Rinzai Zen, is by 'becoming the *kōan*' or becoming completely one with the *kōan*. The solution of the Cypress Tree of Jōshū, for instance, consists in one's *becoming* the Cypress Tree. The solution of Hakuin's One Hand consists in one's *becoming* the 'sound of one hand clapping.' But what is, more concretely, the meaning of man's 'becoming a *kōan*'? 'Becoming a *kōan*' would seem to imply an existential process. What, then, is the inner mechanism of this process?

Nothing provides a better answer to this basic question than our considering the way in which the famous *kōan* of Jōshū's *Mu* (No! or Nothing) has traditionally been employed in the Rinzai sect as the best possible means for disciplining students. The *kōan* itself, which is widely known as "Jōshū's Dog' or 'Jōshū's Mu-Word,' reads as follows:[16]

> A monk once asked Master Jōshū: 'Has the dog the Buddha-nature?'
> The Master replied: '*Mu* (Ch.: *Wu*)!'

The 'first dimension' understanding of this *kōan*, that is, the philosophical 'meaning' of this *kōan*, will now be clear without a lengthy explanation. Against the background of Mahayana metaphysics upholding the view that the Buddha-nature (i.e., the Absolute) is universally inherent in all things, the monk asks Jōshū whether even an animal like the dog has the Buddha-nature or not, trying thereby to fathom the depth of Jōshū's grasp of Zen. As usual, the Master smashes to pieces the conceptual level on which the monk stands in his question, by representing to him directly the *Mu*, the supra-conceptual reality itself. The Absolute, he seems to indicate, transcends the dog's 'having' or 'not-having' it. The problem of 'having' or 'not-having' simply does not exist in the dimension in which Jōshū stands. Such a problem can be raised only at the level of intellectual bifurcation. But as long as one remains attached to the level of bifurcation, the real solution of the problem is unattainable. Thus Jōshū, instead of giving an answer, whether affirmative or negative, to the monk's question, abruptly thrusts under the very nose of the monk the Buddha-nature itself in the form of Nothingness, i.e. the primordially Undifferentiated. The *Mu* in this sense plays exactly the same role as the Cypress Tree or the 'sound of one hand clapping.'

It may be worth mentioning in passing that there is another, more elementary – or shall we say, more primitive – dimension to this anecdote in its pre-*kōan* status. In its original version, before it was given the definite form of a *kōan* and before it began to be used as such, it had been a longer anecdote of a more dogmatic nature, in which Jōshū is pictured as giving two contradictory answers, Yes and No, to exactly the same question asked by two different monks on two different occasions. As a good sample of pre-*kōan* anecdotes, I shall reproduce here the first part of the original version in which Jōshū takes the negative position:[17]

> A monk asked Jōshū: 'Has the dog the Buddha-nature or not?'
> Jōshū: 'No!'
> Monk: '(According to a Buddhist Sutra), all sentient beings are endowed with the Buddha-nature. How, then, is it possible that the dog has no share in the Buddha-nature?'
> Jōshū: 'It is because the dog exists by its own *karma*.'

The last statement of Jōshū may be explicated in our own language as follows. The Buddha-nature (which is omnipresent) is totally nullified by the fact that through the canine *karma* (i.e., through its intrinsic ontological proclivity toward actualizing itself as a dog) the Buddha-nature has assumed the form of an individual dog. As long as there is on our part the awareness of an individually differentiated dog, there is no trace of the supra-temporal and supra-spatial Awareness of the Undifferentiated. Whether this interpretation is right or not, it is certain that the whole anecdote touches upon an aspect of Buddhist dogma, and that Jōshū's *Mu* in this particular setting is to be taken as an ordinary No, denying the existence of the Buddha-nature in the dog, which would mean at the very most that, as Dōgen remarks, the Buddha-nature, being in itself an absolutely Undelimited, does *not* and can *not* exist in its original purity as something delimited. Thus the anecdote already in its pre-*kōan* status clearly points to what will consitute in the *koan*-status the above-mentioned 'first dimension.'

As we have repeatedly pointed out, however, such an understanding is nothing but an unnecessary intellectual entanglement from the point of view of the 'second dimension'. In this latter dimension, the *Mu* must fulfill an entirely different function. The anecdote in the capacity of a *kōan* must work as a psychic technique, and the *Mu* is to operate as a driving force inducing a total transformation of the very psychic mechanism of the Zen student.

Instead of trying to work out the meaning of the *kōan*, the student is strictly commanded to go on contemplating the *Mu* until his whole subjectivity becomes dissolved and transformed into the *Mu*. What he has to do is to face the ungraspable *Mu* without thinking about it. 'Do not', so admonishes the Master Mumon[18] (Ch.: *Wu Mên*), the celebrated compiler of the *Mu Mon Kan*, 'do not mistake the *Mu* for absolute emptiness or nothingness. Do not conceive it in terms of "is" or "is not", either.' In other words, Jōshū's *Mu* is not to be taken as a negation of the existence of the Absolute in the dog. The problem is above and beyond existence or non-existence of anything whatsoever. In an entirely different dimension of the mind the *Problem* must be transformed into 'something like a red-hot iron ball which you have swallowed and which you cannot disgorge no matter how hard you may try'.[19]

Settling into a state of deep, one-pointed concentration, the student must continue gazing at the *Mu*, tenaciously and intensely, repeating at the same time the word *Mu*, silently or loudly, to himself until his whole body-and-mind, losing itself, gets into a particular state indicated by the word *Mu*; that is to say, until he attains the same level of consciousness at which Jōshū himself is supposed to have uttered the word 'Mu!', beyond the bifurcation of consciousness into subject and object. It cannot be doubted that intoning the single word *Mu* in such a state of intense concentration produces almost the same psychological effect as the recitation of a *mantra*. But the peculiar semantic ontent of the word *Mu* ('nothing' – NOTHING) also contributes a great deal toward inducing in the student a special psychological state in which the subject and the object have coalesced into an absolute unity of pure Awareness. For the student who may have started by objectifying the *Mu*, setting it up before him as 'something' to be gazed at, must sooner or later realize that the very semantic structure of *Mu* renders it impossible to be grasped as an object, that it can be grasped only by his revolutionizing his own consciousness, by opening up for it an entirely new dimension in which the *Mu* is actualized in its metaphysical reality, in its 'suchness,' as NOTHING in the sense of the absolutely undifferentiated plenitude of Being. He will then realize that 'he' is no longer there, that there is neither 'I' nor 'not-I', but *Mu* just *Mu*, without a speck of duality.

Such is in a broad outline the instrumental ('second dimension') aspect of the *kōan*. Even such a brief account will have clarified how differently one and the same *kōan* appears as we consider it in terms of its two different dimensions. In the 'first dimension' the *Mu* is the noumenal, the metaphysical, the actualization of which is in itself and by itself Zen metaphysics. In the 'second dimension,' on the contrary, the *Mu* is a method, something by means of which the Zen student disciplines himself toward unveiling what we have earlier called the 'depth level' of his consciousness. But this brings to light at the same time a close tie connecting these two 'dimensions' of the *kōan* with one another. For it is only in the very 'depth level' of consciousness which thus becomes unveiled by the methodological use of the *Mu* that the *Mu* as the noumenal becomes actualized here and now.

In the present section we have attempted to give an exposition of the Zen meditational technique as it has been historically developed by the Sōtō and Rinzai sects. In so doing our principal aim has been to shed further light on the fact (which we established in the earlier sections) that *zazen* or sitting in meditation is in Zen not a technique for emptying the mind in the sense of inducing a total mental blankness; that, on the contrary, it involves the activation of a most intense and concentrated working of the mind on a certain level of consciousness where the subject and object are not differentiated from each other; and finally that such a working of the mind deserves to be regarded as a very peculiar type of 'thinking'. This is most obvious in the Rinzai use of the *kōan* method, but in the '*zazen*-only' method of the Sōtō school too, what we have earlier described as 'depth-thinking' is, albeit in a less obvious form, unmistakably at work.

Notes

1. On Rinzai and 'Ri. /ai Record' see Essay I, Note ?. Rinzai Zen was brought to Japan in the twelfth century by Eisai (1131-1215) who thereby became the historical origin of the development of the Rinzai school in Japan. As we shall see later, this school is still flourishing in the country with the number of the temples amounting to 6000.

2. Essay I, sec. V.

3. Daie Sōkō (Ch.: Tai Hui Tsung Kao, 1089-1163), a famous Zen Master of the Sung dynasty. His 'Epistles' have come down to us under the title of *Ta Hui Shu*.

4. Shōsan Suzuki (1579-1655), originally a samurai and a writer of popular stories, later became a Zen monk and created a very peculiar type of Zen based on his earlier experiences.

5. Of the Rinzai school, 1619-1690, famous for his sermons in colloquial Japanese.

6. Yakusan Igen (Ch.: Yao Shan Wei Yen, 751-834).

7. Dōgen: *Shōbōgenzō* (*op. cit.* Iwanami Series of Japanese Thought XII-XIII) Tokyo 1970-1972, Vol. I. p. 127.

8. Daie Sōkō see above, Note 3.

9. *Shōbōgenzō* (*op. cit.*).

10. Nangaku Ejô, 677-744.

11. On Daie and his 'Epistles', see above, Note 3.

12. On the problem of the 'meaninglessness' of Zen sayings see Essay IV.

13. Jōshū Jūshin (Ch.: Chao Chou Tsung Shên, 778-879), an outstanding Master of the T'ang dynasty. The *kōan* here discussed, which is the *kōan* No. 37 of the *Mu Mon Kan*, has been analyzed in Essay I, sec. VI.

14. Hakuin Ekaku (1686-1769). A remarkable Zen Master, calligrapher and painter, Hakuin systematically rearranged the principal *kōans* that had come down to his time and revived the *kōan* method in Zen discipline. He is admired as the founder of the so-called modern Rinzai school of Zen.

15. See above, Note 5. The quotation is from the *Sayings of Master Bankei* (in *Sayings of Various Zen Schools*, Chikuma Series of Japanese Thought, vol. X, ed. Karaki, 1969, Tokyo, p. 270).

16. *Mu Mon Kan*, No. 1.

17. This part of the anecdote is reproduced here as it is quoted by Dōgen in his *Shōbōgenzō*. The full original anecdote is found in the *Sayings of Jōshū*.

18. Mumon Ekai (Ch.: Wu Mên Hui K'ai, 1183-1260). His words quoted here are from his Commentary on the *kōan* in question.

19. Also from the same Commentary.

Essay VI

THE INTERIOR AND EXTERIOR
IN ZEN

Note: Eranos lecture for the year 1973, published in Eranos-
Jahrbuch XLII, 1975, Leiden.

I Painting and Calligraphy in the Far East

The problem of the distinction and relation between the interior and exterior, or the internal and the external world, has played an exceedingly important role in the formative process of Far Eastern spirituality. The idea has in fact greatly contributed toward the development, elaboration and refinement of many of the most characteristic aspects of Far Eastern culture in such various fields as religious thought, philosophy, painting, calligraphy, architecture, gardening, swordsmanship, tea ceremony, etc.

I shall, by way of preliminaries, begin by giving a few conspicuous examples from the fields of painting and calligraphy before I go into the discussion of how the same distinction between the interior and exterior has been dealt with in Zen Buddhism.

One of the earliest and most important theoreticians of Chinese painting, Hsieh Ho of the 5th century, who in his *Ku Hua Pin Lu* ('An Appreciative Record of Ancient Paintings) established the famous 'Six Principles' of painting, precisely raised the problem of the interaction between the interior and exterior under the title of 'Spiritual Tone Pulsating with Life', *ch'i yün shêng tung*. This principle – which is the first of the six – indicates that in any good painting there must be a perfect, harmonious correspondence realized between the inner rhythm of man and the life rhythm of external Nature in such a way that, as a result, an undefinable spiritual tone pervades the whole space of the picture, vitalizing the latter in the most subtle way and imparting metaphysical significance to the objects depicted, whatever they might be. When a painter succeeds in actualizing this principle, his work will be filled with a peculiar kind of spiritual energy expressing itself in the rhythmic pulsation of life. It will be a work of the all-pervading rhythm of cosmic Life itself, in which the spirit of man will be in direct communion with the inner reality of Heaven and Earth.

The *ch'i yün* or 'spiritual tone' is thus realizable only through an active participation of man in the work of painting with the whole of his spiritual vitality. It is not to be ascribed to the natural *ch'i yün* of the things depicted. Landscape paintings in black and white (that are usually given as examples of the actualization of this principle) could be very misleading in this respect. A distant mountain looming out of the mist, for instance, or a torrent pouring down a rocky valley under cloudy peaks, etc., might easily give us the impression that the *ch'i yün* of the painting is but a reflection or transposition of the *ch'i yün* that is there in the external world of Nature. The fact is, however, that even such homely objects as stones, grass, and vegetables – a cucumber, for example, or an eggplant – may pictorially be represented with no less *ch'i yün* than a grand-scale landscape with mountains and streams, if only the painter knows how to concentrate his spiritual energy upon seeing into the nature of the thing he intends to paint, to harmonize his spirit, so to speak, with the spirit of the thing, and then to infuse into his work through the power of his brush. If he succeeds in doing this, then, as a result, the spirit of the object will be rendered in such a way that it moves, alive, on the paper in perfect consonance with the pulsation of the inner spirit of the artist.

Let us now try to reconstruct the whole process with a view to bringing to light the underlying dialectic of the interior and exterior. Let us suppose that a Far Eastern painter now intends to draw a black and white picture of a bamboo. He is not primarily interested in representing the likeness. For he is first and foremost concerned with penetrating into the inner reality of the bamboo and letting its very 'spirit' flow out of his brush as if it were a natural effusion of the bamboo.

In the tradition of Far Eastern aesthetics, a complete self-identification of the painter with the 'soul' of his motif, i.e., his becoming perfectly at one with the spiritual essence of his motif, is considered an absolutely necessary condition for any high achievement in this sort of painting.

In order to become thoroughly at one with the object he

wants to depict, the painter must first achieve a complete detachment from the agitations of the mind which unavoidably disturb his spiritual tranquility. For only in the profound stillness of a concentrated mind can the artist penetrate into the mysterium of the all-pervading cosmic Lfe and harmonize his spirit with the working of Nature. Hence the importance attached to the practice of 'quiet sitting' among Far Eastern painters as a pre-condition of producing good paintings. Mi Yu Jên, a famous landscape painter of the Sung dynasty, for example, says: 'The (external) things do not touch or excite me when I sit down quietly, cross-legged like a monk, forgetting all troubles and harmonizing myself with the vast blue emptiness'.[1]

Now, to hark back to our example of a painter intending to draw a picture of a bamboo, the first thing he must do is try to realize through meditation a spiritual 'state of non-agitation', a state of deep inner silence, thus making his mind entirely free and untroubled.

Then, with such a 'purified' mind, he meets the bamboo: he gazes at it intently, gazes beyond its material form into its interior: throws his own self wholly into the living spirit of the bamboo until he feels a mysterious resonance of the pulse-beat of the bamboo in himself as identified with his own pulse-beat. Now he has grasped the bamboo from the inside: or, to use a characteristic expression of Oriental aesthetics, he has 'become the bamboo'. Then, and then only, does he take up the brush and draw on the paper what he has thus grasped, without any conscious effort, without any reflection. What kind of work will it be? Let us try to analyze the result of such an activity in terms of the interior and exterior.

(1)   To begin with, the bamboo that has been depicted in this manner is necessarily an immediate expression of the inner rhythm of his own spirit which has harmonized itself with the life-rhythm of the bamboo. It is a landscape of his spirit in the sense that it is a pictorial self-expression of his spiritual reality. In this sense the picture of the bamboo is an externalization of the internal.

(2)   Since, however, what has been grasped at the outset by the painter through a kind of existential empathy is the inner reality of the bamboo (which is in itself a natural object, i.e., a thing of the external world), the picture may and must

also be regarded as a self-expression of the external world through the artist's brush. Each brush-stroke makes itself felt as beating with, and being expressive of, the pulsation of the inner life of the bamboo. Nature externalizes its own 'interior' through the artistic activity of the painter.

(3)   Thus we observe here a double externalization of the internal: the painter externalizes his 'interior', i.e., his mental state or spiritual reality, while Nature on its part externalizes through the brush of the painter its 'interior', i.e., the inner rhythm of life which pervades the whole universe and which runs through Nature.

It is remarkable that what is thus analyzable into a process of double externalization takes place in reality as a single and unique act. That is to say, the very act of the artist expressing his interior is in itself nothing other than the act of Nature expressing its own interior. As a result we have what we have referred to above as *ch'i yün shêng tung* or the 'Spiritual Tone Pulsating with Life'.

In the Far Eastern art of calligraphy we can observe the process of the externalization of the internal in a much simpler and more straightforward way. It is no accident that throughout the history of Chinese culture painting and calligraphy have always been closely connected. In fact the two arts have developed in China in a most intimate association with each other, so much so that they have often been considered one art. For the Far Easterner calligraphy is the painting of the mind.

But calligraphy differs from painting in that the 'objects' in the former are nothing but ideograms, i.e., signs or symbols that are abstract in nature and that are therefore in themselves and by themselves totally devoid of the life-rhythm which characterizes natural objects. They are, so to speak, cold and lifeless things. The lifeless, dead signs become alive and begin to beat with the pulsation of living beings only when they are imbued with the spiritual energy of a calligrapher. In other words, they become aesthetically expressive only through the creative activity of the brush in a master hand. The ideograms are awakened from the slumbering state of pure abstraction and spring into palpitating life through the infusion of the spirit of an artist into them. Then the ideo-

grams are no longer abstract signs: they are external manifes-
tations of the human mind.

In the process of this transformation we witness the same
externalization of the internal which we observed in the typical pattern of Far Eastern painting, but which is observable in
a far less ambiguous way than in the case of painting. This is
mostly due to the fact that the strokes of which the Chinese
characters are composed, taken separately and by themselves, are devoid of meaning. Each component stroke –
vertical, horizontal, slanting, turning upward or downward,
or a dot – does not mean anything except that a whole composed of them, that is, a character, does have a definite
meaning.

The most remarkable thing about this, however, is that
each of the strokes which, as a component element of a
character, does not signify anything definite, suddenly transforms itself into something fully significant and expressive in
the art of calligraphy. For, when executed by a master calligrapher, each single stroke is an immediate self-expression of
the artist's state of mind. No brush-stroke is made without
expressing something of his mind. The brush faithfully obeys
and reflects every movement of the mind of the man who uses
it. And every movement of the brush is a direct disclosure of
the inner structure of his mind at every instant. It is not
without reason that in the Far East calligraphy is considered
the portrait of the mind or self-portrait of the calligrapher.
And as such it has always been appreciated as a very special
kind of spiritual art.

It is however, of utmost importance for our purpose to
remark that what is meant by the dictum: 'Calligraphy is the
painting of the mind' is not simply that the psychological
details of the writer are disclosed as the brush moves on the
surface of the paper. For it will be but natural that the lines
and strokes executed by a man in a mood of melancholy
should tend to become droopy and feeble. A man who happens to be happy and gay naturally writes characters filled
with vigor and vitality. Lines drawn by a man whose mind is
agitated or terrified are almost necessarily unstable and
trembling. What is far more important from the viewpoint of
Far Eastern calligraphy is that a work should be a self-
expression of a high-minded person, that it should be an

external manifestation of the inner states of a spiritually disciplined man. Calligraphy cannot be a spiritual art as the 'painting of the mind' except when it is an immediate externalization of a highly disciplined 'interior'.

By this I am referring to the fact that in the traditional form of Far Eastern calligraphy there is what may most appropriately be called 'calligraphic enlightenment'. After years and years of strenuous effort and rigorous training – and that not only in the technique of using the brush but in purifying the mind and trying to attain a profound inner tranquility – there comes to the calligrapher a decisive moment at which he feels the whole of his spiritualized 'interior' suddenly flowing out of himself through the tip of his brush as if it were something material, actualizing itself on the paper in the form of successive characters. In such a situation, *he* is utterly incapable of doing anything; it is rather his 'interior' that dictates as it wills the movement of the brush. Only after having once gone through such a 'moment' of calligraphic enlightenment is the man a real calligrapher; up to that moment he has simply been a student, an apprentice, not a master, no matter how masterly and dexterous he might be in executing beautiful or forceful brush-strokes. And it is on such a level of spiritual discipline that calligraphy becomes a typical Far Eastern art as the 'externalization of the internal'.

In fact, in every work of Far Eastern calligraphy, executed by one who has once gone through such an experience, we invariably observe the spiritual state of the man directly and naturally expressing itself in external forms. This is most easily to be seen in Zen calligraphy. But in other branches of calligraphy too, the externalization of the internal is clearly observable, no matter how different the content of the 'internal' may be in each case.

The most basic form of Japanese calligraphy, the *hiragana*-writing of *waka*-poetry, for example, has nothing to do with Zen. And the calligraphic beauty of Japanese script is markedly different from that of Chinese characters. In Japanese calligraphy the beauty is primarily formed by gracefully flowing lines. The slow, rhythmic and graceful flow of the lines is felt by the Japanese to be a direct external expression of the inner *poésie*; it is *poésie* itself, the inner *poésie* of the calligrapher itself in the form of the external *poésie* of flowing lines. The lines themselves are profoundly poetic; they *are* poetry. And in this sense, Japanese calligraphy is also a fine illustration of the externalization of the internal, because here too the 'internal' is a strictly and rigorously disciplined one, albeit in quite a different way from the 'internal' of Zen calligraphy.

I have now briefly dealt with the problem of the interior and exterior in connection with the two typical forms of Oriental art just in order to bring home the important role this distinction has played in the formation of spiritual culture in the Far East. With these preliminaries we may now turn to our specific subject: the distinction and relation between the interior and exterior in Zen Buddhism.

II Pseudo-Problems in Zen

It would seem that the distinction between the interior and exterior is a kind of intrinsic geometry of the human mind. As Gaston Bachelard[2] once remarked, 'the dialectics of outside and inside' belongs to the most elementary and primitive stratum of our mind. It is a deep-rooted habit of our thinking. In fact we find everywhere the opposition of the interior and exterior. 'Inside the house' versus 'outside the house', 'inside the country' versus 'outside the country', 'inside the earth' versus 'outside the earth', 'inner (i.e., esoteric) meaning' versus 'outer (i.e., exoteric) meaning', the ego or mind as our 'inside' versus the external world or Nature as our 'outside', the soul as our 'inside' versus the body as our 'outside', etc., etc. The everyday ontology reposing upon the contrasting geometrical images of the interior and exterior thus forms one of the most fundamental patters of thinking, by which our daily behavior is largely determined. 'It (i.e., the dialectics of inside and outside) has', says Bachelard, 'the sharpness of the dialectics of *yes* and *no*, which decides everything. Unless one is careful, it is made into a basis of images that governs all thoughts of positive and negative'.[3]

Zen also often talks about the interior and exterior. In Zen teaching and training much use is made of the distinction between them, in the majority of cases the 'interior' referring to the mind or consciousness and the 'exterior' to the world of Nature against which the human ego stands as subject aganst object. Examples abound in Zen documents. Thus to give a few examples taken at random from the *Lin Chi Lu* 'The Sayings and Doings of Master Lin Chi (J.: Rinzai, d 867)'.[4]

> If you desire to be like the old masters, do not look outward. The light of purity which shines out of every thought you

conceive is the *Dharmakāya* (i.e., ultimate Reality) within yourselves.

I simply wish to see you stop wandering after external objects.

Do not commit yourselves to a grave mistake by convulsively looking around your neighbourhood and not within yourselves . . . Just look within yourselves.[5]

The extraordinary importance of this distinction in Zen Buddhism will be brought home by merely reflecting upon the fact that the practice of meditation (*dhyāna*) which is uncontestedly the very core and essence of Zen is usually understood to consist in stopping our mind from running after 'outward' things and turning it 'inward' upon its own 'inner' reality.

And yet, strictly speaking from the Zen point of view, the problem of the interior and exterior is but a pseudo-problem, in no matter what form it may be raised, because, seen with the eyes of an enlightened man, the interior and exterior are not two regions to be distinguished from one another. The distinction has no reality: it is nothing but a thought-construct peculiar to the discriminating activity of the mind. For one who has seen with his spiritual eye what the Hua Yen metaphysics indicates as the unimpeded interpenetration of the noumenal and the phenomenal, and then, further, the interpenetration of the phenomenal things among themselves, it will be meaningless and even ridiculous to speak of the interior standing against the exterior.

The problem of the interior and exterior is thus a pseudo-problem because in raising this problem we establish forcibly, as it were, two independent domains, make them stand opposed to each other, and discuss the relation between them, while in reality there is no such distinction to be made. It is a pseudo-problem because it is a problem that has been raised where there is none, and because one discusses it as if it were a real problem. The whole matter is, to use a characteristic Zen expression, 'causing unnecessary entanglements where in reality there are none'.

It is to be remembered, however, that Zen utilizes many pseudo-problems – besides that of the interior and exterior – for specific purposes. A pseudo-problem could be used as an expedient, a means of teaching leading toward the dissipation of false thinking. Poison as an antidote for poison. The classical documents of Zen are in this sense filled with pseudo-problems.

In fact almost all the questions that are recorded in the famous *kōan* collections and other Zen records as having been addressed each by a disciple or a visiting monk to some accomplished master are pseudo-problems.

'Has the dog the Buddha-nature?' (i.e., Is an animal like the dog possessed of an innate capability to be enlightened and become a Buddha?)

'Who is Chao Chou?' (a question addressed to Master Chao Chou himself.)

'What is the significance of the First Patriarch of Zen coming all the way from India to China?' (i.e., What did Bodhidharma bring from India? What is the very essence of Buddhism?)

'Who are you?' or 'Who am I?'

From the standpoint of an accomplished master (like, for example, Chao Chou), questions of this sort are simply meaningless: they are 'unnecessary entanglements'.

In actuality, however, these and similar pseudo-problems are intentionally and consciously utilized in Zen. And the way they are utilized is very characteristic of, and peculiar to, Zen. Let me first briefly explain this point.

In ordinary conversation or dialogue the man who asks a question expects from the beginning a reasonable answer from the man to whom he addresses himself, an answer that will be concordant with his question. This common pattern of question-answer in no way applies to the Zen dialogue known as *mondō*.

In a Zen context, a question is presented not in order to be answered but to be rejected outright. He who asks: 'Has the dog the Buddha-nature?' in expectation of a reasonable answer is a man who has absolutely no understanding of Zen. The monk who, having already attained some knowledge of Zen, asks his master: 'Has the dog the Buddha-nature?', aims exclusively at witnessing with his own eyes, or with the whole of his body-mind, how the master shatters this very question. In the midst of an existential tension between man and man, the disciple observes how the master nullifies on the spot the pseudo-problem, and by observing it he tries to gain a glimpse of the spiritual state of his master and thereby gain a chance, if possible, to attain to the same state. Or, in case the monk who asks the question happens to be a man of enlightenment, he wants thereby to fathom the depth of the master's spiritual awareness.

In any case, such a pattern of question-answer structurally presupposes the existence of dimensional discrepancy between the master who answers (A) and the disciple who asks (B). In other words, it stands on the supposition that A and B stand in two different dimensions of spiritual awareness. A is not supposed to give an answer to B's question, standing on the same level of awareness as B. The question is uttered on the level of B, while the answer to it is given on the level of A – this is the normal form of Zen *mondō*. Otherwise expressed, the answer given by A does not constitute an answer to B's question in the ordinary sense. Rather, the real answer in an authentic Zen *mondō* is that which discloses and nullifies at the same time the spiritual discrepancy lying between A and B.

There is, thus, no knowing what will come out from A as an answer to B's question.

A monk once asked Yün Mên:[6] 'Where do Buddhas come from?'
(i.e., What is the ultimate truth of Buddhahood?)
Yün Mên replied: 'Lo! The East Mountain goes flowing over the water!'

A monk asked Chao Chou:[7] 'What is the true significance of Bodhidharma's coming from India to China?' Chao Chou replied: 'The cypress tree in the courtyard!'

The answer in each of these cases is apparently nonsensical enough to confuse and confound B. The answer is often given in the form of a sharp blow with a stick, a kick, a slap in the face, a shout, etc. But in no matter what form it may be given, verbal or non-verbal, the basic structure remains always the same: namely, by bringing to naught the discrepancy between A and B, a life-and-death attempt is made on the part of A to let *B* witness and, if possible, experience the spiritual dimension in which stands *A* himself.

Here is another example which is relevant to our main subject.

A monk asked Chao Chou: 'Who is Chao Chou?'
The master replied: 'East Gate, West Gate, South Gate, North Gate!'

This answer which in an ordinary context would naturally be sheer nonsense, *is* in this particular context a real and excellent answer.[8]

There are cases in which the answer given by *A* looks as if it stood on the same level as the question of *B*. Then the whole situation is liable to become very misleading. Take for example the celebrated *Wu* (J.: *Mu*) of Chao Chou.

A monk once asked Chao Chou: 'Has the dog the Buddha-nature?', to which the master replied: 'No (*wu*)!' If we were to suppose that this answer was given at the level at which the monk uttered his question, then this 'No!' would most naturally mean: 'No, the dog has no Buddha-nature'. And Chao Chou's intention would thereby utterly be missed. In reality his answer aims primarily at invalidating not only the pseudo-problem raised by the monk, but also the existential consciousness itself of the monk: it aims at nullifying at one blow the spiritual discrepancy between Chao Chou and the monk. And such is the most authentic form of answers given to all pseudo-problems in Zen contexts.

Zen does not consider the raising of pseudo-problems meaningless and useless. Quite the contrary. It is through the seemingly round-about way of pseudo-problems being raised and, once raised, being violently nullified on the spot that the student is led to Zen experience in many cases. This process corresponds to what I have clarified earlier from a metaphysical point of view.[9] There I have analyzed the process by which the absolutely inarticulate Nothingness becomes articulated into a sensibly concrete form, and then the latter is negated on the spot, i.e., at the very moment of articulation, the original Nothingness being thereby disclosed for just an instant, in the twinkling of an eye. What is at issue in the present passage has exactly the same structure. Here, too, a pseudo-problem is first presented by *B* in his spiritual dimension; then it is nullified by *A* on the spot, at the very moment it is presented, with a blow, verbal or otherwise, issuing from the spiritual dimension of *A*, in such a way that *A*'s inner state is disclosed, naked, to the eye of *B*.

As I stated at the outset, the problem of the interior and exterior is also one of the typical pseudo-problems. Zen begins by making a clear-cut distinction between the interior and exterior, puts the two into sharp contrast, and then all of a sudden shocks the beginners by making a categorical statement that in reality there is no such distinction.

In describing the experience of *satori* or enlightenment, Zen masters often use the expression: 'the interior and exterior becoming smoothed out into one whole sheet'. Not infrequently the state of awareness at the moment of *satori* is described as a 'state of an absolute, internal and external unity'. Thus Master Wu Mên,[10] to give one typical example, in giving suggestions to the disciples as to how they should 'pass the *kōan* of Chao Chou's *Wu* (or in Japanese *Mu*, "No!")', makes the following remark:

> If you want to pass this barrier, transform the whole of your mind-and-body into one single ball of Doubt and concentrate upon the question: What is this 'No'? Concentrate upon this question day and night . . . Just continue concentrating upon this problem; you will soon begin to feel as if you had gulped a red-hot iron ball which, stuck into the throat, you can neither swallow down nor spit out. (While you are in such a desperate state) all unnecessary knowledges that you have acquired and all false forms of awareness will be washed away one after another. And as a fruit gradually ripens, your time will ripen, and by a natural process your interior and exterior will finally become smoothed out into one whole sheet.

Since, properly speaking, there has been from the very beginning no real distinction, the 'interior and exterior being smoothed out into one whole sheet' is nothing but a false description of reality. There is however, no denying that the expression contains some amount of truth when it is considered a description of what is actually experienced in the course of Zen training.

In fact, from the point of view of a man who has not yet attained *satori*, his interior and exterior are obviously two different domains of experience. I see this table. The 'I' which is the seeing subject is separated from the table which is the object seen. The one is the interior and the other the exterior. The instantaneous process by which the distinction loses its reality so that the interior and exterior become transformed into an absolute metaphysical unity, is faithfully reproduced by this peculiar Zen expression: 'The interior and exterior become smoothed out into one whole sheet'.

Thus the problem of the distinction and relation between the interior and exterior, although it is admittedly a pseudo-problem, does possess in Zen Buddhism the possibility of being developed theoretically as a meaningful philosophical problem. In embarking upon this task, we evidently cannot start from the standpoint of a master who has fully attained enlightenment. For in his spiritual dimension there is no place even for raising such a question; the problem simply does not exist for such a man. It is therefore only as a problem for men of non-enlightenment who are on their way toward enlightenment that the problem of the interior and exterior acquires in Zen the right to be treated as an important problem, theoretical as well as practical. Yet, in dealing with this problem in this sense, a penetrating eye must be kept open, surveying the whole extent of the problem from its beginning till the end. And such an eye must necessarily be the eye of a man who has already attained enlightenment.

Our situation becomes in this way somewhat complicated. For in order to deal with the problem of the interior and exterior from the viewpoint of Zen, we have to start from the naïve world-experience of an ordinary man for whom the external world is clearly distinguished from his mind as two separate entities, and, at the same time, we must remain aware of how the problem of the relation between the interior and exterior is ultimately to be resolved in the experience of enlightenment. This is the procedure we are going to follow in what remains of the present Essay.

III Experience of Satori

I would like to start the discussion of our problem by considering an anecdote concerning the first encounter of Tung Shan
Shou Ch'u[11] with Master Yün Mên. At that time Tung Shan
was still a young student of Zen. Later he became one of the
most distinguished masters of the T'ang dynasty.

When Tung Shan came to Yün Mên for instruction, the
latter asked him: 'Where do you come from?' The *mondō*
starts from this point.

> Tung Shan: 'I come from Ch'a Tu (J.: Sato)'
> Yün Mên: 'Where did you spend the summer?'
> Tung Shan: 'At such-and-such a place in the Province of Hu
> Nan'.
> Yün Mên: 'I forgive you thirty blows with my stick (which you
> well deserve).
> You may now retire'.

The next day Tung Shan came up to Yün Mên again and
asked: 'What wrong did I do yesterday to deserve thirty
blows?' Thereupon the master gave a cry of sharp reproof:
'You stupid rice-bag! Is that the way you wander all over the
country?'[12]

There is something typically Zen in this dialogue between
Tung Shan and Yün Mên. But why indeed did Tung Shang
deserve in the eyes of the master thirty blows with a stick? Let
us for a moment ponder upon this problem.

'Where do you come from?' This is one of those innocent-
looking questions which are often addressed by a Zen master
to a newly-arrived monk. By the answer given, whether verbal or non-verbal, the master can immediately see through
the newcomer. Without any further questioning, he now
knows at what stage of spiritual training the monk stands.

Whatever answer the latter may give, or even before he opens his mouth to utter a word, the very mental attitude of the monk in answering the question discloses to the eyes of the master how the monk looks at the relation between himself and the so-called 'external' or objective world.

'Where do you come from?' These simple words which would at the first glance look like quite a conventional question, thus carry in a Zen context extraordinary weight, for the question concerns the very ground of one's own being, the real location of one's own existence. Otherwise expressed, 'Where do you come from?' is a question that may very well be reformulated in terms of the interior and exterior. 'Do you originally come from the inside or the outside?' That is to say, 'Where is your home?' or 'Where do you really live?'

Suppose I say: 'I come from Tokyo', taking the words of the master ('Where do you come from') to be asking about the geographical location of the place from which I have come. According to the Zen documents, innumerable monks have fallen into this pitfall. 'But what kind of "Tokyo" do you mean?' The master usually does not take pains to ask such a question in such a form. But, if verbally formulated, the attitude of the master would necessarily assume this form. And no sooner is this second question asked by the master, whether implicitly or explicitly, than the external 'Tokyo' becomes on the spot internalized. 'Tokyo' thus internalized would exactly be the thing which Zen usually refers to by a more characteristic expression: 'your original Face which you had even before your parents were born'.

The common-sense statement that I come from Tokyo as an external, i.e., geographical place, is in a Zen dialogue totally meaningless. The very fact of my coming-from-Tokyo must be understood in a spiritual sense, i.e., as something taking place in the dimension of spiritual awareness. Every step I take in this 'coming' is for Zen a step in self-realization. The Zen master is not primarily interested in external geography: what is really important to him is my internal geography, that is to say, to what extent I have realized my coming-from-Tokyo as a spiritual event.

However, we must not commit the mistake of regarding the internalized Tokyo as an 'internal' place standing against the 'external' world. For an internal place understood in such a way would simply be another external place. What is really meant is a spiritual domain where the reality is witnessed in its original undifferentiation before it is bifurcated into the interior and exterior.

The young Tung Shan deserved thirty blows with a stick because he took Yün Mên's question in terms of external geography: because his answer had little to do with his internal geography, and, of course, much less with the spiritual domain of undifferentiation which lies beyond even the very distinction between internal and external geography.

Thus it will be clear that Zen begins by establishing a distinction between the interior and exterior, but that this distinction itself is to be considered something that must ultimately be superseded.

Let us now go back once again to the starting-point, and reconsider the whole process by which the initial distinction between the interior and exterior becomes nullified and the two ontological regions become 'smoothed out into one whole sheet'.

In analyzing what we might properly call Zen experience (i.e., the personal realization of the state of enlightenment) in terms of the relation between the interior and exterior, we find two theoretical possibilities. We may describe them as:

(1) The interior becoming exterior, or the externalization of the internal.

(2) The exterior becoming interior, or the internalization of the external world.

In the first case (which is often popularly referred to by saying: 'Man becomes the thing'), one suddenly experiences one's 'I' (the internal) losing its own existential identity and becoming completely fused into, and identified with, an 'external' object. Man *becomes* a flower. Man *becomes* a bamboo. This experience, however, does not establish itself as an authentically Zen experience unless man goes further until the single flower or bamboo with which he has been identified, is in his spiritual awareness seen to contain the whole world of Being. At such a stage the 'I' expands to the ultimate limits of the universe. That is to say, the 'I' is no longer an *I* as an independent entity: It is no longer a subject standing against the objective world.

In the second case, i.e., the internalization of the external, what has heretofore been regarded as 'external' to one's self becomes suddenly taken into the mind. Then everything that happens and is observed in the so-called 'external' world comes to be seen as a working of the mind, as a particular self-determination of the mind. Every 'external' event comes to be seen as an 'internal' event. Man feels himself filled with an undeniable realization that he, his mind-and-body, has become completely transparent, having lost its existential opaqueness that would offer resistance to all things coming from the 'outside'. Man feels himself – to use an expression of Master Han Shan (J.: Kanzan, 16th century) – as 'one great illuminating whole, infinitely lucid and serene'. His mind now is to be likened to an all-embracing mirror in which the mountains, rivers and the earth with all the splendor and beauty of Nature are freely reflected. Thus the 'external' world is re-created in a different dimension as an 'internal' landscape. The mind of man in such a state, however, is no longer the individual mind of an individual person. It is now what Buddhism designates as the Mind.

These two (apparently opposite, but ultimately and in reality identical) interpretations of Zen experience require more detailed elucidation. This will be done presently.

But before going into further details, I would devote a few pages to the discussion of a peculiar kind of spiritual experience which is typical of Zen and which in fact presents in miniature the very structure of *satori* or enlightenment in terms of the fundamental relation between the interior and exterior.

The correspondence between the interior and exterior, leading ultimately to the complete unification of the two, whether we approach it in terms of the first possibility or the second that have just been briefly touched upon, can clearly be observed in the most concise and concentrated form in the experience of 'living' a certain decisive instant at which a momentary communion is realized between interior and exterior. Just a click is produced on a special spiritual plane, and enlightenment is already there, fully actualized.

The particular manner in which this 'click' as a spiritual event arrives to man is well illustrated by the celebrated anecdote recounting how Master Hsiang Yen (J.: Kyōgen)[13] experienced *satori* for the first time in his life. After many years of desperate and futile efforts to attain enlightenment, Hsiang Yen, in a state of utter despair, came to the conclusion that he was not destined in this life to see into the secret of Reality, and that, therefore, it was better for him to devote himself, instead, to some meritorious work. He decided to become a grave keeper to a famous master, built for himself a reed-thatched hermitage, and lived there in complete seclusion from others. One day, whilst sweeping the ground, a small stone rapped against a bamboo. All of a sudden, quite unexpectedly, the hearing of the sound of the stone striking a bamboo awakened in his mind something which he had never dreamt of. It was the 'click' of which mention has just been made. And it was the attainment of enlightenment. The awakening came to him as an experience of his own self and the whole objective world being all smashed up into a state of undifferentiation.

Upon this Hsiang Yen composed the following famous *gāthā*:

> The sharp sound of a stone striking a bamboo!
> And all I had learnt was at once forgotten.
> No need there had been for training and discipline.[14]
> Through every act and movement of everyday life
> I manifest the eternal Way.
> No longer shall I ever fall into a hidden trap.
> Leaving no trace behind me I shall go everywhere.

It is recorded that many a man of Zen came to this kind of Awakening by the stimulation of quite an insignificant – so it would look to outsiders – sense perception: the call of a bird, the sound of a bell, the human voice, the sight of a flower blooming, etc. When the mind is spiritually matured, anything can serve as the spark to set off the explosion of the inner energies in a way hitherto undreamt of. The Buddha is said to have suddenly experienced the Awakening when by chance he looked at the morning star. Master Wu Mên[15] (J.: Mumon) had struggled for six years with the above-mentioned *kōan* of Chao Chou's 'No!' One day, as he heard the beating of the drum announcing mealtime he was suddenly awakened. The famous Japanese Zen master Hakuin[16] had his Awakening when he heard the sound of a temple bell announcing the dawn as he was sitting in deep meditation one cold winter night. He is said to have jumped up with overflowing joy. Master Ling Yün[17] had undergone a most rigorous training without, however, being able to attain enlightenment. While on a journey, he sat down to have some rest and without any definite intention turned his eyes toward a village lying far-off under the mountain. It was springtime. Quite accidentally his eyes were caught by peaches in full bloom there. All of a sudden he realized that he was an enlightened man. Examples of this sort can be given almost indefinitely.

What happened to these people? For the purpose of elucidating this point, let us try to reconstruct the process by which Master Hsiang Yen was finally led to enlightenment by hearing the sound of a small stone striking a bamboo.

Hsiang Yen was sweeping the ground. He was absorbed in the work. His mind emptied of all disturbing thoughts and images, with absolute concentration, he was sweeping the ground, without thinking of anything, without being conscious even of his own bodily movement. As is natural with a man rigorously trained and disciplined in meditation, his act of sweeping the ground was itself a form of a practical *samādhi*. It is not that the sweeping of the ground has the symbolic significance of the purification of the mind. The very absorption of the whole person – the mind-and-body – in the activity of sweeping the ground has exactly the same function as that of being absorbed in profound meditation. It is the actualization of what Zen usually calls the state of the 'no-mind' (*wu-hsin*, J.: *mu-shin*).

In such a state there is no consciousness of the earth, fallen leaves, and stones as 'external' objects. Nor is there consciousness of the 'I' who is sweeping the ground as the 'internal' source of action. Already in this state of practical *samādhi* or 'no-mind', Zen is fully realized. Since there is no consciousness of the 'I' as distinguished from the things, there is here no distinction between the interior and exterior. There is only Hsiang Yen. Or there is only the world. Yet Hsiang Yen in such a state, while being Hsiang Yen, *is* the All. Hsiang Yen and the world are thus completely at one. This, however, is not yet the state of enlightenment.

In order that all this be realized specifically as 'enlightenment', this absolute unity of the interior and exterior must necessarily be brought into the incandescent light of consciousness in its original absolute simplicity. In the case of Master Hsiang Yen, the spark was provided by the sound of a small stone which he swept against a bamboo. By this sensestimulation he is awakened from the *samādhi*. All of a sudden he becomes aware of the earth and the leaves on the ground: he becomes aware of the rake in his hand, the movement of his hands, and arms; he becomes aware of his own self, too. The whole world including himself comes back to him. However, for Hsiang Yen it is not the mere emergence of the external world out of nowhere. Nor is it the resuscitation of his old self. It is rather the emergence or resuscitation of a reality prior to its bifurcation into the interior and exterior. In other words, Hsiang Yen at that very instant realized in a flash the fact that the interior and exterior had already been 'one whole sheet' while he had been absorbed in sweeping the ground, and that such was the original mode of being of Reality. The moment of enlightenment as understood by Zen comes when man regains the awareness of the subject and object on a spiritual plane transcending the subject-object bifurcation.

Thus when Master Hsiang Yen in the midst of *samādhi* heard the sound of a small stone striking a bamboo, he was himself the sound of the stone hitting against the bamboo. And the sound was the whole universe. When Hakuin was awakened from meditation by the sound of a temple bell ringing, it was the sound of himself ringing that he heard. The whole universe was the sound of the bell. And Hakuin himself was the sound of the bell listening to the sound of the bell. In the same way, when Ling Yün was enlightened by the sight of peaches blooming afar, he was the peach blossoms. The universe was the fragrance of the peaches, and he himself was the fragrant universe.

What is actually experienced and realized in cases like these may perhaps be best described as the sudden realization of the ontological transparency of all things, including both the things existing in the 'external' world and the human subject which is ordinarily supposed to be looking at them from the outside. Both the 'external' things and the 'internal' of man divest themselves of their ontological opaqueness, become totally transparent, pervade each other, and become submerged into one.

It is no accident that in Zen as well as in many other traditions of mysticism such a situation is often described in terms of the essential luminosity of being. 'Light' is but a metaphor for the particular nature of things seen in the supra-sensible and supra-intellectual dimension of the mind. But the metaphor is so appropriate that many mystics have really experienced the mutual relation between the human 'I' and the things of the 'external' world and the mutual relation between the different things themselves as an interpenetration of different lights. The subject and object, the interior and exterior, are here seen as two different lights which, though each remains an independent light, freely penetrate each other without the least obstruction from either side, so that the two merge into one all-pervading Light illuminating itself as a purely luminous whole.

IV The Externalization of the Internal

With these preliminaries we are now in a position to turn to the discussion of the above-mentioned two theoretical possibilities of interpreting what we may properly call Zen experience or the Zen vision of Being: namely (1) the externalization of the internal and (2) the internalization of the external. I treat these two apparently opposite ways as 'theoretical' possibilities, because whichever way one may choose one is sure to be led to exactly the same result. Whether you externalize the internal or internalize the external, you will end up by arriving at one and the same vision of Being. As a matter of historical fact, however, there are Zen masters who took the first of these two ways, and there are others who chose the second. Let us first discuss the externalization of the internal.

The externalization of the internal in a Zen context starts from the loss of the ego consciousness on the part of man in his encounter with an 'external' object. Losing the consciousness of the empirical ego-subject – which is according to Buddhism precisely the thing which is responsible for veiling our spiritual eyes and which thus prevents us from recognizing the metaphysical ground of Being – man gets submerged in the object. 'Man *becomes* the thing' to use again the popular Zen expression. 'Man *becomes* the bamboo' for example, or 'man *becomes* the flower'. Master Dōgen in a celebrated passage of his work, *Shōbōgenzō*[18] says:

> Delusion consists in your establishing the ego-subject and acting upon objects through it. Enlightenment, on the contrary, consists in letting the things act upon you and letting them illumine yourself. .... In looking at a thing, put the whole of your mind-body into the act; in listening to a sound,

put the whole of your mind-body into the act (in such a way that your ego may become lost and submerged in the thing seen or heard). Then, and then only will you be able to grasp Reality in its original suchness. In such a case, your spiritual grasp of the thing will be quite different from a mirror reflecting the image of something or the moon being reflected on the surface of water, (for the mirror and the thing reflected therein, or the water and the moon, still remain two entities, each maintaining its own identity.) (In the case of the spiritual unification of yourself and a thing, on the contrary,) if either one of the two makes itself manifest, the other completely disappears, the latter being submerged in the former. (That is to say, in the situation here at issue in particular, the 'I' disappears completely and the thing only remains manifest.) Now to get disciplined in the Way of the Buddha means nothing other than getting disciplined in properly dealing with your own I. To get disciplined in properly dealing with your own I means nothing other than forgetting your own I. To forget your own I means that you become illumined by the 'external' things. To be illumined by the things means that you obliterate the distinction between your (so-called) ego and the (so-called) egos of other things.

It will be clear that a deep, spiritual empathy with all things in Nature is what characterizes the externalization of the internal as experienced in the form of the total submersion of the human ego in an object, the submersion being so complete and total that the word 'object' loses its semantic basis. In the more limited field of aesthetic enjoyment, this kind of empathy is commonly experienced when, for instance, one is intently listening to an enchanting piece of music.

Music heard so deeply
That it is not heard at all, but you are the music
While the music lasts . . .

(T.S. Eliot: Four Quartets).

As Professor William Johnston[19] aptly remarks: 'In this typical, intense moment, music is heard so deeply that there is no longer a person listening and music listened to; there is no I opposed to music: there is simply music without subject and object'. In other words, the whole universe is filled with music: the whole universe *is* music. We can express the same thing in a somewhat different form by saying that the 'I' has died to itself and has been reborn in the form of music. In this kind of aesthetic experience Zen may be said to be already realized, whether one calls it Zen or not. Zen, however, requires that one should be in exactly the same state with regard to everything, not only while listening to music. One should become a bamboo. One should become a mountain. One should become the sound of a bell. That is what Zen means by the expression: 'seeing into the nature of things'.

It is, however, of utmost importance to remember in this connection that one's merely losing oneself and 'becoming' music, bamboo, flower or any other thing, does not constitute Zen experience in the fullest sense of the term. While one is in the state of complete oneness with the 'object', whatever it may be, which is realized in one's being totally absorbed in the contemplation of the thing, one is at most on the threshold of Zen. Strictly speaking, this state is not yet Zen. It may develop into Zen experience, as it may become something else. Enlightenment as the Zen tradition understands it is still far from being actualized.

Suppose I am intently gazing at a flower, for example. Suppose further that I have, in so doing, lost myself and entered into the flower in the manner explained above. I have now become the flower. I *am* the flower. I am living as the flower. From the viewpoint of Zen, however, this should not be considered the final stage of the spiritual discipline. Zen emphasizes that I should go on further until I reach what is designated in the traditional terminology of Oriental philosophy as a state prior to subject-object bifurcation. That is to say, my existential submersion into the flower must be perfect and complete to such an extent that there remains absolutely no consciousness of myself, nor even of the flower. This spiritual state of absolute unification which, psychologically is a kind of unconsciousness, is to be realized as the total disappearance of the flower or music as well as of the 'I', There is in such a state no flower, no music, just as there is no trace of the 'I'. What is really actualized here is Something which is absolutely undifferentiated and undivided; it is Awareness pure and simple with neither subject nor object.

But even this is not yet the ultimate stage to be reached in Zen discipline. In order that there be the experience of enlightenment, man must be awakened from this pure

Awareness. The absolutely undivided Something divides itself again as the 'I' and, for instance, the flower. And at the precise moment of this bifurcation, the flower suddenly and unexpectedly emerges as an absolute Flower. The painter paints this absolute Flower in his picture. The poet sings of this Flower in his poem. A flower has now re-established itself as the Flower, the absolute Flower. The latter is a flower blooming in a spiritual atmosphere which is essentially different from that in which blooms an ordinary flower. And yet the two are one and the same flower. This situation is what Dōgen refers to when he remarks that the 'mountains and rivers (as they appear in the state of enlightenment) must not be confused with ordinary mountains and rivers', although they are the same old mountains and rivers.

Nothing presents the process by which this Zen world-view becomes established, better – and in a manner more typical of Zen – than the oft-quoted saying of Master Ch'ing Yüan.[20] He said:

> Thirty years ago, before this aged monk (i.e., I) got into Zen training, I used to see a mountain as a mountain and a river as a river.
> Thereafter I had the chance to meet enlightened masters and, under their guidance I could attain enlightenment to some extent. At this stage, when I saw a mountain: lo! it was not a mountain. When I saw a river: lo! it was not a river.
> But in these days I have settled down to a position of final tranquillity. As I used to do in my first years, now I see a mountain just as a mountain and a river just as a river.

Here we see the characteristic Zen view of Reality neatly analyzed into three distinctive stages.

(1) The initial stage, corresponding to the world-experience of an ordinary man, at which the knower and the known are sharply distinguished from one another as two separate entities, and at which a mountain, for example, is seen by the perceiving 'I' as an objective thing called 'mountain'.

(2) The middle stage, corresponding to what I have just explained as a state of absolute unification, a spiritual state prior to subject-object bifurcation. At this stage the so-called 'external' world is deprived of its ontological solidity. Here the very expression: 'I see a mountain' is strictly a false

statement, for there is neither the 'I' which sees nor the mountain which is seen. If there is anything here it is the absolutely undivided awareness of Something eternally illuminating itself as the whole universe. In such a state, a mountain of course is not a mountain. The mountain seen in such a state is simply 'ineffable' – or 'beyond language and thought' – because it is 'nothing'. By rational reflection upon the experienced fact one would only say that the mountain is no-mountain.

(3) The final stage, a stage of infinite freedom and tranquillity, at which the undivided Something divides itself into subject and object in the very midst of the original oneness, the latter being still kept intact in spite of the apparent subject-object bifurcation. And the result is that the subject and object (the 'I' and the mountain) are separated from one another, and merged into one another, the separation and merging being one and the same act of the originally undivided Something. Thus at the very moment that the 'I' and the mountain come out of the Something, they merge into one another and become one: and this one thing establishes itself as the absolute Mountain. Yet, the absolute Mountain, concealing in itself a complex nature such as has now been described, *is* just a simple mountain. The above-mentioned Cypress-Tree-in-the-Courtyard of Master Chao Chou is a typical example of this kind of 'external' thing. And such is in fact the nature of the externalization of the internal as we understand it in Zen.

V The Internalization of the External

Now we return to the reverse of what we have just discussed, i.e., the internalization of the external, the spiritual process by which the world of Nature (the so-called 'external' world) becomes internalized and comes to be established as an 'internal' landscape. As I have indicated earlier, the underlying spiritual event itself is in both cases one and the same. How could it be otherwise? For there cannot be two different Zen experiences that would stand diametrically opposed to each other. Throughout its history Zen has always been one, but it has produced divergent forms principally at the level of theorization. Diversity has also appeared with regard to the ways man actually experiences the moment of enlightenment and what happens thereafter. The internalization of the external which we are going to discuss, differs only in this sense from the externalization of the internal.

In the case of the externalization of the internal which we have just examined, what strikes the keynote is a pervading empathy on the part of man with all things in Nature. The basic formula is: Man loses his 'I', dies to himself, fuses into an 'external' thing, then loses sight of the 'external' thing, and finally becomes resuscitated in the form of that particular 'external' thing as a concrete manifestation of the whole world of Being. Man, in short, *becomes* the thing, and *is* the thing: and by being the thing is the All.

In the case of the internalization of the external, on the contrary, man comes to a sudden realization that what he has thought to be 'external' to himself is in truth 'internal'. The world does not exist outside me: it is within myself, it is me. Everything that man has hitherto imagined to be taking place outside himself has in reality been taking place in an interior space. The real problem, however, is: How should we understand this 'interior space'? Does the human mind constitute an interior space in which all things exist and happen as 'internal' things and 'internal' events? We are thus directly led to the problem of the Mind as it is understood by Zen.

The famous *kōan* of Hui Nêng's Flag-Flapping-in-the-Wind[21] may be adduced here as a suitable illustration of the case.

After having attained enlightenment under Master Hung Jên,[22] the Fifth Patriarch, Hui Nêng went to the South and stayed in Kuang Chou or Canton. There, one day, he was listening to a lecture on Buddhism in one of the temples. Suddenly the wind rose and the flag at the temple gate[23] began to flap. It was then that the incident related in the *kōan* occurred. The *kōan* reads as follows:

> While the Sixth Patriarch was there, the wind began to flap the flag. There were two monks there, who started an argument about it. One of them remarked, 'Look! The flag is moving'. The other retorted: 'No! It is the wind that is moving'. They argued back and forth endlessly, without being able to reach the truth.
> (Abruptly Hui Nêng cut short the fruitless argument) by saying: 'It is not that the wind is moving, it is not that the flag is moving. O honorable Brethren, it is in reality your minds that are moving!' The two monks stood aghast.

Here we have, so it would seem, the most obvious case of the internalization of the external. The wind blows in the mind. The flag flaps in the mind. Everything happens in the mind. Nothing remains outside the mind. The flag flapping in the wind ceases to be an event occurring in the external world. The whole event (and implicitly the whole universe) is internalized and re-presented as being in the interior space. In reality, however, the structure of the 'internalization' here at issue is not as simple as it might appear to those who read this *kōan* without any previous acquaintance with Zen teaching. Let us elucidate this point from a somewhat different angle.

In the same *Wu Mên Kuan*[24] there is a passage in which Chao Chou, while still a student, asks his master Nan Ch'üan: 'What is the Way (i.e., the absolute Reality)?' and gets the answer: 'The ordinary mind – that is the Way', This well-known dictum: 'The ordinary mind – that is the Way' is given a poetic interpretation by Master Wu Mên in his commentary upon this *kōan*. It runs:

> Fragrant flowers in spring, the silver moon in autumn,
> Cool breeze in summer, white snow in winter!
> If the mind is not disturbed by trivial matters,
> Every day is a happy time in the life of men.

What, then, is this 'ordinary mind' in which flowers bloom in spring, the moon shines in autumn, a refreshing breeze blows in summer, and the snow is white in winter? These characteristic things of the four seasons are presented by Wu Mên as an internal landscape of the 'ordinary mind', just as the flapping of the flag was presented by Hui Nêng as the internal flapping of the mind.

It will be clear to begin with that the 'mind' here spoken of is the mind of an enlightened man, the enlightened mind. The 'ordinary' mind of Nan Ch'üan is not, in this sense, an ordinary mind. Quite the contrary. Far from being the empirical consciousness of the ego-substance as normally understood by the word, what is meant by the 'ordinary mind' is the Mind (technically called the 'no-mind') which is realized in a spiritual state prior to or beyond the subject-object bifurcation, the mind that has expanded to the fullest limits of the whole universe. It is not the *ordinary* mind as the locus of our empirical consciousness. What is meant is the Reality, the very ground of Being, which is eternally aware of itself.

The strange fact about this Mind, however, is that it does not (and cannot) function in a concrete way except as completely identified with our empirical consciousness. The Mind is something noumenal which functions only in the phenomenal. It is precisely in this sense that Nan Ch'üan calls it the 'ordinary mind'. And it is only in this sense that the flapping of a flag or the blooming of flowers in spring may be described as an 'internal' event. Thus understood, nothing in fact exists outside the 'mind', nor does anything occur outside the 'mind'. Whatever exists in the so-called external world as a phenomenon is but a manifestation-form of the 'mind' the noumenal. Whatever occurs in the external world is a movement of the 'mind', the noumenal. This is what we mean by the term 'mind' with a capital *M*.

The structure of the Mind thus understood is complicated because it is, thus, of an apparently self-contradictory nature: on the one hand, it is entirely different from the empirical consciousness in that it is of a super-sensible, and super-rational dimension of Being, but on the other hand it is completely and inseparably identified with the empirical consciousness. Nan Ch'üan's 'The ordinary mind – that is the Way' refers to this latter aspect of the mind.

There is an ancient Zen dictum which runs: 'The mountains, the rivers, the earth – indeed everything that exists or that happens – are without a single exception of your own mind'. Commenting upon this statement Master Musō[25] of the late Kamakura period in Japan makes the following remark. There are monks, he says, who tend to think that such daily activities as eating, drinking, washing their hands, putting-on and putting-off their garments, going to bed, etc., are all mundane acts having nothing to do with Zen discipline; they think that they are seriously engaged in Zen discipline only while they sit cross-legged in meditation. Such people, according to Master Musō, fall into this grave mistake 'because they recognize things outside the mind', that is, because they believe that the world exists outside their minds. Those are men who do not understand the real meaning of the dictum: 'The mountains, the rivers, and the earth are your own mind'.[26] Otherwise expressed, these people are completely ignorant of the nature of the Mind which is being activated at every moment as the 'ordinary' minds of individual men.

> A monk once asked Master Chao Chou: What kind of thing is my mind?'
> To this Chao Chou replied by asking the monk: Have you already eaten your meal?'
> The monk: 'Yes, I have'.
> Chao Chou: 'Then wash your rice bowl!'

The monk feels hungry, and he eats his meal. Having finished eating, he washes the rice bowl. Chao Chou indicates how the Mind is being activated in the midst of all these natural, daily activities. That is to say, in each of the minds which function through the most commonplace doings, the Mind is being unmistakably activated. The 'ordinary mind' is thus a locus of

an infinite spiritual energy, which, once its individual determination is removed, will instantaneously expand itself to the
farthest limits of the whole universe.

From the viewpoint of such accomplished masters as Nan
Ch'üan and Chao Chou, the 'ordinary mind' has nothing
extraordinary about it. For them the 'ordinary mind' is just an
ordinary mind. But there is at its back the awareness of the
Mind. It is an ordinary mind that has been reached through
the awareness of the 'no-mind', just as the ordinary mountain
about which we talked earlier in discussing the externalization of the internal, is just an ordinary mountain that has been
reached after it has gone through the stage of a no-mountain.
In other words, the 'ordinary mind' of a Nan Ch'üan is not our
empirical consciousness as originally given. It is the 'ordinary
mind' that has been realized through the actual experience of
enlightenment.

The old Zen records abound in examples showing how
difficult it was for Zen students to grasp this point.

> A monk once asked Master Chang Sha:[27] 'How is it possible to
> transform (i.e., internalize) the mountains, rivers and the
> great earth, and reduce them to my own mind?'
> Chang Sha: 'How will it be possible, indeed, to transform the
> mountains, rivers and the great earth, and reduce them to my
> own mind?'
> Monk: 'I do not understand you'.

In this well-known *mondō*, the monk is questioning the validity of the dictum: 'All things are the Mind'. In so doing he is
evidently taking the position of naive realism. For him, the
'mind' is the ordinary mind *before* it has gone through the
stage of the Mind. It is empirical consciousness standing
against the mountains and rivers as 'objects' external to it.
Chang Sha's answer is a rhetorical question, meaning that it is
utterly impossible to bring the 'external' world into the
interior space of such a mind. The monk could not understand
the point.

The fact that the 'mind' as understood by Chang Sha himself is not an internal world standing opposed to the external
world, is clearly shown by the following famous *mondō*.

> A monk asked Chang Sha: 'What kind of thing is my mind?'
> Chang Sha: 'The whole universe is your mind'.

The monk: 'If it is so, I would have no place to put myself in'.
Chang Sha: 'Quite the contrary: this precisely is the place for
you to put yourself in'.
The monk: 'What, then, is the place for me to put myself in?'
Chang Sha: 'A boundless ocean! The water is deep,
unfathomably deep!'
The monk: 'That is beyond my comprehension'.
Chang Sha: 'See the huge fishes and tiny fishes, swimming up
and down as they like!'

There is obviously a fundamental lack of understanding between the monk and Chang Sha. For the monk is talking
about the mind, his own individual, empirical consciousness,
whereas Chang Sha is talking about the Mind. Rather than
emphasizing the actual identity of the empirical mind and the
cosmic Mind, the master here intentionally distinguishes the
former from the latter and tries to make the monk realize that
what he considers to be *his own* mind is in reality Something
like a boundless ocean of unfathomable depths, in which
fishes, big and small, i.e., all things that exist, find each its
proper place, enjoying boundless existential freedom.

The same idea has been given a poetic expression by Master Hung Chih[28] in the following way:

The water is limpid, transparent to the bottom,
And the fishes are swimming leisurely and slowly.
Immense are the skies, boundlessly extending,
And the birds are flying far, far away.

And Dōgen:[29]

The fishes go in the water. They swim on and on without ever
reaching the boundary of the water.
The birds fly in the sky. They fly on and on without ever
reaching the boundary of the sky.

Nothing in fact could describe the 'internal' landscape of the
Mind more beautifully than these words. And it is only in the
metaphysical dimension of the Mind that the 'mountains,
rivers, and the great earth' can be said to be 'inside the mind'.
For every single thing is here this or that aspect of the Mind,
and every single event is this or that movement of the Mind.
And such is the internalization of the external as Zen understands it.

In ending, however, I must bring back your attention to what I emphasized at the outset: namely that the problem of the interior and exterior is after all but a pseudo-problem from the viewpoint of Zen. Once the distinction is made between the interior and exterior, the problem of how they are related to each other may and perhaps must – be developed in terms of the externalization of the internal and the internalization of the external. But, strictly speaking, there is no such distinction: the distinction itself is a delusion. Here let me quote again a *kōan* which I have quoted earlier without giving any explanation.

> A monk once asked Master Chao Chou:'Who is Chao Chou?'
> Chao Chou replied: 'East Gate, West Gate, South Gate, North Gate!'

That is to say, Chao Chou is completely open. All the gates of the City are open, and nothing is concealed. Chao Chou stands right in the middle of the City, i.e., the middle of the Universe. One can come to see him from any and every direction. The Gates that have once been artificially established to separate the 'interior' from the 'exterior' are now wide-open. There is no 'interior'. There is no 'exterior'. There is just Chao Chou, and he is all-transparent.

Notes

1. Quoted by Osvald Sirén in his *The Chinese on the Art of Painting*, Schocken Book, New York, 1936, p. 68.

2. Gaston Bachelard: *The Poetics of Space*, trans. by Maria Jolas, Beacon Press, Boston, 1969, Chap. IX entitled 'The Dialectics of Outside and Inside'.

3. *Ibid.*, p. 211.

4. Lin Chi (Rinzai) and the *Lin Chi Lu* (J.: *Rinzai Roku*) have been mentioned several times in the preceding pages.

5. The English translation is by Daisetz Suzuki, *Essays in Zen Buddhism*, Third Series, Rider, London, 1970, p. 49, pp. 50-51, p. 51.

6. Yün Mên (J.: Ummon, 864-949), an outstanding Zen master in the T'ang dynasty. This *kōan* has been elucidated in Essay V, sec. IV.

7. This question-answer has become a very famous *kōan* (*Wu Mên Kuan*, No. 37); widely known in the Zen world as the Cypress-tree of Chao Chou, it is explained in detail in Essay II, sec. II, Essay III, sec. V.

8. The meaning of this will be made clear at the end of this Essay.

9. Essay III.

10. Wu Mên (J.: Mumon, 1183-1260), the compiler of the *Wu Mên Kuan* (J.: *Mu Mon Kan*) or 'The Gateless Gate'. The words here quoted are found in his Commentary on Case No. 1 of the *Wu Mên Kuan*. The *kōan* itself has been elucidated earlier (Essay V, sec. V).

11. Tung Shan Shou Ch'u (J.: Tōzan Shusho, datcs unknown), the chief disciple of Yün Mên, not to be confused with Tung Shan Liang Chieh (J.: Tōzan Ryōkai, 807-869), the co-founder of Ts'ao Tung (J.: Sōtō) Sect. He is known particularly for his answer: 'Three pounds of flax!' which he gave when asked by a monk: 'What is the Buddha?' (see Essay II, sec. II).

12. Reproduced from *Ch'uang Têng Lu* (J.: *Dentō Roku*) XXIII.

13. Hsiang Yen Chi Hsien (J.: Kyōgen Chikan, dates unknown), the leading disciple of Wei Shan Ling Yü (J.: Isan Reiyū, 771-853) in the T'ang dynasty. He is widely known precisely for the incident here related.

14. i.e., From the very beginning, I have been in the state of enlightenment, although I have not been aware of the fact.

15. For Master Wu Mên, see above, Note 10.

16. Hakuin Ekaku (1686-1769), the greatest representative of the Rinzai (Lin Chi) school of Zen in Japan, known for his newly-devised *kōan* of 'Listen to the sound of one hand clapping' (see Essay V, Note 14).

17. Ling Yün Chih Ch'in (J.: Reiun Shigon, dates unknown), a famous Zen master of the T'ang dynasty.

18. On Dōgen (1200-1253) and his *Shōbōgenzō*, see Essay I, Note 3. The passage here quoted in translation is from a chapter entitled *Genjō Kōan* (Iwanami Series of Japanese Thought XII-XIII: *Dōgen*, Tokyo, 1970-1972, vol. I, pp. 33-36).

19. *The Still Point – Reflections on Zen and Christian Mysticism*, Perennial Library, Harper & Row, New York, 1971, p. 21.

20. Ch'ing Yüan Wei Hsin (J.: Seigen Ishin), an outstanding master in the Sung dynasty (11th century).

21. Hui Nêng (J.: Enō, 683-713), the Sixth Patriarch of Zen Buddhism in

Toward A Philosophy of Zen Buddhism

China. His appearance marks a decisive turning point in the historical development of Zen. Zen, which had up to this time remained largely Indian, became completely sinicized by his activity. The anecdote here related is recorded in the *Wu Mên Kuan,* No. 29. I have analyzed this anecdote in Essay I, sec. V.

22. Hung Jên (J.: Gunin, 605-675).

23. A flag hung out at a temple gate was usually the announcement that a lecture or sermon was being given.

24. No. 19.

25. Concerning the 'National Teacher' Master Musō, see above, Essay II, sec. I.

26. Musō Kokushi: *Muchū Mondō Shū,* II.

27. Chang Sha Ching Ch'en (J.: Chōsha Keishin, dates unknown), a famous Zen master of the T'ang dynasty (9th century), a disciple of Nan Ch'üan. See Essay I, sec. V.

28. Hung Chih Chêng Chüeh (J.: Wanshi Shōgaku, 1091-1157), one of the greatest masters of the Sung dynasty. What is here quoted in translation are the closing words of his celebrated explanation of the spirit of *zazen*-practice.

29. The words are found in the *Shōbōgenzō* (Chap. *Genjō Kōan, op. cit.,* I, p. 37).

Essay VII

THE ELIMINATION OF COLOR IN FAR EASTERN ART AND PHILOSOPHY

Eranos lecture for the year 1972, published in Eranos-Jahrbuch XLI, 1974, Leiden.

I The Colorful and the Colorless World

Though sensibility to color and its beauty is something commonly shared by all men, irrespective of their geographical, historical, ethnic and cultural differences, each nation or each culture is remarkably characterized by inborn likes and dislikes for certain colors and color combinations. And this comes out in many different forms, as one of the most conspicuous of which we may mention the negative and positive attitude taken toward the aesthetic value of color.

I would start by drawing attention to the fact that the negative attitude toward color is characteristic of the Far Eastern aesthetic experience, whether it be in the field of painting, poetry, drama, dancing or the art of tea. I shall discuss in the present Essay some aspects of Oriental philosophy that will theoretically account for the remarkable natural inclination that is observable in Chinese and Japanese culture toward the subduing or suppression of color leading ultimately to a total elimination of all colors except black and white. I shall try to clarify further that even 'black' and 'white' in such a situation cease to function as colors, and that they function rather as something of a totally different nature.

Many Westerners who have had some real aesthetic acquaintance with the Far East tend to represent its art in the form of black-and-white ink painting. The art of ink painting in China and Japan is in fact the best illustration of the negative attitude toward color which I have just referred to as being most characteristic of Far Eastern art. For in this monochromic world of artistic creation, the inexhaustible profusion and intricacy of the forms and colors of Nature are reduced to an extremely simplified and austere scheme of black outlines and a few discrete touches or washes of ink here and there, sometimes in the glistening black, sometimes watered down to vaporous gray. In the background there may be a haziness of faint gray; more often than not the background is a blank, white space, i.e. bare silk or paper left untouched by the brush. There is consequently no titillation and gratification here of the sense of color.

What then is the real charm of paintings of this sort? We know that it is not only the Orientals themselves that are attracted by the special 'beauty' of the black-and-white. We know in fact that many art connoisseurs in the West have shown an enthusiastic appreciation of Far Eastern ink-painting. How are we to account for this fact? This is in brief the main problem which I should like to discuss in the following Essay. In so doing, however, I shall approach the problem not from the technical point of view of an art critic, which I am not. I shall rather try to bring to light the basic ideas that underlie the elimination of color. I shall deal with this latter problem as a problem of a peculiar type of aesthetic consciousness, as a peculiar spiritual phenomenon revealing one of the most fundamental aspects of Far Eastern culture.

Speaking of a peculiar type of Japanese poetry known as *haiku*, which is said to be the most reticent form of poetic expression in the world, consisting as it does of only seventeen syllables arranged in three consecutive units of 5/7/5 sylla-bles, R.H. Blyth once wrote: '*Haiku* is an ascetic art, an artistic asceticism'.[1] The phrase 'an artistic ascetiscism' not only characterizes *haiku*; as is clear, it applies equally well, or perhaps even better, to the art of black-and-white ink paint-ing. It is important to remember, however, that this artistic asceticism, i.e., the suppression of externals and the reduction of all colors to black and white, manifests its real aesthetic function only against the background of a highly refined sensibility for colors and their subtle hues. In other words, the true profundity of the beauty of black-and-white is disclosed only to those eyes that are able to appreciate the splendors of sumptuous and glowing colors with all their delicate shades and tints. Otherwise, the ultimate result of the achromatiza-tion here in question would simply be utter absence of color in a purely negative sense, which would not be apt to excite any aesthetic emotion.

Due perhaps to the climatic conditions of the country and the colorful and picturesque appearance of its Nature, the Japanese had developed from most ancient times a remarkable sensibility for colors and hues which go on changing with the revolving seasons of the year.[2] In matters of color, as Y. Yashiro observes, Nature in Japan is comparable to a gorgeous brocade resplendent with infinitely varied colors. These colors of Japanese Nature, Yashiro goes on to say, are of a dazzling beauty; they are beautiful enough to intoxicate our aesthetic sense. Yet, on the other hand, the brilliance of the colors is characteristically counterbalanced by what we might designate as a chromatic 'reticence', a kind of natural restraint, quiet soberness (popularly known in the West as *shibui*), spreading like thin mists over the colors, matting their naked flamboyance and subduing their unrestrained external gorgeousness. These characteristics of Nature in Japan are said to have positively contributed toward the formation of the typical, aesthetic sensitiveness of the Japanese to color and its delicate nuances.[3]

However this may be, the fact that the Japanese in olden times were endowed with a very peculiar color sensibility is shown by a number of concrete, historical evidences. I shall give here two remarkable examples. The first one is taken from the aesthetic culture of the Heian Period (794-1185).

The Heian Period (meaning literally a period of Peace and Tranquility) in which the Fujiwara family stood at a splendid height of prosperity and domination around the imperial court in Kyoto, was the first peak in the history of Japan with regard to the development of aesthetic sensibility. It is to be remarked that the unusually keen aesthetic sensibility of the Fujiwara courtiers centered around the beauty of color. They were extremely color-conscious. The Heian Period was literally a 'colorful' period. And during the tenth, eleventh, and twelfth centuries, the heyday of Fujiwara culture, the aesthetic sensibility attained to an unprecedented degree of elaboration, elegance, and refinement. This is best observable in the use, choice and combination of colors for the robes worn by the court ladies.

Unfortunately no real specimens of those Heian robes survive, but the lack of material evidence is well compensated for by the innumerable references to the court robes and their

224   *Toward A Philosophy of Zen Buddhism*

color in contemporary literature as well as by the pictorial representation of gentle scenes of court life in the narrative scrolls of later ages, notably in the picture scroll of the famous *Tale of Genji*. Costumes were in most cases described with meticulous care both verbally and pictorially because the garment a person wore was considered in the Heian Period a most immediate expression of his or her personality. 'The garment *was* the person; it was the direct symbol of his or her personality'.[4] It is important for our purpose to note that this symbolic function of the garment was exercised almost exclusively by the aesthetic effects produced by colors and their combination.

The prose literature of this period – the romantic stories by court ladies, their diaries and essays – mentions the names of different colors, the number of which amounts to more than one hundred and seventy.[5] It is no exaggeration to say that the prose literature of that period constitutes in itself a flowery field of colors.

All these colors used to be combined in various ways through the most elaborate and sophisticated combination of clothes and their linings, undergarments and upper garments, so that they might constitute layers of color harmonies. The matching of various colors was in fact an art of highest refinement to be displayed within the limits of the well-established and generally accepted code of aesthetic taste. When silk robes are laid one upon another, the lower colors are more or less faintly seen through the color above, which could result in the creation of an indescribably delicate new color. Thus to give a few concrete examples, the color called *kōbai*, 'pink-plum' was in itself an independent color evocative of the pink color of blooming plum blossoms. But what was called 'pink-plum-layer' was a different color produced by two color layers, the outer layer being pink or white and the inside layer the dark red of sappan-wood. Further, the 'fragrant-pink-plum-layer' was still another color produced by an outer layer of deep 'pink-plum' and an inside layer of very light 'pink-plum'. Or to give another example the *yamabuki*, 'yellow-rose' was, as the appellation itself shows, bright yellow reminiscent of the natural color of the flower of a Japanese plant known by that name. But the *hana-yamabuki*, 'flowery-yellow-rose', also called 'evening yellow-

rose', was a compound color formed by an outer layer of light
dead-leaf-brown and an inside layer of bright yellow. And
yamabuki-nioi, 'yellow-rose-fragrance' was a standardized
color layer to be used for the costume of court ladies, the
uppermost layer being bright yellow having underneath a
number of layers of increasingly light yellow and the final
undergarment being deep blue.

More important still for the color-conscious women of the
Heian Period, however, was the stratification of harmonious
colors coming from the very make-up of their formal costume. The court ladies wore the so-called *jūni-hitoé* meaning
'twelve-layer' garment. It consisted of an outer robe of
gorgeous brocade and embroidery and twelve or even more
silk undergarments of different colors and shades which were
arranged in such a way that each robe was slightly smaller and
shorter than the one below it, so that a beautiful color
stratification might be visible at the neck and the outer edges
of sleeves.

Quite naturally the ladies themselves and the noblemen in
the imperial court had as a rule an extremely sharp and severe
critical eye for color harmonies. Even the slightest fault in the
combination of colors could hardly escape their notice. In a
passage of the Diary of Lady Murasaki, widely known as the
authoress of the *Tale of Genji*, we find an observation made
by herself, which is quite interesting in this respect. One day,
so she writes, when all the court ladies in attendance on the
Emperor had taken special care with their garments, a certain
lady proceeded to the Imperial presence. Everybody without
exception noticed that there was a fault in the color combination at the openings of her sleeves. It was not really a very
serious error, Lady Murasaki adds, but the color of one of her
undergarments was a shade too pale.[6]

I have gone into these details about the Heian costume in
order to show in the first place the degree of elegant
refinement reached by the Japanese of those days in the
development of sensibility for chromatic colors and their
aesthetic value. Enough has been said, I believe, to corroborate the statement made earlier that the Heian Period was
literally a 'colorful' period in the cultural history of Japan. In
terms of the distinction, also made earlier, between the positive and the negative attitude toward color, Heian culture

may rightly be said to be characterized by the definitely positive attitude taken by the courtiers of that age. The observation of this fact will naturally be conducive to another observation which is of greater importance for our present purposes; namely that the elimination of color which is unanimously considered one of the distinguishing marks of Far Eastern aesthetics is backed by a passionate love of the beauty of colors and hues.

We must also observe in this connection that even in the midst of this flamboyantly colorful world created by the aesthetic sense of the Heian aristocrats there is almost always perceivable a kind of soberness, quietude and stillness, coming either from the very quality of the colors chosen or from the peculiar ways they are combined one with the other – or perhaps from both – so that the colors in most cases appear delicately subdued and toned down.

In this sense we may say that in this early period a marked tendency toward the subdual of colors is already observable. But 'black' itself was in the eyes of the Heian courtiers, a dull, gloomy, unpleasant, and ominous color. It reminded them of death, and, at best, of abandoning the pleasures of the world and entering the monkhood. The effect it was apt to produce was generally nothing but dark emotions like sadness, grief, melancholy. Not infrequently the black-dyed robe is described as something ugly, lowly and poor, or odious and abominable. Even in such a world, however, there were among people of the highest aesthetic sophistication some whose color taste was refined to such an extent that they could go against and beyond the common-sense standard of taste and find in black the deepest stratum of beauty as the ultimate consummation of all colors or as the direct expression of the sublimation and purification of all emotions realized by one who had penetrated the unfathomable depth of the sadness of human existence. In the *Tale of Genji* we sometimes are suprised to find the aesthetic eye of Lady Murasaki already turned toward the supreme beauty of a dark, colorless world far beyond the 'colorful' frivolities of sensuous pleasures.[7]

The Japanese taste for the exuberance of glowing color and the splendours of sumptuous decoration reached its second peak in the Momoyama Period which lasted from 1573 to

1615. Lavish display of colors and designs had never been so boldly made before in the history of Japan. In contrast to the too delicate aesthetic refinement of the Heian court aristocracy verging on effeminacy, the Momoyama, a period of warriors, produced a culture saturated with their robust and vigorous spirit. It was a culture of virile vitality. The aesthetic taste of the age, quite in keeping with the warrior spirit, and backed by the unprecedented material prosperity of the merchant class, found its most adequate expression in the magnificent structure of the castles and palaces and in the gorgeousness of their interior decoration. In fact the creative energies of this period were most lavishly spent on the construction of huge fortress-castles and palaces.

Nobunaga (1510-1551), the first military dictator of the period, erected his famous Azuchi castle. Hideyoshi (1536-1598) who succeeded him and who brought the splendor of the period to its apex, built among others his most sumptuous castle on Momoyama (meaning literally Peach Hill) in 1594, known as the Peach Hill Palace, from which the period itself derived its name.

Both Nobunaga and Hideyoshi had the celebrated artists of the age decorate the walls and sliding panels of their castles in the most magnificent manner. At the head of those colorists stood Eitoku Kanō (1543-1590) who was asked to undertake the grand-scale decoration of these castles. Eitoku Kanō, the founder of what is known as the Kanō school of Japanese painting, with his bold brushwork, large designs and the decorative use of patterns of dazzlingly brilliant colors, truly represents the so-called Momoyama style. As the result of the assiduous work of Eitoku and his numerous disciples, the broad surface of the walls of the huge audience halls in the castles and the sliding panels were covered by abstract areas and decorative patterns of crimson, purple, lapis, emerald and blue on backgrounds of pure gold, amidst which stood out trees, birds and rocks painted with a certain amount of realistic detail – a flowery mosaic of rich colors. The halls were further glorified by folding screens representing various aspects of Nature, animate or inanimate, painted in a profusion of sumptuous colors glowing with hues of lapis lazuli, jade, vermilion, oyster-shell white, etc.

Thus the Momoyama Period is predominantly a 'colorful' age, even more brilliantly colorful than the Heian Period, equally characterized by the positive attitude toward color, though in a very different way from the latter. And yet – and this is the most important point to note for the purposes of the present Essay – just at the back of this gorgeous display of flaunting colors there was a totally different world of powerful black-and-white painting. We must remember that the Japanese by that time had already passed through the sober Kamakura Period (1192-1333) in which Zen Buddhism thrived, emphasizing the importance of realizing the existence of a formless and colorless world of eternal Reality beyond phenomenal forms and colors. After the end of the Kamakura Period and before the advent of the Momoyama Period the Japanese had also passed through the Muromachi Period (1392-1573) in which many a first-rate painter produced masterpieces of black-and-white painting in the spirit of the austere restraint which is typical of Zen, and under the direct influence of the poetic ink-painting of the Sung Period in China. Most of these Muromachi paintings, done by Zen monk-painters, were of such a nature that they roused in the minds of the beholders an undefinable but irresistible longing for the colorless dimension of existence which these paintings so well visualized.

Thus there is nothing strange in the fact that in the grandiose castles of the Momoyama Period there were private chambers of the non-colorful style standing in sharp contrast to the lavishly ornate official halls and corridors. In fact most of the famous colorists of the age who usually painted in the gorgeous Momoyama style were also well-trained in monochrome painting, the most notable example being Tōhaku Hasegawa (1539-1610), originally of the Kanō school, who left masterpieces of both colorful and black-and-white painting and who ended up by founding a new school of his own.

Viewed in this light, the Momoyama Period may be said to have been an age marked by the taste for the display of color, which was backed by the taste for the elimination of color. Far more telling in this respect than the pictorial art is the very peculiar elaboration of the art of tea through the aesthetic genius of the tea-master Rikyū (1521-1591).

Under the passionate patronage of that very warrior-dictator, Hideyoshi, who, as we have just seen, liked so much the splendor of flaunting colors and gorgeous forms and who had his castle so luxuriously decorated, Rikyū the tea-master perfected a particular art of tea known as *wabi-cha*, literally the tea of *wabi*, or the art of tea based on, and saturated through and through with, the spiritual attitude called *wabi*. The tea of *wabi* was according to the author of the celebrated *Book of Tea*, 'a cult founded on the adoration of the beautiful among the sordid facts of everyday existence'.[8] The tea of *wabi* brings us into the domain of the elimination of color.

Wabi is one of the most fundamental aesthetic categories in Japan, and its taste casts its grayish shadow over many aspects of Japanese culture; for *wabi* is not a mere matter of aesthetic consciousness, but it is a peculiar way of living, an art of life as much as a principle of aestheticism.

Wabi is a concept difficult to define. But at least is it not impossible to have a glimpse of its structure by analyzing it into a limited number of basic constituent factors. For the sake of brevity I shall here reduce them to three and explain them one by one: (1) loneliness, (2) poverty, and (3) simplicity.

(1) The first factor, loneliness or solitude, living alone away from the dust and din of mundane life, must be understood in a spiritual or metaphysical sense. The idea of fugitiveness which is suggested by the word, if taken in terms of ordinary human life, would simply mean being-unsociable, which is exactly the contrary of what is aimed at by the art of tea. For the art of tea is intended to be enjoyed by a group of men temporarily gathered together for the purpose of drinking tea together. The loneliness in this context must rather be taken in the sense so admirably illustrated by the Zen master Sengai (1750-1873) in his *Song of Solitary Life*[9] which reads:

I come alone,
I die alone;
In between times
I'm just alone day and night. (In classical Chinese)

This I who comes to this world alone
And passes away from this world alone –
It's the same I who lives in this humble hut all alone. (In Japanese)

The meaning of 'being alone' is explained by Sengai himself in another place as follows. 'What I call alone / Is to forget both alone and not-alone, / And again to forget the one who forgets: / This is truly to be alone'.

(2) The second factor, poverty ('being poor') must also be taken in a special sense. It means primarily living in the absolute absence ɔf all ornate materials, existing in a vacant space far removed from the luxury of rich furniture. Physically it *is* a life of poverty. But this material poverty must be an immediate and natural expression of poverty in a spiritual sense. It must be material poverty sublimated into a metaphysical awareness of the eternal Void or Emptiness. Otherwise poverty would simply be sheer indigence and destitution having nothing to do with aesthetic experience.

(3) The third factor, simplicity, is closely connected with the two preceding factors. The tea-room of the so-called Rikyū style, originally designed by this tea-master for the purpose of creating the art of *wabi*, is outwardly nothing but a mere cottage too small to accommodate more than five persons, or even less. The interior is of striking simplicity and chasteness to the extent of appearing often barren and desolate. No gaudy tone, no obtrusive object is allowed to be there. In fact the tea-room is almost absolutely empty except for a very small number of tea-utensils each of which is of refined simplicity. Quietude reigns in the tea-room, nothing breaking the silence save the sound of the boiling water in the iron kettle – the sound which to the Japanese ear is like the soughing of pine-trees on a distant mountain.

From the point of view of color, the essential simplicity of the tea-room may best be described as the state of colorlessness. The tea-room is not exactly or literally colorless, for everything in this world does have color. To be more exact, we had better in this context make use of the commonly used Japanese phrase: 'the killing of colors', that is, to make all colors subdued and unobtrusive to the limit of possibility. It is but natural that the extreme subduing or 'killing' of colors should ultimately lead to a state verging on monochrome and sheer black-and-white. The monochrome is here a visual presentation of the total absence of color. But we should not forget that the absence of color is the result of the 'killing' of color. That is to say, under the total absence of color there is a vague reminiscence of all the colors that have been 'killed'. In this sense, the absence of color is the negative presence of color. It is also in this sense that the external absence of color assumes a positive aesthetic value as the internal presence of color. Thus there is something fundamentally paradoxical in the aesthetic appreciation of colorless or black-and-white, and that not only in the art of tea but also in Far Eastern art in general.

Nothing illustrates this paradoxical relation between the absence and the presence of color better than a celebrated *waka*-poem by Lord Teika of the Fujiwara family[10] (1162-1241), which is constantly quoted by the tea-men as their motto. The poem reads:

> All around, no flowers in bloom are seen,
> Nor blazing maple leaves I see,
> Only a solitary fisherman's hut I see,
> On the sea beach, in the twilight of this autumn eve.

The tea master Jyō-ō (1503-1553), who initiated Rikyū into the *wabi* type of tea, is said to have been the first to recognize in this poem a visualization of the very spirit of the *wabi*-taste. It is to be remarked that the poet does not simply state that there is nothing perceivable. He says, instead, 'no flowers in bloom are seen, nor blazing maple leaves I see'. That is to say, brilliant colors are first positively presented to our mental vision to be immediately negated and eliminated. What takes place here is in reality not even an act of negating colors. For the negation of colorful words in this context represents a metaphysical process by which the beautiful colors are all brought back to the more fundamental color, that is, the color which is not a color. And Nature is poetically re-presented in the dimension of the colorless color which is symbolized by a fisherman's hut standing all alone on the beach in the twilight gray of the autumn evening. Thus the desolate wilderness of the late autumn depicted in this poem does not constitute a picture in monochrome understood in a superficial sense. It is, on the contrary, a sensuous presentation of the spirit of *wabi* understood as an art of 'killing' colors in order to bring them up to the dimension of the absolute Emptiness.

That the above is not an arbitrary interpretation of the poem on my part is testified by a famous passage in the *Nambō Records*,[11] a book in which a monk called Nambō Sōkei, who was one of the leading disciples of Rikyū, gives us a fairly systematic exposition of the principles of the *wabi*-taste tea as he learnt it from his teacher. In the passage in question, quoting the *waka*-poem which we have just read, Nambō notes that, according to what Rikyū has told him,

> Jyō-ō used to remark that the spirit of the *wabi*-taste tea is exactly expressed by Lord Teika in this poem.
> The splendor of colorful flowers and tinted maple leaves (mentioned in this poem) are comparable to the gorgeousness of the formal, drawing-room tea. But as we contemplate quietly and intently the brilliant beauty of the flowers in bloom and tinted maple leaves, they all are found ultimately to be reduced to the spiritual dimension of absolute Emptiness which is indicated by the 'solitary fisherman's hut on the sea beach'. Those who have not previously tasted to the full the beauty of flowers and tinted leaves will never be able to live in contentment in a desolate place like a fisherman's hut. It is only after having contemplated flowers and tinted leaves year after year that one comes to realize that 'living in a fisherman's hut' is the sublime culmination of the spiritual Loneliness.

The paradoxical relation between the absence and the presence of color is equally well exemplified in a somewhat different form in a different field, in the Noh drama, a typical Japanese art that flourished in the Muromachi Period between the Kamakura and the Momoyama Period. The Noh costumes were and still are of the most gorgeous kind, made usually of colorful brocades with glittering gold, shimmering silver, and brilliant colors. In terms of color, the Noh drama is undeniably a world of chromatic exuberance. Under the surface of this polychromic splendor, however, the vision of a genius like Zeami (1363-1443), the real founder of Noh as an art, was directed toward the world of black-and-white. For him the flower of Noh drama and dancing was to bloom in its full in a dimension of spiritual depth where all these colors would be reduced to a monochromic simplicity.[12] For the ultimate goal of expression in the Noh drama is again the world of eternal Emptiness. In the metaphysical vision of Zeami, the last stage of training to be reached by the Noh actor after having gone through all the stages of strenuous spiritual discipline was the stage of what he calls 'coolness' where the actor would be beyond and above all flowery colors, a world of Emptiness into which all phenomenal forms of Being have been dissolved.

The fantastic gorgeousness of color in Noh costumes is also counterbalanced and effaced by the austere restraint shown in the bodily movement of the actor. The sobering effect of extreme restraint in the expression of emotion, which is not lost sight of even for a moment, is such that all colors lose their nakedly sensuous nature and turn into exquisite tones of subdued richness – subdued to the utmost limit of reticent expression. On the Noh stage movement represents stillness, and the stillness is not mere immobility in a negative sense. For in the peculiar atmosphere of spiritual tension, silence speaks an interior language which is far more eloquent than verbal expression, and non-movement is an interior movement which is far more forceful than any external movement. Thus beyond the external brilliancy of color which the Noh drama actually displays on the stage, the unfathomable depth of the eternal Colorlessness is evoked before the eyes of the spectator.

What, then, is this Colorless? And why Colorlessness rather than Colorfulness? I shall try to answer this question in the following pages by explaining the inner structure of the world of black-and-white.

II The Black-and-White Art

I have in the preceding section tried to explain through some conspicuous examples culled from the cultural history of Japan that the black-and-white or colorlessness in the aesthetic consciousness of the Far East is not a mere absence of chromatic colors; that, on the contrary, it is directly backed by an extremely refined sensibility for the splendor of colors; and that the colorlessness must be rather understood as the consummation of the aesthetic value of all colors.

I shall now turn to the problem of the inner structure of black-and-white and the particular philosophy of beauty underlying the monochromic forms of art that have developed in China and Japan.

I shall begin by quoting a remarkable statement made by Yün Nan T'ien (1633-1690), a well-known Chinese painter of the 17th century, i.e. the Ch'ing Period, on the significance of extreme simplicity in painting.[13] He says:

> Modern painters apply their mind only to brush and ink, whereas the ancients paid attention to *the absence of brush and ink*. If one is able to realize how the ancients applied their mind to the absence of brush and ink, one is not far from reaching the divine quality of painting.

The 'absence of brush and ink' may in a more theoretic form be formulated as the principle of non-expression. The principle stems from the awareness of the expressiveness of non-expression, that is to say, the expressive absence of expression. It applies to almost all forms of art that are considered most characteristic of far Eastern culture. In the case of the pictorial art the principle of non-expression is illustrated in a typical form by black-and-white ink drawings done by a few brush strokes or some light touches of ink on a white ground, the serenity of the white space being in many cases even more expressive than the exquisitely expressive lines and glistening ink.

Of course a drawing, as long as it remains a drawing, cannot entirely dispense with lines or touches of ink. The 'absence of brush and ink' is in this sense nothing but an unattainable ideal for those painters who want to actualize the principle of expression through non-expression. However, one can at least come closer and closer to the absolute absence of expression in proportion to the ever increasing inner accumulation of spiritual energy. Hence the great achievements in the field of ink painting in the Sung and Yüan Period in China and the Kamakura and Ashikaga Period in Japan, when Zen Buddhism attained its ascendancy in the two countries. And hence also the development, in the tradition of this form of pictorial art, of the technique known as the 'thrifty brush' and the 'frugality of ink'. These two phrases originate from the realization of the fact that, in order to express the serentiy of the mind in its absolute purity and in order to depict the reality of things as they really are – in their natural Suchness, as Zen Buddhism calls it – the painter must eliminate from his drawing all non-essential elements by using as few brush strokes as possible and by sparing the use of ink to the utmost limit of possibility.

As the result of the stringent application of this principle, many artists painted in soft ink watered down to an almost imperceptible vapor of gray. The outstanding painter in the Sung Period, Li Ch'êng, for instance, is said to have, 'spared ink as if it were gold'. Lao Jung of the Yüan Period is said to have 'spared ink as if it were his own life'. The kind of ink painting represented by these masters is traditionally known as 'mysteriously hazy painting' (*wei mang hua*). According to the testimony of his contemporaries Lao Jung used to paint in such a way that the whole space was veiled in a dim haze; one felt as if something were there, but nobody could tell what it was.

This is perfectly in keeping with the spirit of Taoism which, together with Zen, greatly influenced the development of ink painting. Lao Jung's work is no other than a pictorial presentation of the Way (*tao*) as described in Lao Tzŭ. In the *Tao Tê Ching* we read:

Even if we try to see the Way, it cannot be seen. In this respect
it may be described as 'dim and figureless'.
Even if we try to hear it, it cannot be heard. In this respect it
may be described as 'inaudibly faint'.
Even if we try to grasp it, it cannot be touched. In this respect it
may be described as 'subtle and minute'.
In these three aspects, the Way is unfathomable. And the
three aspects are merged into one.[14] (That is to say, the Way
can be represented only as a dim, hazy, and unfathomably
deep One).

The Way is utterly vague, utterly indistinct.
Utterly indistinct, utterly vague, and yet there is in the midst of
it a sign (of Something).
Utterly vague, utterly indistinct, and yet there is Something
there.[15]

If the 'mysteriously hazy painting' of a Lao Jung aims at a
pictorial presentation of the Way, the Absolute, as Lao Tzŭ
describes it here, the ink painting could theoretically be
developed in two different directions: firstly toward depicting
the absolute Nothing which the Way is in itself, and secondly
toward depicting this absolute Nothing as it functions as the
ultimate metaphysical ground of Being. The author of *Tao Tê
Ching* himself describes the Way as a contradictory unity of
Nothing and Something. Thus:

Deep and bottomless, it is like the origin and ground of the ten
thousand things . . . .
There is absolutely nothing, and yet it seems as if Something
were there.[16]

If the painter chooses the first direction, he will naturally end
up by drawing the Nothing in its absolute nothingness, that is,
actually not drawing anything at all. Then, a piece of white,
blank paper or silk, untouched by the brush will have to be
regarded as the highest masterpiece of pictorial art. It will be
interesting to note that in fact there did appear some painters
who put this principle into practice. As a result we have in the
history of Japanese painting what is known as the 'white-
paper-inscription' (*haku-shi-san*) which consists in leaving
the paper absolutely blank and only inscribing at the top some
verses that are intended to interpret the picture which is
supposed to be underneath. This curious type of 'white paint-

ing' is said to have been inaugurated by a Japanese teaman in the late Tokugawa Period, Yōken Fujimura.[17] But going to such extremes is inevitably conducive to the suicide of painting as painting. For, as long as one depends upon graphic means, one cannot, by *not* drawing anything, aesthetically evoke the vision of the Emptiness of a Lao Tzŭ or the Nothingness (*śūnyatā*) of Mahayana Buddhism.

The only possible way to take for the painter appears thus to be the second one mentioned above; namely to approach the absolute Nothing from the point of view of its being the ultimate metaphysical ground of the phenomenal world. The basic idea underlying this approach is suggested in the most concise form by the following two verses of the distinguished poet-painter of the Northern Sung Period, Su Tung P'o (J.: So Tō Ba, 1036-1101):

> Where there is nothing found, there is found everything,
> Flowers there are, the moon is there, and the belvedere.

The majority of those who paint in 'water-and-ink' depict something positive in black ink on a white ground – a flower for example, a tree, a bird, etc., or often a whole landscape. In so doing, the painter sometimes seizes the precise metaphysical instant at which the figures of phenomenal things arise to his mind in the state of contemplation, emerging out of the depths of the formless and colorless ground of Being. It is in fact a spiritual event. A fine example of painting as a spiritual event of this kind is the celebrated landscape painting known as the *Haboku Sansui* (i.e. literally the Broken-Ink Mountain and Water) of Sesshū (1420-1506). Sesshū was an extraordinary Japanese Zen monk in the Muromachi Period, who was at the same time the most distinguished ink painter of the age. *Haboku* or 'broken-ink' is a peculiar technique of ink painting which is more properly to be called the 'splashed ink' technique.[18] Briefly explained it consists in that the painter first draws the main points of his motif in extremely pale watery ink, and then, before the ink gets dry, quickly and boldly flings over the wet surface vivid blots of black ink and draws a few lines of deep black.

Necessarily in this work of Sesshū nothing is depicted with a clear-cut outline. The whole landscape consists of indistinct forms, varying ink tones, vapors and the surrounding emptiness. In immense distances of the background, beyond veils of mist, craggy pillars of mountains loom against the sky, vague and obscure, like phantoms. In the foreground a rugged wall of a cliff with thick bushes (painted with a few brush strokes in rich and thick ink) is seen rising sheer from the river bank. Under the cliff a small house is discernible. On the water, which is finely suggested by the absence of ink, floats a solitary boat, perhaps a fisherman's boat. The remaining surface of the paper is left entirely bare. But the empty areas obviously play in this landscape a role at least as important as – if not more important than – the splashed blots of ink. For it is only amidst the surrounding cloudy space that the positive side of the picture (consisting of a few black strokes and splashes) turned into a metaphysical landscape crystallizing a fleeting glimpse of the world of phenomena as it arises out of a realm beyond the reach of the senses. It is, on the other hand, by dint of the figures actually depicted in black ink that the blank space ceases to be bare silk or paper, transforms itself into an illimitable space, and begins to function in the picture as the formless and colorless depth of all phenomenal forms and colors.

As another excellent example of the use of a wide blank space of a similar nature we may refer to the equally celebrated ink painting attributed to the Chinese painter Mu Ch'i (J.: Mokkei) of the 13th century, 'The Evening Bell from a Temple in the Mist'. It is a rare masterpiece of ink painting. A wide, dim space – a suggestion of the Infinite – occupies a greater part of the paper. The depicted forms are reduced to a minimum: a small corner of the roof of a house, the faint silhouette of a temple in the aerial distance, the shadowy woods emerging and disappearing in the mist, the lower parts of the trees entirely lost in the twilight. In contrast to the dynamism of ink splashes in the Broken-Ink Landscape of Sesshū, the equally hazy landscape of Mu Ch'i is of a static nature. A profound cosmic quietude reigns over the land-scape. One might say that the dynamism of Sesshū's painting depicts the very instant of the forceful emergence of the phenomenal world out of the eternal Emptiness, whereas Mu Ch'i depicts here the essential stillness of the phenomenal world reposing in the bosom of the all-enveloping Silence.

But in either case, what is evoked by the blank space is the same Great Void which is the ultimate source of all things. The blank space, in other words, visualizes a metaphysical or spiritual space which is absolutely beyond time. It evokes a timeless space, the timeless dimension of things. And this is true even of the Broken-Ink Landscape of Sesshū in which, as I have just said, the 'emergence' of the phenomenal world is depicted. For the emergence here in question is not a 'temporal' emergence, but it is the metaphysical and a-temporal emergence of things in a spiritual Space which in Mahayana Buddhism is often referred to by the word Mind.

Not all ink paintings, however, are done in such a vaporous and diffused manner. Quite the contrary, the contours of the things are often very clearly delineated with expressive lines, now heavy and thick, now agile and light. But the fundamental relation between the depicted figure and the empty background remains essentially the same. For the heightened impression of the positive presence of an object enhances, in its turn, the impression of the illimitability of the cosmic and metaphysical space which would engulf into its depths the phenomenal form that has emerged out of itself.

The peculiar relation which I have just mentioned between the heightened presence of an object depicted and the blank space enveloping it is most easily observable in paintings done in the 'thrifty brush' style. Look at the famous 'Mynah-Bird on a Pine-Tree' by Mu Ch'i, a monochrome picture of a solitary bird in deep black perched on the rugged trunk of an aged pine-tree which is drawn in extremely dry and astringent ink. The background is again a blank space which, by dint of the forceful presence of the black bird in the foreground, turns into the cosmic Loneliness of ultimate Reality itself. And the piercing eye of the bird – which is the very center of the picture – seems to be penetrating into the deepest dimension of Reality lying beyond the very existence of the bird itself.

This picture of the 'Mynah-Bird on a Pine-Tree' will remind us of the oft-quoted *haiku*-poem of Bashō (1664-1694) who is in Japan popularly known as the peerless '*haiku*-saint'. The poem reads:

On a branch of a withered tree
A raven is perched –
This autumn eve.

This is indeed a verbal painting in black-and-white, the black
figure of a solitary raven perching on a dead branch against
the background of the illimitable Emptiness of an autumn
eve. Here again we have an instance of a perfect visualization
of the cosmic Loneliness out of which arise the lonely figures
of the phenomenal world – not through brush and ink this
time, but by the evocative power of words. The externalized
forms of Being are essentially lonely, no matter how brilliantly colorful they might be as pure phenomena. This essential loneliness of phenomenal things is best visualized by
black-and-white. This must be what was in the mind of the
haiku-poet Bashō when he characterized the basic attitude of
verse-making peculiar to his own school in distinction from
that of all other schools, by saying: 'The *haiku* of the other
schools are like colored paintings, whereas the works of my
school must be like monochrome paintings. Not that in my
school all works are invariably and always colorless. But
(even when a verse depicts things beautifully colored) the
underlying attitude is totally different from that of other
schools. For the matter of primary concern in my school is the
spiritual subduing of all external colors'.

It will be only natural that *haiku* poetry whose basic spirit is
such as has just been explained, should attach prime importance to the 'absence of brush and ink', to use again the Yün
Nan T'ien's expression. In other words, *haiku* – at least that of
the Bashō school – cannot subsist as a poetic art except on the
basis of the clear awareness of the aesthetic value of empty
space. For a *haiku* is a poetic expression of a fleeting glimpse
into a trans-sensible dimension of Being through a momentary grasp of an illuminating aperture that the poet finds in a
sensible phenomenon. The latter can be sketched by words,
but the trans-sensible dimension, the Beyond, allows of being
expressed only through what is not expressed. *Haiku* expresses these two dimensions of Being at one and the same time by
positively depicting the phenomenal forms of Nature. Hence
the supreme importance of the blank space which is to be
created by non-expression.

The artistic use of blank space is observable in almost all forms of art in the Far East. The technique of non-motion in the Noh drama to which reference has been made earlier is an apt example. Non-motion, or the absolute absence of bodily movement is nothing other than empty space actualized on the stage by the actor through the cessation of motion. It is an instant of external blankness into which the entire spiritual energy of the actor has been concentrated. The technique of non-motion is considered the ultimate height to which the Noh dancing can attain. To express intense dramatic emotions through the exquisite movement of the body in dancing is still comparatively easy. According to Zeami, only the perfectly accomplished actor after years and years of rigorous technical training and spiritual discipline, is able to actualize on the stage the most forceful expression of emotion by the extreme condensation of inner energy into a sublimated absence of action. The actor does not move his body. He remains absolutely still, as if crystallized into an image itself of Timelessness. In this extraordinary density of spiritual tension, without dancing he dances; he dances internally, with his mind. And against the background of this non-action, even the slightest movement of the body is as expressive as a tiny dot of black ink on the surface of white paper in ink painting.

Much more could be said on the significance of dramatic blank space in the theory of Noh as developed by Zeami and his followers. Still more could be said on the role played by blank spaces in various forms of Far Eastern art as well as in other more practical fields of human life in the Far East. For the purposes of the present Essay, however, enough has already been said on this aspect of our problem. Let us now turn to the more positive side of the matter, namely the significance of the positively depicted forms as distinguished from the empty background.

Let us recall at this point that the spirit of Far Eastern art in its most typical form consists in expressing much by little; it is an art which aims at producing the maximum of aesthetic effect by the minimum of expression verging on non-expression. Thus in ink painting just a few brush strokes and the resulting summary lines and ink washes can evoke the weighty presence of a thing far more impressively than a minute, faithful reproduction of its color and the details of its external form. What is the secret of this type of art? The right answer to this question will be given by our elucidating the inner structure of the things as they are pictorially represented with the least possible number of lines and strokes, and with the elimination of all colors except black.

It will have been understood that monochrome ink painting in China and Japan is a peculiar art centering round the aesthetic appreciation of the spiritual atmosphere which it evokes. In this art Nature and natural objects play a predominant part. In fact the most typical form of brush-and-ink work is landscape painting. And the pictorial representation of landscapes and various natural objects is done by means of lines and ink tones.

The word 'landscape painting' in this context, however, needs a special comment. For the word 'landscape' does not necessarily mean a whole landscape. It is to be remembered that there is no *nature morte* in the traditional conception of painting in the Far East.[19] The concept does not exist. Many pictures that would in the West normally be put into the category of *nature morte* are regarded in the East as landscape paintings. It is of little importance here whether a 'landscape' painting represents a whole landscape or only a flower, grass, or fruit. What is actually drawn may be a single bamboo, for instance. It is in reality not a single bamboo. Before the eyes of the beholder, the single bamboo expands itself into a dense grove of bamboo, and still further into the vast expanse of Nature itself. It is a landscape painting. Or, to give another example, a solitary autumn flower is seen quietly blooming against a white background. It is not a mere picture of a single flower, for the depicted flower conjures up the presence of Nature infinitely extending beyond it. And by so doing, the flower discloses to our inner eye the cosmic solitude and quietude of all solitary existents in the world. Even a fruit or vegetable can in this sense constitute the subject of a landscape painting. The most celebrated picture of 'Six Persimmons' attributed to Mu Ch'i is a good example. In its extreme simplification of the form of persimmons drawn in varying tones of black ink, it is a pictorial representation of the vast cosmos. The underlying philosophy is Hua Yen metaphysics which sees in one thing, in every single thing, all other things contained. R.H. Blyth gives this philosophic view a brief but beautiful poetic expression when he says that each thing 'is with all things, because . . . when one thing is taken up, all things are taken up with it. One flower is the spring, a falling leaf has the whole of autumn, of every autumn, of the timeless autumn of each thing and of all things'.[20]

As we have noted earlier, monochrome painting depends exclusively on two factors: (1) line and (2) ink tone. By definition it eliminates all chromatic colors that go to make Nature flamboyant in the dimension of our sensory experience. Necessarily and inevitably Nature becomes transformed in a peculiar way when it is represented as a world consisting only of lines and ink tones.

In the tradition of Oriental ink painting, drawing a natural object in brush-lines is directly conducive to the spiritualization of Nature. The Oriental brush made of hard and soft bristles is of such a nature that it faithfully reflects the varying moods of the man who uses it and the various degrees of the depth of his mind. Furthermore, it must be remembered that in China and Japan the brush-stroke technique is most intimately related with the technique of drawing spiritualized lines that developed in the art of calligraphy – the most abstract of all Oriental arts, exclusively interested in an immediate expression of the depth of the spiritual awareness of the man. Thus in drawing pictures by brush-lines the painter is able to infuse the object he has chosen to depict with the inner energy of his own, just as he does in writing ideographic characters.

The brush-strokes can be sudden, rugged, and vehement. They can also be soft and supple, serene and quiet. The painter sometimes draws an object with a fluid sinuous line of an indescribable suavity and sweetness. Sometimes his lines are alert, quick and fiery; sometimes, again, slow and heavy. Each line has its own speed and weight. The weight of the line is determined by the amount of power with which the brush is pressed against the paper. The pressure of the brush, coupled with the speed of its movement, faithfully reflects the spiritual undulations of the painter.

As for the ink tones, another basic factor of monochrome painting, sufficient explanation has already been given in an earlier section of this Essay concerning its spiritualizing function. Thus the Far Eastern art of ink painting is definitely a spiritual art.

It will readily be admitted that, as an essentially spiritual art, this kind of painting requires the utmost concentration of the mind. The concentration of the mind is required first of all by the peculiar nature of Oriental paper used for this art. Oriental paper is no less sensitive than the Oriental brush in the sense that it absorbs water and ink easily and quickly. Even the slightest drop of water, not to speak of ink, soaks instantaneously into it and leaves an indelible trace on its surface. Strictly speaking, 'painting' is here impossible. Unlike Western oil painting, in which colors can be piled up in layers, an ink painting is a work that must be finished once and for all. Every stroke is the first and the last stroke. Absolutely no retouch is possible. If a line gets broken in its flow, for example, it is broken for ever; it cannot be continued, for the movement of the spirit has stopped as the line has stopped. There is thus no time for deliberation in the process, no room for subsequent corrections and alterations. As Chang Yen Yüan (9th century, the T'ang Period) remarks in his famous and important book on the fundamentals of Chinese painting 'He who deliberates and moves the brush, intent upon making a picture, misses the art of painting, while he who cogitates and moves the brush without such intentions, reaches the art of painting. His hand will not get stiff; his heart will not grow cold; without knowing how, he accomplishes it'.[21]

This intense concentration of the mind is demanded of the painter not only for the technical or practical reason arising from the nature of Oriental paper. It is required also for another important reason, the discussion of which will directly lead us toward the more philosophical aspect of our subject. As in Western painting, Oriental ink painting starts from, and is based upon, a close observation of the things of Nature. The observation, however, does not consist here in a strictly objective, scientific and methodical observation of Nature. The observation of things which is demanded in the typically Oriental type of painting is a complete penetration of the eye of the painter into the invisible reality of things until the pulse-beat of his soul becomes identical with the pulse-beat of cosmic Life permeating all things, whether large or small, organic or inorganic. Such an observation of things is possible only by means of an intense concentration of all the inner forces of the soul – a state of the mind in which observation is identical with introspection, that is to say, in which the observation of the external world is at the same time the act of penetration into the interior of the mind itself.

In a passage of 'Scattered Notes at a Rainy Window' (*Yü Ch'uang Man Pi*), which is considered the most important writing on Chinese aesthetics in the Ch'ing Period, the author, Wang Yüan Ch'i remarks:

> The idea must be conceived before the brush is grasped – such is the principal point in painting. When the painter takes up the brush he must be absolutely quiet, serene, peaceful and collected and shut out all vulgar emotions. He must sit down in silence before the white silk scroll, concentrate his soul and control his vital energy . . . When he has a complete view in his mind, then he should dip the brush and lick the tip.[22]

It is important to observe in this connection that for the Far Eastern painter everything is inspirited; everything in this world has a spirit within itself. The painter concentrates first and foremost on penetrating into the 'spirit' of the thing which he wants to paint. The 'spirit' of a thing is the primordial origin of its phenomenal appearance, the innermost ground of its being, lying beyond its external color and form. It is this inscrutable spiritual force, the life-breath, the deepest essence of the thing, that is considered to make a painting a real piece of art, when the inspired painter has succeeded in transmitting it through brush and ink. Even a single stone must be painted in such a way that its pictorial reproduction reverberates with the pulsation of the life-spirit of the stone.

This innermost spirit of things is variously named in different fields of thought in China and Japan. In the classical theories of painting it is called the 'bone-structure'. The 'bone-structure' of stone, for example, is the depth-form which the stone assumes in the primordial stratum of its existence. It is the most fundamental form of the stone which the painter must discover by years of close observation-introspection through the painstaking process of elimination of all subordinate elements and external factors one after another until he reaches the utmost limit of simplification at which alone is the 'spirit' of the stone revealed to his mind in a flash of illumination.

In the theory of *haiku*-poetry, the 'spirit' here in question is called *hon-jō*, the 'real nature' of a thing. Explicating a central idea taught by Bashō, one of his representative disciples[23] says:

> Our master used to admonish us to learn about the pine-tree from the pine-tree itself, and about the bamboo from the bamboo itself. He meant by these words that we should totally abandon the act of deliberation based on our ego. . . . What the master meant by 'learning' is our penetrating into the object itself (whether it be a pine-tree or a bamboo) until its inscrutable ssence (i.e. its *hon-jō*) is revealed to us. Then the poetic emotion thereby stimulated becomes crystallized into a verse. No matter how clearly we might depict an object in a verse, the object and our ego would remain two separated things and the poetic emotion expressed would never reach the true reality of the object, if the emotion is not a spontaneous effusion out of the (*hon-jō*) of that very object. Such (discrepancy between the emotion and reality) is caused by the deliberate intention on the part of our ego.[24]

Likewise, in the same book:

> Concerning the right way of making *haiku*, I have heard our master say: As the light (of the deep reality) of a thing flashes upon your sight, you must on the instant fix it in a verse before the light fades out.
> Another way of making *haiku* is what the master has described as 'shaking out of the mind the instantaneous inspiration onto the exterior form of a verse'. This and all other similar ways taught by the master have this idea in common that one should go into the interior of the thing, into the spirit of the object, and immediately fix through words the real form of the thing before the emotion cools down.[25]

Thus, to come back to the art of ink painting, the most important point is that one should penetrate into the innermost reality of an object or a whole landscape, and seize the life-breath which is animating it. But the penetration of the artist here spoken of into the spirit of a thing cannot be achieved as long as he retains his ego. This is the gist of what

Bashō taught about the art of *haiku*-poetry. One can delve deeply into the spirit of a thing only by delving deeply into his own self. And delving deeply into one's own self is to lose one's own self, to become completely egoless, the subject getting entirely lost in the object. This spiritual process is often referred to in the East by the expression: 'the man becomes the object'. The painter who wants to paint a bamboo must first become the bamboo and let the bamboo draw its own inner form on the paper.

What I have referred to in the foregoing as the 'inner form', 'innermost reality', 'bone-structure', 'spirit' etc. of a thing corresponds to what is called *li* in Chinese philosophy. The term *li* played a role of tremendous importance in the history of Chinese philosophy, first in the formation of the Hua Yen metaphysics in Buddhism, and later in the philosophical world-view of Neo-Confuciansim in the Sung Period. The philosophy of Chu Hsi (J.: Chu Tzǔ, 1139-1200), for example, may best be characterized as a philosophical system developed around the central concept of *li*.

For lack of time and space I cannot go into the discussion of this concept now. Suffice it here to say that for Chu Tzǔ the *li* is the eternal principle transcending time and space, immaterial, indestructible, and super-sensible. In itself the *li* is the meta-physical ('above form', *hsin êrh shang*), but it inheres in everything physical ('below shape' *hsin êrh hsia*); i.e. every physical object in existence, whether animate or inanimate. That is to say, every sensible object that exists in this world has inherent in it a metaphysical principle governing from within all that is manifested by the object in the dimension of its physical existence. The *li* of a thing is, in short, the deepest metaphysical ground of the thing, which makes the thing what it really is – the 'is-ness' or 'such-ness' of the thing as the Buddhists would call it.

In a famous passage of his 'Commentary on the Great Learning' (*Ta Hsüeh*), Chu Tzǔ emphasizes the supreme importance of our realizing the *li* of everything by means of what he calls the 'investigation of things'. He says:

> If we want to bring our knowledge to the utmost limit of perfection, we must take up all things and thoroughly investigate the *li* of each individual thing one after another. This is

possible because, on one hand, the human mind is endowed with a penetrating power of cognition and because, on the other, there is nothing under Heaven that is not endowed with *li*. Our knowledge usually remains in the state of imperfection only because we do not penetrate into the depth of the *li* of the things.

Thus the foremost instruction of the 'Great Learning' consists in urging every student to go on deepening the cognition of the *li* of all things in the world, taking advantage of the knowledge of *li* which he has already acquired, until his cognition of the *li* reaches the limit of perfection. After years of assiduous and unremitting effort, the student may suddenly become enlightened in a moment of illumination. Then everything will become thoroughly transparent to him: the outside and inside of all things, the fine and coarse of every single object, will be grasped in their reality. At the same time the original perfection of the reality of his own mind and its magnificent activity will also become apparent to him.[26]

Thus according to Chu Tzǔ, the *li* exists in the interior of every individual man, but the same *li* exists also in each one of all physical objects under Heaven so that in the most profound dimension of existence man and Nature are one single reality, although in the physical dimension each thing is an independent entity separated from all the rest. Because of this structure of reality, man is able – at least theoretically – to return to the original unity of the internal *li* and the external *li*, through sustained effort in combining introspective meditation and a searching investigation into the *li* of each individual object in the world. The very moment at which this unity of the internal *li* and the external *li* is realized is for Chu Tzǔ the moment of supreme enlightenment corresponding to *satori* in Zen. A man who has achieved this is a 'sage' in the Neo-Confucian sense.

Later, in the Ming Period, Wang Yang Ming (1472-1527), the celebrated philosopher of that time, tried out this method of attaining sagehood advocated by Chu Tzǔ. The interesting incident is related by Wang Yang Ming himself in his *Ch'uan Hsi Lu*, 'Record of the Transmission of Instructions'. He and one of his friends decided one day to carry out Chu Tzǔ's teaching. As an easy and practical starting-point, the two friends agreed to try to grasp the *li* of a bamboo that happened to be there in the courtyard. They set to work at once. Day and night they concentrated their mind upon the bamboo, trying to penetrate into its inner spirit. The friend fell into a nervous breakdown in three days. Wang Yang Ming himself who held out longer than his friend could not continue the 'investigation' of the *li* of the bamboo more than seven consecutive days. His body became completely worn out, his mental energy exhausted, and the bamboo had not yet disclosed its *li* to him. He gave up in utter despair, murmuring to himself: 'Alas, we are not endowed with the capacity to become sages!'.[27]

In fairness to this remarkable thinker I would add that Wang Yang Ming later achieved enlightenment by means of pure contemplation and meditation. But to go into this subject would lead us too far away from our present problem.

It is in any case clear that the failure suffered by Wang Yang Ming was due to his inability at this earlier stage of his life to 'become the bamboo', to use again that peculiar expression. In the field of painting and poetry we know the existence of many artists who could accomplish this spiritual feat.

The remarkable painter-poet of the Sung Period, Su Tung P'o, to whom reference has earlier been made, has, for example, left a number of interesting accounts in both prose and poetry of his friend Wên Yü K'o (Wên Tung, 1018-1079) who was widely acclaimed by his contemporaries as a rare genius in the art of painting bamboos. In a short poem which our poet composed and inscribed over a picture of bamboos by Wên Yü K'o, he says:

When Yü K'o paints bamboos,
He sees bamboos; not a man does he see.
Nay, not only is he oblivious of other men;
In ecstasy, oblivious of his own self,
He himself is transformed into bamboos. Then,
Inexhaustibly emerge out of this mind bamboos, eternally fresh and alive.[28]

In another place, a prose essay in which he describes the art and personality of Wên Yü K'o, he says:

In order to paint a bamboo, the painter must start by actualizing the perfect form of the bamboo in his mind. Then taking up the brush, he concentrates his inner sight upon the bamboo in his mind. And as the image of what he really wishes to paint

clearly emerges, he must, at that very instant, start moving the
brush in pursuit of the image like a falcon swooping at a hare
that has just jumped out of the bush. If the concentration
relaxes even for a moment the whole thing is gone. This is
what Yü K'o taught me.[29]

The image of the bamboo which Yü K'o says the painter must
follow in a fiery swiftness of execution is the essential form
that manifests itself in his concentrated mind out of the *li* of
the bamboo. Quite significantly Su Tung P'o uses the word *li*
as a key-term of his aesthetic theory. Everything in the world,
he says, has in its invisible depth as 'eternal principle' (*ch'ang
li*).[30] A painting which is not based on the intuitive apprehension of the 'eternal principle' of the object it depicts is not, for
a Su Tung P'o, worthy to be considered a real work of art, no
matter now minutely and faithfully the picture may transmit
the likeness of the external shape and color of the thing.

It will have been understood that in this kind of pictorial art,
the elimination of color is almost a necessity. Color-sensation
is the most primitive form of our cognition of external things.
In the eyes of the Far Eastern artist or philosopher color
represents the surface of Nature. For one who wants to break
through the veils of the physical exteriority of things and
concentrate his mind on the eternal *li* existing in their interior
as well as in his own mind, the seduction of color is a serious
hindrance in the way of his apprehension of the innermost
nature of the things, and in the way of his realization of his
original unity with all things in the most profound layer of
spiritual life.

From this becomes understandable also the very special
function of black in Oriental painting. In colored paintings,
black functions ordinarily as the obstruction of chromatic
colors. It indicates the end of all other colors, and consequently the end of the life-breath pervading Nature. In ink
painting, on the contrary, black *is* life; it is the infinite possibility of expression and development. Black here is not sheer
black. For in its negation of all colors, all colors are positively
affirmed.

When a red object is actually painted red, the object
becomes immovably fixed in that particular color. According
to the typically Oriental way of thinking, however, red con-

tains in itself all other colors; and precisely because it contains in itself the essential possibility of being actualized in any other color, is it here and now manifesting itself as red. Such a world, in which every single color is seen to contain in itself all other colors so that each color appears as the point of convergance of all colors, such a world of infinite color possibilities can best be painted in black -- at least, in the view of the Far Eastern painter.

In the latter part of this Essay, I have exclusively dealt with the problem of the positive aspect of ink painting, that is, the problem of the positive representation of natural objects in this kind of Oriental art. In bringing this Essay to a final close, I would recall once again the importance of the negative aspect of 'painting without painting anything', the aspect of expressing by non-expression what is not actually expressed.

Ike-no Taiga (1723-1776), a representative Japanese painter in the Edo Period, was once asked: 'What do you find most difficult in painting?' 'Drawing a white space where absolutely nothing is drawn – that is the most difficult thing to accomplish in painting' was the answer.

Notes

1. R.H. Blyth: *History of Haiku*, vol. I (Tokyo, 1963). H. Blyth, known as the author of a number of works on Zen Buddhism, *Haiku*, and some other aspects of Japanese culture, had a good understanding of the spiritual tradition of Japan. He died in 1964.

2. See Yukio Yashiro: *Nihon Bijutsu-no Tokushitsu* ('The Characteristic Features of Japanese Art'), (Tokyo, 4th ed. 1954), p. 235.

3. *Ibid.*, p. 236.

4. Yoshio Araki: *Genji Monogatari Shōchō Ron* ('Symbolism in the *Tale of Genji*') in the Journal *Kaishaku to Kanshō* (vol. 142, Tokyo, 1948).

5. See Aki Ihara: *Heianchō Bungaku-no Shikisō* ('The Chromatic Aspects of Literature in the Heian Period'), (1967, Tokyo), p. 8.

6. *Murasaki-Shikibu Nikki* ('The Diary of Lady Murasaki'), Iwanami Series of Classical Japanese Literature, Vol. 14, (Tokyo, 1961), pp. 507-508. This passage is more fully quoted in English by Ivan Morris: *The*

World of the Shining Prince – Court Life in Ancient Japan (a Peregrine Book, Oxford, 1969), p. 206. This latter book gives a fine description of the general characteristics of Heian culture. On the textile arts and costume decoration in Japan, Helen B. Minnich's *Japanese Costume* (Rutland and Tokyo, 1963) is the best work available in English.

7. On the special aesthetic significance of black in the *Tale of Genji*, see Aki Ihara, (*op. cit.*; cf. Note 5), pp. 203-235, a chapter entitled *Sumizome-no Bi* ('The Beauty of the Black-Dyed Robe'); also p. 23.

8. Kakuzō Okakura: *The Book of Tea* (Dover Publications, New York, 1964), p. 1. The book was originally written and published in 1906.

9. Daisetz T. Suzuki: *Sengai, The Zen Master*, ed. by Eva Van Hoboken (Faber & Faber, London, 1971), pp. 23-24.

10. Fujiwara Teika, son of Fujiwara Shunzei, was a *waka*-poet of the highest rank in the early Kamakura Period. His work represents the very spirit and style of the *Shinkokin-shū* Anthology. The poem here discussed is found in this Anthology.

11. The authenticity of *Nambō Roku* has very much been discussed. But the importance of the book as a theoretic treatise on the *wabi* art of tea remains the same, whether it be a real work of Nambō or not. The passage is quoted from *Kinsei Geidō Ron*, Iwanami Series of Japanese Thought, No. 41, (Tokyo, 1972), p. 18.

12. See Shōzō Masuda: *Noh-no Hyōgen* ('Expression in Noh') (Tokyo, 1971), pp. 27-28.

13. The statement is in reality an inscription on a picture. I quote it from Osvald Sirén: *The Chinese on the Art of Painting* (*op. cit.*), p. 199. The italics are mine.

14. *Tao Tê Ching*, XIV.

15. *Ibid.*, XXI.

16. *Ibid.*, IV.

17. See Yukio Yashiro: *Nihon Bijutsu-no Tokushitsu* (*op. cit.*), pp. 143-144.

18. For more detail on this problem, see Ichimatsu Tanaka: *Japanese Ink Painting – Shūbun to Sesshū*, Heibonsha Survey of Japanese Art, No. 12 (New York and Tokyo, 1972), pp. 173-174.

19. See Shōgo Kinbara: *Tōyō Bijutsu* ('Oriental Art') (Kawade, Tokyo, 1941), pp. 102-103.

20. Blyth: *Haiku*, vol. I, *Eastern Culture* (Hokuseidō, Tokyo, 5ed., 1967) Preface p. 8.

21. Quoted from Oswald Sirén, *op. cit.*, p. 24.

22. *Ibid.*, p. 203.

23. Dohō Hattori (1657-1730), author of the *San Zōshi* ('Three Booklets') in which he noted down Bashō's remarks on *haiku* and its spirit.

24. *Aka Zōshi* 'Red Booklet' (one of the 'Three Booklets'), quoted from the Iwanami Series of Classical Japanese Literature Series, No. 66. (Tokyo, 2nd., 1972) pp. 398-399.

25. *Ibid.*, p. 400-401.

26. 'Commentary on the Great Learning', Chapter V.

27. *Ch'uan Hsi Lu*, Part III.

28. Translated from the text given in *So Tōba*, Shūei-sha Series of Classical Chinese Poetry, No. 17, (Tokyo, 1964), pp. 249-250.

29. Translated from the text given in *So Tōba Shū* (Collected Writings of Su Tung P'o), Chikuma Series of Chinese Civilization, No. 2, (Tokyo, 1972), p. 131.

30. *Ibid.*, p. 88.

Index

For easy reference, Chinese names are generally indexed in both their Chinese and Japanese forms. Japanese pronunciations are given in parentheses after most Chinese names. Letter-by-letter alphabetization is used; thus *sheng ti* precedes Shen Hsui.